Adults Abused As Children

Steps 1 through 12
from the 12 Step Anonymous Perspective

Ellin Chess

Testimonials for
Adults Abused As Children Steps 1 through 12, from the 12 Step Anonymous Perspective

"El Chess's book has been immensely helpful as I've traveled the 12 Step journey of recovery from extreme emotional neglect throughout my childhood. I've read many books on healing from childhood trauma and abuse. This book is by far one of the best! It really stands out because it stays true to the spirit of the 12 Steps without minimizing the fact that healing from child abuse is VERY DIFFERENT than recovery from all the various addictions that other 12 Step groups focus on."

– Lloyd

"To help us navigate an often painful and sensitive subject as this, *Adults Abused As Children* has detailed chapters with helpful practices, study questions, practical tools, affirmations, and more. Informative, well thought-out, and inspiring. Her writing encourages me to gently look within and begin to heal my inner self."

– Kat E.

"This book is very supportive with recovery related to being abused as a child. The Journal Questions at the end of each Step provide potential 'hooks' into my childhood and memories. Having just gone through the Journal Questions for the 4th Step, I found them to be from a positive to neutral perspective, even though they are openings for me to look back into my horrid past. The questions were neither negative nor scary. I learned that some character traits I developed for survival in my childhood, can be remapped as an adult. I find this most helpful in threading out bits and pieces of my history. I have found much-needed pieces for my healing through this book, ones I have not found anywhere else."

– Carol

"An excellent book on healing from childhood abuse through the 12 Steps. One of the things I learned is that there is no hierarchy of trauma in the different types of abuse. None are better or worse than others. I no longer compare my abuse with others nor minimize my experience. This understanding has shed a whole new light on my thinking."

– Bruno

"I am just beginning to unravel how incredibly helpful the information in this book is for my healing. It has taken a few reads through it to realize this. I appreciate the stories and depth of the topics. I find the prompts for writing, affirmations, and prayers for each Step effective and comforting. I discovered the many, many different ways to approach the 4th Step inventory as being crucial for "looking inside myself" as an adult. This book continues to encourage me to use the 10th Step as a wonder-full resource for healing from my childhood abuse. The book is such a gift to me."

– Sandy

"The ritual of opening this, my first book on healing from my childhood abuse, had me swelling with satisfaction. The notes I've written give me great peace. I understand more and more about myself. I am grateful for this book. Thank you."

– Angelique

Adults Abused As Children

Steps 1 through 12
from the 12 Step Anonymous Perspective

AN UPLIFTING STEP-BY-STEP GUIDE

Ellin Chess

© 2022, 2024 by Ellin Chess

All rights reserved. No part of this book may be reproduced in any written, electronic, recording, or photocopying form without prior written permission of the publisher. The exception would be in the case of brief quotations embodied in critical articles or reviews and pages where permission is specifically granted by the publisher.

No liability is assumed for damages that may result from the use of the information contained within.

Okay Enterprises
adultsabusedaschildren.com
facebook.com/ellinchess/

Ellin Chess
708 Gravenstein Highway North #424; Sebastopol, CA 95472
707.861.0144
admin@adultsabusedaschildren.com

Editing: Lynn Goodwin
Cover and Interior Design: Lorna Johnson Print
Cover Photo: Adobe Stock Photography
Author Photographs: Star Dewar, Star Shots Photography

Publisher's Cataloging-in-Publication data

Names: Chess, Ellin, author.

Title: Adults abused as children : steps 1 through 12 from the 12 step anonymous perspective / Ellin Chess.

Description: Sebastopol, CA: Okay Enterprises, 2022.

Identifiers: LCCN: 2022912586 ISBN: 978-0-9675399-8-0 (print) | 978-0-9675399-9-7 (ebook)

Subjects: LCSH Adult child abuse victims--Rehabilitation. | Post-traumatic stress disorder--Treatment. | Psychic trauma--Treatment. | Twelve-step programs. | Self help. | BISAC SELF-HELP / Abuse | SELF-HELP / Personal Growth / Self-Esteem | SELF-HELP / Post-Traumatic Stress Disorder (PTSD) | SELF-HELP / Twelve-Step Programs | BODY, MIND & SPIRIT / Healing / Prayer & Spiritual | BODY, MIND & SPIRIT / Inspiration & Personal Growth | FAMILY & RELATIONSHIPS / Abuse / Child Abuse

Classification: LCC RC569.5.C55 .C44 2022 | DDC 158--dc23

Ordering Information:
Books may be purchased in quantity by contacting the publisher directly:
Okay Enterprises in Sebastopol, CA by calling 707.861.0144.

Dedication

This book is dedicated to all adults who were abused as children and to the kids inside us who were abused when we were children.

To my little Tellie — I'm sorry. I love you.

To Gay, one of us who didn't make it, and all others who left us too soon.

To children everywhere who are still being abused...we see you whole and well.

To Source.

Contents

A Note on Anonymity i

Appreciations iii

Author's Notes. v

Author Summary of the 12 Steps for Adults Abused As Children viii

Author Summary of the 12 Spiritual Principles of the 12 Steps xii

The 12 Steps of ADULTS ABUSED AS CHILDREN ANONYMOUS. xv

The 12 Traditions of ADULTS ABUSED AS CHILDREN ANONYMOUS. xvii

Preface. xxi

Overview of the ADULTS ABUSED AS CHILDREN ANONYMOUS PROGRAM 1

What is ADULTS ABUSED AS CHILDREN ANONYMOUS? . . 3

Vision and Mission Statements of ADULTS ABUSED AS CHILDREN ANONYMOUS 5

Working the Program of ADULTS ABUSED AS CHILDREN ANONYMOUS 7

Introduction — Our Past Abuse 11

    What is Child Abuse? 12

    Some Types of Child Abuse 13

    Some Effects of Child Abuse 15

Resources to Help Us 23

    Feelings, Memories, and Self-Care Strategies 24

    Self-Care Strategies 25

    Affirmations 28

    Tips, Tricks, and Tools for Working the 12 Steps 31

Meeting Information for ADULTS ABUSED AS CHILDREN ANONYMOUS **45**

Suggested Meeting Format for ADULTS ABUSED AS CHILDREN ANONYMOUS **47**

    Meeting Opening Statement 47

    Meeting Guidelines 49

    Meeting Agreements. 50

    12 Steps of ADULTS ABUSED AS CHILDREN ANONYMOUS 51

    The 12 Traditions of ADULTS ABUSED AS CHILDREN ANONYMOUS 54

    Introductions and Announcements 57

    Now You Are Ready to Hold the Meeting 57

    After the Meeting — Closing Statement: 60

    Optional: Closing Prayer 61

Step 1 Through Step 12 . . . . **63**

The Wording in the 12 Steps **65**

Step 1 . . . . **69**
We admitted we were powerless over the past abuse – that our lives had become unmanageable.

    Introduction 73

    The First Word Is "We" 75

    Kinds of Abuse 76

    Powerlessness 78

    Admitting 79

    Unmanageability 82

    Step 1 Summary 88

    Step 1 Affirmations 89

    Step 1 Journal Questions 90

    Step 1 Prayer 91

Step 2 95
Came to believe that a Power greater than ourselves
could restore us to sanity.

    Introduction 99

    Beliefs 100

    Came to Believe 105

    What Is a Power Greater Than Ourselves? 107

    Restoration 110

    Restored to Sanity 112

    Step 2 Summary 116

    Step 2 Affirmations 118

    Step 2 Journal Questions 119

    Step 2 Prayer 120

Step 3 123
Made a decision to turn our will and our lives over to the care
of *God as we understood Him*.

    Introduction 127

    What Does It Mean to Turn Over Our Will? 129

    Surrender 134

    We Love Ourselves 141

    Our Understanding of a Higher Power 144

Making a Decision —
We Discover that We Have Choices 146

Step 3 Summary 150

Step 3 Affirmations 151

Step 3 Journal Questions 152

Step 3 Prayer 153

Step 4 157

Made a searching and fearless moral inventory of ourselves.

Introduction 161

What Is an Inventory? 165

Why Do an Inventory? 167

We Assess Our Moral Inventory 170

Things to Note When Doing an Inventory 173

We Are Nonjudgmental 175

Ways of Writing an Inventory 177

We Inventory the Past and the Present 180

We Are Not Alone 184

We Are Fearless 186

Unmanageability Motivates Us 189

We Search Within 192

We Hide Who We Are 194

We Deny 196

Spiritual Principles 199

Feelings and Memories May Appear 202

Self-Enhancing Character Traits 207

Self-Diminishing Character Traits 209

Step 4 Summary 212

Step 4 Affirmations 214

Step 4 Journal Questions 215

Step 4 Prayer 217

Step 5 . . . . **221**

Admitted to God, to ourselves, and to another human being the exact nature of our wrongs.

Introduction 225

Wrongs 230

Exact Nature 235

Structure for Admitting 238

How to Do a 5th Step 240

Admit from an Adult Perspective 241

Admit to God and to Ourselves 245

Admit to Another Human Being 249

Sponsorship 252

Service 254

Step 5 Summary 256

Step 5 Affirmations 260

Step 5 Journal Questions 261

Step 5 Prayer 263

Step 6 267

Were entirely ready to have God remove all these defects of character.

Introduction 271

The Principle of Readiness 274

Becoming Ready 277

Let Go. Let God. 279

God Removes Defects 282

We Allow Removal 288

Our Defects of Character 291

List of Some Character Defects 294

List of Some Character Assets 296

Step 6 Summary 298

Affirmations for New Behaviors 301

Step 6 Affirmations. 303

Step 6 Journal Questions 304

Step 6 Prayer 306

Step 7. 309

Humbly asked Him to remove our shortcomings.

Introduction 313

Humility 316

Our Relationship with God 321

Ask for Help 323

Remove Shortcomings 330

Step 7 Summary 336

Step 7 Affirmations. 339

Step 7 Journal Questions 340

Step 7 Prayer. 341

Step 8. 345

Made a list of all persons we had harmed, and became willing to make amends to them all.

Introduction 349

Make a List 352

Harm. 360

Harm to Ourselves 362

Self-care 368

Harm to Others. 371

Became Willing. 375

Make Amends. 380

Forgiveness. 388

Self-forgiveness 390

All Persons We Harmed. 393

Step 8 Summary 397

Step 8 Affirmations. 401

Step 8 Journal Questions 402

Step 8 Prayer 403

Step 9. 407

Made direct amends to such people whenever possible, except when to do so would injure them or others.

Introduction 411

Benefits of Step 9 414

How to Begin 416

Making Amends 420

Three Kinds of Amends. 422

Making Direct Amends to Others 425

Making Indirect Amends to Others 429

Making Amends to Myself. 432

Making Living Amends 437

Amends that Could Harm 439

Step 9 Summary 445

Step 9 Affirmations. 448

Step 9 Journal Questions 449

Step 9 Prayer 451

Step 10. 455

Continued to take personal inventory and when we were wrong and when we made progress, promptly admitted it.

Introduction 459

Continuing the Inventory 461

Personal Inventory 465

Step 10 Daily Guide. 468

When to Do an Inventory 473

Promptly Admitting When We Were Wrong
and When We Made Progress 477

Benefits of Step 10 481

Step 10 Summary 483

Step 10 Affirmations 485

Step 10 Journal Questions. 486

Step 10 Prayer. 488

Step 11 . . . . **491**

Sought through prayer and meditation to improve our conscious contact with God, *as we understood Him,* praying only for knowledge of His will for us and the power to carry that out.

Introduction 495

God, *As We Understood Him* 498

Seeking 501

Improving Our Conscious Contact 503

Making Contact Through Prayer 508

Making Contact Through Meditation 521

Benefits of Prayer and Meditation. 524

Praying for Knowledge of God's Will 529

Praying for Power 532

Step 11 Summary. 536

Step 11 Affirmations 539

Step 11 Journal Questions 541

Step 11 Prayer 543

Step 12 547

Having had a spiritual awakening as the result of these Steps, we carried this message to others and practiced these principles in all our affairs.

Introduction 551

A Spiritual Awakening as a Result of These Steps . . . 554

Step 12 Is Written in the Past Tense 563

Spiritual Practice 565

Asleep and Awake 568

Carrying the Message 571

The Spiritual Principles of The 12 Steps 578

Practicing the Principles 579

In All Our Affairs 582

Service 584

Step 12 Summary 588

Step 12 Affirmations 595

Step 12 Journal Questions 597

Step 12 Prayer 599

About the Author............................605

Appendix...................................607

The 12 Steps of Alcoholics Anonymous®...........608

The 12 Traditions of Alcoholics Anonymous®.......610

Permissions................................619

Affirmations: Step 1 Through Step 12..............621

Journal Questions: Step 1 Through Step 12.........635

Prayers: Step 1 Through Step 12 655

How to Get Involved and Start Your Own Meeting....667

Index......................................669

A Note on Anonymity

I wrote this book as an adult abused as a child who has worked through these 12 Steps as a spiritual path for my healing.

It is my desire to have others, with similar backgrounds, have access to this life-changing way of healing.

I did not write this book as a member of any anonymous program, including **ADULTS ABUSED AS CHILDREN ANONYMOUS.**

— Ellin Chess, Author of **Adults Abused As Children**

Appreciations

Thank you to the following people who helped birth this book: The seeds for this book were planted by Source in 1985. I said YES I would tell. This volume is the result of my commitment.

The original crew in 1995:
Judy, who birthed the first draft with me with unbridled devotion by interviewing me as I went through all 12 Steps. Mindy, who painstakingly typed up the printed version from the audio tapes. Her service was invaluable.

The crew in 2022:
Windi Braden was brilliant as my collaborator. She interviewed me, distilled the information, and expressed it in print with amazing accuracy and effectiveness. To work with Windi was a joyful, grace-filled experience!

Editorial and publishing team:
Ruth Schwartz, experienced wisewoman and publishing manager, aka the Wonderlady; Lorna Johnson, cover and interior layout master; Star Dewar, photographer extraordinaire; and Lynn Goodwin, developmental editor of the highest order. Thank you all!

To my children, Gary and Drew, who have always supported me in everything I do.

And especially to Tye, my beloved husband and best friend, who believes in me and my efforts in all ways!

Author's Notes

I'm so glad you're reading this book! My promise to you is: if you follow and apply yourself simply from where you are right now in your life, to working these 12 Steps, you will feel empowered and experience life in ways you've always desired.

This path is a journey of healing from the effects of childhood abuse. We take small steps toward what we want in life. The 12 Steps work!

Writing this book has been an act of completing a commitment I made to my Higher Power when I was three years old. At that time, I had a near-death experience after an event caused by one of my perpetrators. When I was on the other side, I was asked to come back and "tell." I said "yes." This book is the result of the "telling." What I want more than anything is to give hope to other adults abused as children!

In many ways, my childhood is still a mystery to me. I didn't expect what happened to me. I could never make sense of it. I could not have anticipated what our planet would be like today, either. I thought my experience of being human would be different. This book will interest those of us who want to shift the ways we experience our lives.

Abuse of power is rampant worldwide. Fear and hatred abound. Bloody deeds are justified. Many of us are abdicating our responsibility for our lives to others as we wonder why we're so unhappy.

I sought a path for myself that resonates with me and has the possibility for the vision I have held. The 12 Steps for adults abused as children are a way that works. I have been practicing this path since 1981 with amazing success. It delivers what I want: peace of mind, hope, personal transformation, and a way to make a difference.

There are many paths that offer opportunities for developing myself to become the kind of person I want to be. I chose the 12 Step path for its universal approach to spirituality, which encourages me to have a Higher Power of my understanding.

As an adult abused as a child, I found that I thrive within a structure to navigate the day. The 12 Steps offer such a structure with solutions that follow universal principles. I witness the results in myself and those around me who follow them, as well.

I am convinced that any one of us who sincerely desires a life we love can attain it through working the 12 Steps. On this path, I have been learning what my part in my adult life is. The possibility of my being human is open to being created. Each day, I practice how I want my life to be. For this, I am responsible.

Our foundation as children did not include self-esteem, emotional security, or feeling safe. However, as adults, we can take control of our lives in ways never imagined. We can ask our Higher Power to guide us and let us know what is ours to do to facilitate the healing of our past. We no longer have to live lives as victims. We follow the guidance we receive to the best of our ability. We succeed one day at a time. Our lives are not fixed; they are open to being created.

One of the most important aspects of this book is that it takes the focus off our childhood abuse and the abusers, and puts it on us! The results include more ease in our lives, more peace of mind, and more joy. We live our lives according to who <u>we</u> are now.

I invite you, the reader, to consider this 12 Step path to heal what's left over from your abusive childhood and stands in the way in your adult life. I offer you the opportunity to have what you want in your life, as I have been blessed to have in mine.

– El Chess

Author Summary of the 12 Steps for Adults Abused As Children

This is the **author's** interpretation of the 12 Steps.

Step 1:

We admitted we were powerless over what happened to us as children. We admitted what it was like and what our part was. We experience challenges that remain in our lives because of our childhood abuse.

Step 2:

Because we were not experiencing our adult lives as we wanted to, and our efforts alone were not sufficient to accomplish this, we decided to believe that a Power greater than ourselves could help us.

Step 3:

We decided to turn to a Higher Power of our own understanding, and allow this Power to work in our lives and within us. As we let go of what we cannot control, we make progress toward experiencing happiness and inner peace.

Step 4:

To experience life differently as an adult, we were willing to be realistic about our part in the past. We became honest about our part in the present. We discovered who we had become as we explored our attitudes, beliefs, actions, and character traits. We determined whether each was moving us closer to what we wanted or perpetuating the unmanageability of our lives. We wrote down what we uncovered without judgment. Discovering where we are is the first step to determine where we want to go and how to get there.

Step 5:

We admitted to ourselves where we had erroneous thinking, where we had acted incorrectly as adults, and how these errors had impacted our lives. Through examining our thoughts and actions, the aspects that were not for our highest good, were revealed to us. As we release these aspects, we allow new possibilities to emerge. We trust our Higher Power and another person by sharing what we have learned with them.

Step 6:

As we looked within, we saw how we blocked our progress. We acknowledged where we were not yet ready or willing to release our resistance. We ask our Higher Power to remove those personal characteristics which hold us back.

Step 7:

In the process of admitting, believing, surrendering, searching, owning and releasing what is in our way, we saw what was lacking within us. As we discover where we come up short, we shift our attitudes and actions, and open up to allow our Higher Power to help us.

Step 8:

Through our honest search within, we discovered how we have negatively impacted ourselves and others. We held ourselves accountable for our part and were willing to "correct the damage" we caused, especially to ourselves. We remember that we want to experience life differently and to do this we need to "clean our slate."

Step 9:

After we had assessed what we needed to do to "clean the slate," we took action to accomplish this. Changing our attitude or viewpoint can be an effective way to prevent us from repeating harm.

Step 10:

We continued to assess our part in our lives on a regular basis. We admitted when we were on a path that was not for our highest good. In addition, we noted when we were on a path that moved us forward. As we make these assessments, we "clean the slate" when appropriate, and acknowledge ourselves as well, when we make progress.

Step 11:

We remembered that by ourselves, we could neither actualize nor manifest the lives we wanted. We experience personal transformation through connecting to our Greater Power as we seek to know what is ours to do and experience the power to do it.

Step 12:

We continued to live in spiritual alignment with what we learned through working these 12 Steps. In this way, we make a positive difference everywhere we go in the world.

Author Summary of the 12 Spiritual Principles of the 12 Steps

Step 1:

Powerlessness. I experience discomfort. I seek peace.

Step 2:

Faith. I have faith in my process of restoration.

Step 3:

Surrender. I release what's getting in my way of my healing.

Step 4:

Honesty. I look within.

Step 5:

Trust. I am accountable for who I have become.

Step 6:

Readiness. I am willing to be transformed.

Step 7:

Humility. I am willing to be human.

Step 8:

Willingness. I am willing to be complete with my past.

Step 9:

Restitution. I am willing to forgive and be forgiven.

Step 10:

Accountability. I continue to grow and heal.

Step 11:

Spirituality. I connect with my Higher Power.

Step 12:

Service. I share my growth and healing.

The 12 Steps of ADULTS ABUSED AS CHILDREN ANONYMOUS

Step 1:
We admitted we were powerless over the past abuse — that our lives had become unmanageable.

Step 2:
Came to believe that a Power greater than ourselves could restore us to sanity.

Step 3:
Made a decision to turn our will and our lives over to the care of God **as we understood Him.**

Step 4:
Made a searching and fearless moral inventory of ourselves.

Step 5:
Admitted to God, to ourselves, and to another human being the exact nature of our wrongs.

Step 6:
Were entirely ready to have God remove all these defects of character.

Step 7:

Humbly asked Him to remove our shortcomings.

Step 8:

Made a list of all persons we had harmed, and became willing to make amends to them all.

Step 9:

Made direct amends to such people whenever possible, except when to do so would injure them or others.

Step 10:

Continued to take personal inventory and when we were wrong and when we made progress, promptly admitted it.

Step 11:

Sought through prayer and meditation to improve our conscious contact with God, **as we understood Him,** praying only for knowledge of His will for us and the power to carry that out.

Step 12:

Having had a spiritual awakening as the result of these Steps, we carried this message to others, and practiced these principles in all our affairs.

The 12 Traditions of ADULTS ABUSED AS CHILDREN ANONYMOUS

Tradition 1:
Our common welfare should come first; personal progress for the greatest number depends upon **ADULTS ABUSED AS CHILDREN ANONYMOUS** unity.

Tradition 2:
For our group purpose there is but one ultimate authority— a loving God as He may express Himself in our group conscience. Our leaders are but trusted servants; they do not govern.

Tradition 3:
Adults abused as children, when gathered together for mutual aid, may call themselves an **ADULTS ABUSED AS CHILDREN ANONYMOUS** group, provided that, as a group, they have no other affiliation. The only requirement for **ADULTS ABUSED AS CHILDREN ANONYMOUS** membership is a desire to heal from the past abuse.

Tradition 4:
Each group should be autonomous, except in matters affecting another group or **ADULTS ABUSED AS CHILDREN ANONYMOUS** as a whole.

Tradition 5:

Each group has but one primary purpose — to carry its message to the adults abused as children who still suffer. We do this by practicing the 12 Steps of **ADULTS ABUSED AS CHILDREN ANONYMOUS** ourselves.

Tradition 6:

An **ADULTS ABUSED AS CHILDREN ANONYMOUS** group ought never endorse, finance, or lend our name to any outside enterprise, lest problems of money, property, and prestige divert us from our primary purpose.

Tradition 7:

Every **ADULTS ABUSED AS CHILDREN ANONYMOUS** group ought to be fully self-supporting, declining outside contributions.

Tradition 8:

ADULTS ABUSED AS CHILDREN ANONYMOUS should remain forever non-professional, but our service centers may employ special workers.

Tradition 9:

ADULTS ABUSED AS CHILDREN ANONYMOUS groups, as such, ought never be organized; but we may create service boards or committees directly responsible to those they serve.

Tradition 10:

ADULTS ABUSED AS CHILDREN ANONYMOUS has no opinion on outside issues; hence our name ought never be drawn into public controversy.

Tradition 11:

Our public relations policy is based on attraction rather than promotion; we need always maintain personal anonymity at the level of press, radio, TV, films, and other public media.

Tradition 12:

Anonymity is the spiritual foundation of all our Traditions, ever reminding us to place principles before personalities.

Preface

Created as a healing path and guide, this book is for individuals who were abused and traumatized as children who choose to follow the 12 Steps toward transforming their lives. We become empowered to discover new ways of living with greater joy, peace, and happiness. The 12 Steps are discussed in great detail and can be used by a 12 Step group of **ADULTS ABUSED AS CHILDREN ANONYMOUS.** The 12 Steps can be found on pages xv and 51.

The 12 Traditions of **ADULTS ABUSED AS CHILDREN ANONYMOUS** are a guide for our 12 Step groups to follow to assist in maintaining a safe atmosphere in meetings and to handle the business of the groups. Some of us seek to adapt these Traditions and apply them in our homes and workplaces successfully. The 12 Traditions of **ADULTS ABUSED AS CHILDREN ANONYMOUS** can be found on pages xvii and 54. These steps refer to us as adults, not as children. For example, in Step 6 we focus on our character defects as adults, not as children.

If a group meeting is not available to us, it has been demonstrated that others have gone through the 12 Steps of this program successfully without attending meetings. We read about the Step we're working on and journal about it. We might start or join an online meeting as we hear what others experience as well as sharing our stories. We continue to pray and meditate by ourselves or with others. However, it is highly advised to include a mentor, counselor, or trusted friend as we progress through each Step, as we need non-judgmental feedback, support, and encouragement.

Overview of the ADULTS ABUSED AS CHILDREN ANONYMOUS PROGRAM

What is ADULTS ABUSED AS CHILDREN ANONYMOUS?

ADULTS ABUSED AS CHILDREN ANONYMOUS is a program of 12 Steps for adults abused as children to follow to help us heal from our childhood abuse. The program suggests that we attend group meetings on a regular basis, if possible.

We are supported and organized only by our members. The organization operates without any outside funding. Thus, we are a fellowship of men and women who come together with a common issue: we are adults who were abused as children. We have no fees or dues, no pledges to sign, no promises to make to anyone.

As adults abused as children, we may discover a new action we could take or a new attitude we could adopt by listening to others as they work through the 12 Steps themselves. In addition, our shares may help another. The only requirement is the desire to heal. All of the Steps are a suggested program of healing based on the experiences of those who came before us.

As we work through the Steps, we can choose another member of **ADULTS ABUSED AS CHILDREN ANONYMOUS** to be our sponsor. A sponsor is someone we trust who has already worked the Step we are on and can assist us in understanding it for ourselves as we go through it. We always choose who our sponsor is and we can change sponsors for any reason at any time.

The anonymous aspect of the program reminds us that everything shared from one member to another, in the meeting or outside of it, is held in the strictest confidence. In addition, we realize that although we are each unique in our individuality, we are all equal in the program, with none of us being more important or special than another.

As adults we need a safe place where we can go to feel supported, where we can grow and become better informed about the effects that child abuse has had on our lives. We will discover how our past abuse has shaped who we are today as we begin our path to lasting change and find the healing that we have so longed for. This is the goal of the 12 Step program of **ADULTS ABUSED AS CHILDREN ANONYMOUS.**

Vision and Mission Statements of ADULTS ABUSED AS CHILDREN ANONYMOUS

Vision Statement:

We are a vibrant community of adults abused as children who are now leading healthy and satisfying lives. We represent beacons of hope for all.

Mission Statement:

To empower all adults abused as children to create inner peace and lasting change by using the 12 Steps of **ADULTS ABUSED AS CHILDREN ANONYMOUS.**

To inspire people to share their journey of healing from victim to wholeness.

Working the Program of ADULTS ABUSED AS CHILDREN ANONYMOUS

Newcomers often ask, "How do we work the program of **ADULTS ABUSED AS CHILDREN ANONYMOUS**?" We go through the 12 Steps and learn how to structure our lives so we are able to achieve the healing we want.

The most effective way to begin is to go through each Step, preferably in order, beginning with Step 1. Since each Step builds on the ones that follow, we gain understanding from a previous Step in order to work the Step we're on.

Focusing on the Steps is a tool others have found helpful. We do this by reading literature on a particular Step or about a certain situation, journaling about it, and sharing it with someone else.

As we go through each Step, we see how it applies to our lives today and how it sheds light on what it brings up from the past.

Involving others breaks our tendency to isolate. We practice trust, honesty, and courage when we choose to connect with another person. Making phone calls to another member or trusted friend, attending **ADULTS ABUSED AS CHILDREN ANONYMOUS** meetings, listening to others share their experiences, and sharing our own are ways to include others in our program of healing.

Service, or giving of self, offers us the opportunity to make a difference, as well as giving us a way of expressing our gratitude for all we have received. In the program, we might sponsor another member, call someone who needs support, or volunteer at a meeting.

Maintaining our desire and inner passion for happiness by caring about ourselves is the foundation of the program. This desire motivates, fuels, and directs our thinking and our actions.

Repeating meaningful affirmations, praying, and meditating are effective ways to connect with a Power greater than ourselves. We are reminded that with help, we can change. We welcome personal growth knowing it is the key to these changes and we discover choices we didn't even know we had.

We use all these tools to support our aim of rebuilding our lives one day at a time!

Notes

Notes

Introduction — Our Past Abuse

What is Child Abuse?

Child abuse has been described as maltreatment or neglect resulting in the harm of a child. **Each individual decides whether he or she was abused or not.** No one but us may know what really happened and what it was really like. Only we know if we are an adult abused as a child.

Abuse is abuse is abuse.

An individual's abuse is not less significant, or more significant or traumatic, if it happened only once or if it went on for months or even years. It is not about the length of time or the number of times that it happened for the effects to be dramatic. Regardless of the types of abuse, the **results** of child abuse for adults abused as children are far more similar than they are different. There is no hierarchy of trauma in the types of abuse.

Some Types of Child Abuse

- Abandonment
- Cults
- Emotional
- Mental
- Mind Control
- Narcissism
- Neglect
- Physical
- Psychological
- Religious
- Ritual
- Sexual
- Slavery
- Trafficking
- Witnessing abuse
- Witnessing domestic violence

Abuse of any kind is never the abused person's fault.

Notes

Some Effects of Child Abuse

In our earliest years, our caregivers or the adults in our lives shaped our sense of ourselves and the world around us. They did this through their body language, actions and words, by the way they looked at us, the tone of voice they used, their touch and their willingness to comfort us or not. All of these factors and more shaped us.

The abusive events of our childhoods make us more reactive and less adaptive. Many of us are still living in sheer survival mode, regardless of the present circumstances, and we may not even be aware of it.

When the need arises within us to be nurtured or loved, it is confusing to trust that these needs can and will be met. As children, many of us had to deny them in order to survive. We may have lost sight that these needs still exist for us today.

As children, we most likely felt small or unprepared to handle our lives as they really were. As a result, we may tend to minimize our abuse so that we feel up to meeting life's challenges today.

We may be afraid that if we admit how horrible the abuse was, we'll fall apart, unable to put ourselves back together. To complicate things further, we may be living with another devastating effect — the inability to trust ourselves and others.

We may have learned to be afraid to feel and to trust life because we have endured so much pain, leaving us filled with self-doubt, self-loathing, fear, and anger. As a result, some of us question whether life is really worth living.

It is not uncommon for adults abused as children to develop addictions. An addiction is one of the ways we may have found to help us avoid feelings and escape from reality. We developed thought patterns that supported denial and came to believe that we didn't have what it took to deal with life, especially without using something or someone.

Some of us have resorted to self-battering or self-mutilation as a reaction to the pain within us. It's like we're destroying ourselves, tearing ourselves down one negative act at a time. We need help learning how to channel these strong, destructive emotions in new ways to help us overcome any more harm to ourselves or others.

We may have a distorted perception of ourselves, though it is not necessarily about our self-esteem, but about our ability to know who we are in the world. How we appear to others may be very different from how we appear to ourselves. Our own version may be quite jaded; for example, we might think we are stupid while other people would heartily disagree.

All abuse takes a huge toll on a child's sense of well-being. Regardless of the type of abuse, the effects are sadly similar. As adults, working the 12 Steps has been found to be life-changing in dealing with the effects of child abuse.

Other Common Effects of Abuse for Adults Abused as Children

- A tendency to isolate
- Anxiety and/or excessive worrying
- Behavior that is overly compliant and passive, or very demanding, aggressive, and full of rage
- Difficulty in expressing thoughts and feelings
- Discomfort with physical contact or difficulty connecting with others
- Eating disorders
- Extreme obedience or perfectionism
- Increased fear or avoidance of specific people or situations
- Low self-esteem
- Physical, emotional, or intellectual disabilities
- Recurrent memories of the abuse
- Safety issues
- Sleep pattern disturbances
- Strong feelings of shame or guilt
- Substance use

Lexie reveals:
I revisited my past so i could heal:

I used to smash my head against the floor to try and knock some sense into me, or I would take my fists and punch my thighs until they were black and blue. I might even hit the steering wheel over and over with clenched fists, hurting my hands and breaking blood vessels.

Later on, I learned that I had to set limits for my little one, the child inside me who was still in so much emotional pain. I could no longer allow such self-abuse. My little one had no sense of loving my physical body, but my adult learned to develop such caring. My inner parent provided comfort and nurturing for my little one as I healed.

Because I was raised in an environment of constant intimidation, control and sadistic violence, I gave up the ownership of my body to the abusers. I was violated so often and my need to survive was so great, I lost the ability to know my own body and emotions.

Through working the 12 Steps of **ADULTS ABUSED AS CHILDREN ANONYMOUS,** I have been able to recognize the importance of going back and recounting the experiences, acknowledging my own sensations and feelings. Through the 12 Steps, I have regained ownership of and love for my body. I finally found self-love.

One of the reasons for naming and claiming our past abuse is that it gives us a place to start to find some answers to two questions: How did we become the way we are and how does it still affect us today?

Notes

Resources
to Help Us

Feelings, Memories, and Self-Care Strategies

As we begin our journey through the 12 Steps, it is important to stay alert to feelings of anger, despair, and disappointment. They may result in feeling overwhelmed or experiencing great sadness. We may also experience confusion, humiliation, anxiety, shame, or regret. In addition, we may find ourselves full of relief, excitement, forgiveness, hope, or gratitude! These feelings and others are normal.

It is also important to consider that new realizations or memories may surface. It is not uncommon to start to remember things that we hadn't before, especially with regard to our past and past abuse. Some of us want to know everything that happened; however, some individuals don't want any more memories at all. Some of us call them flashbacks.

Memories can appear as intuition, in dreams, as a sense, as a picture, as a trauma or trigger, as a bodily response, and in other ways unique to each of us. They may also show up when others speak of their own experiences.

As we work the Steps we might feel upset or overwhelmed. It is crucial to remember to take care of ourselves. During these times it is helpful to follow some self-care strategies.

Self-Care Strategies

- Acknowledge where you do have real power
- Call a friend
- Cry
- Do some art; color, for example
- Drink some tea
- Eat a well-balanced meal
- Exercise
- Get a hug
- Get a massage
- Give yourself a pat on the back for having the courage to tell the truth
- Give yourself permission to feel bad
- Give yourself permission to feel good
- Journal, then put the pen down and walk away for a time
- Light a candle and stare at the flame
- Make small decisions to get control of your life back
- Meditate
- Nap
- Pound a pillow
- Pray

- Reach out to someone in the Program
- Read inspirational material
- Remember something you do well
- Remind yourself that your reactions are normal
- Shred paper by hand
- Sit and take some breaths
- Take a bath/shower
- Take a walk
- Take breaks from isolation
- Volunteer to help someone else
- Watch a funny movie

Often, when we're triggered, we need to get our focus back on ourselves in the present. Taking an action on our own behalf does just that. These, and other strategies, allow for our true feelings to arise without us being paralyzed or incited to react in an unhealthy manner. Remember, treating ourselves as if we count is a foundation of our healing.

We must assess for ourselves, while working these 12 Steps, if we need additional support from a professional such as a therapist, clergy, or spiritual mentor. We are encouraged to seek and use whatever support we need, as often as we need it.

Notes

Affirmations

As we work through the 12 Steps, we may find that we need to remind ourselves of who we can be — what kind of a person we want to be or can imagine ourselves to be. Affirmations are easy, effective, and powerful as tools for this purpose.

An affirmation is a positive statement of the experience we want to have. To affirm means to declare something is true, even before we may experience it. We can even think of it as something that could be true, such as, "I am peaceful."

Affirmations afford us the opportunity to choose our intentions and then practice living them out. We have choices in how we think and what we tell our minds to focus on. Our minds will try and follow what we want.

When we say affirmations, hear them, or think about them, our thoughts create our reality. They help to steer us in the right direction.

As we practice saying affirmations, we begin to change how we feel. If we are feeling unworthy of good, we might say to ourselves "I deserve the best that life offers me." **We always make our statements in the present tense.**

The more time we spend with positive thoughts, the easier it is to transform our lives into ones that we desire.

Affirmations are an excellent way to be in conscious control of our thoughts.

If it's convenient, for the greatest benefit, we can look in the mirror and say the affirmations out loud to ourselves. Writing an affirmation can increase its power as well. In addition, they are effective when affirming another person's well-being. We might remind ourselves, "Paul has value too." Or we might repeat, "I accept Maggie as she is."

Maggie affirms:

When I am afraid, I may find myself wanting to be in control. As I notice this, I replace my fearful thoughts and feelings with words of faith. They assist me in fixing my mind on peace and away from anxiety.

Sometimes I repeat, "I respond to life with trust and ease." Then my body relaxes, I let go of tension and shift into a state of calmness.

Affirmations for Healing for Adults Abused As Children

1. Life is getting easier.
2. I see my progress.
3. I am enough as I am.
4. I can make a decision to cooperate with a Higher Power.
5. I trust in Source.
6. I give faith a chance.
7. I treat myself as if I count.
8. When in doubt, I love myself.
9. I lead from my heart.
10. My thoughts are Source-directed.
11. I am serene.
12. I love my body.
13. I claim my freedom now.
14. I release old beliefs.

We may feel moved to create affirmations of our own at any point.

Tips, Tricks, and Tools for Working the 12 Steps

1. **We separate the past from the present.** The feelings and thoughts that come forth when we are triggered are most often left over from our past. They may have much less to do with what's happening in the present moment than we realize. It helps to reorient ourselves to the present by remembering this. We may be able to identify a past belief or an experience that caused the current trigger. It would help us to create a more appropriate belief that is relevant for today.

Sharon shares:
When I'm around someone who's very angry, I can get triggered by my fear of getting hurt or that something bad is going to happen. I get overwhelmed from the sense of danger and it throws me back into a past when my life was filled with such terror.

What helps me is to get back into present time as I physically reorient myself to my surroundings. My past belief says that I am not safe, that I am in danger. So I breathe, put my feet on the ground, look around, and remind myself where I am.

I acknowledge my old belief and change it to...I am safe today. The abusers are no longer here.

2. **We ask ourselves are we coming from strength or weakness when we need to make a decision?** If we find we're coming from weakness (like jealousy, anger or envy) we can press pause, if possible, until we can transition back to a place of strength. We can ask ourselves how we're feeling on a 1 to 10 scale, with 10 being the best. If we find we're between 1 and 5 and it's not an urgent decision, we can wait. We can remind ourselves that we don't have to decide anything at all for the moment. We can wait until we feel stronger to make a decision. If we're between 6 and 10, then we can go ahead with choosing what feels right for us.

3. **We check our motives.** When we get in touch with where we're really coming from and how we are really feeling, we start to uncover more about what causes our upsets. We may mistake the actions or words of others as being the cause of our reactions, but in checking our own motives we may determine it was our fear, anger, or disappointment that precipitated our responses. We learn firsthand what triggers us.

4. **We use another Step to help us work the Step we're on.** If we get stuck or confused on a particular Step, we can go back to a previous Step to gain clarity about what is in our way of moving forward. Often, it's one of the first three Steps we need to review since they are the foundation of our healing.

5. **We look at our choices and options.** Others sharing what worked for them under similar circumstances can be helpful to us. We can check to see if we are headed in the desired direction we want to go by assessing our thinking or our actions. Even if we can't think of any options in the moment, it's comforting to remember that they do exist and can be discovered at a later time.

6. **We remember we're human beings.** Being a human being can be challenging sometimes. We're growing and learning new ways of living our lives in a healthy manner. We're asking ourselves to consider new ideas, maybe for the first time. Surrendering, reviewing our lives, and allowing memories and feelings to surface require courage, support, and appropriate self-care. We've never been at this place before in our lives, so we need to be realistic about our expectations of ourselves.

    We also need to remember that the others in our lives are human beings too. Admitting our humanness is essential for us to succeed in having our lives transformed. None of us is perfect; we do our best, one day at a time.

7. **We make "sandwich calls."** When we have a difficult action to carry out we can make a phone call to a support person before and after we take the necessary action. It is a wonderful experience and an action of self-care to reach out to another and feel the support of someone who believes in us. This support enables us to do things we may not have otherwise done on our own.

8. **We raise our consciousness.** In our lives today, when someone else is being petty, demanding, or aggravating, we can choose a "higher" mind-set than the other person's thinking. We can think and act bigger than what's going on in front of us, and in turn, this may prevent unnecessary conflict or lessen our own discomfort.

   When our actions or thoughts are not what we want them to be, or when we are aware of making an undesirable choice like becoming arrogant or intolerant, we can make a conscious decision to go to a place within for higher, inner wisdom. This deepens our self-compassion and understanding.

   Focusing on gratitude or searching for the blessing in a situation can help us shift our perception, strengthen self-awareness, and allow the transition from small-minded thinking or behavior, to thinking and behaving with integrity and greater respect for everyone involved.

9. **We fake it until we make it.** There are only three things we can control: our attitudes, our thoughts, and our actions. We are growing and learning that we can choose a specific attitude, such as "don't take it personally," when our feelings are hurt. And at the same time, we can also carry out a desired attitude by reshaping our actions and not immediately retreat into ourselves or even sulk when we're hurt. Yet, just as often, we may be able to control our actions in the ways we would want, but we are not yet able to adopt the necessary attitude that supports our actions.

Remaining silent when someone says something hurtful to us and not lashing back at them demonstrates control over our actions. However, we might still harbor bad feelings toward that person. We know what mind-set would help us, such as patience, tolerance, or forgiveness but we just can't feel it or create that for ourselves yet. "Fake it until we make it" buys time for us to shift our inner world so we can express how we want to be in the outer world. It means "pretend as if" we can carry out the desired attitude or action…until we really can.

10. **We separate fact from story.** Accepting what really happened and our interpretation of it, helps give us a clearer picture of the truth of our past. We need to admit "what was so" without adding our reactions or assumptions about it.

    As children, we based our beliefs on what we felt or thought at the time, not necessarily on the reality occurring in the moment.

    Johnnie remembers:

    When I was twelve, I was going to run away from home because of my physically abusive mother. My older brother, who was fourteen, wouldn't let me through the front door to leave.

    At the time, I assumed my older sibling's action was because he loved me and didn't want me to leave, only to find out very soon after, that my brother figured he would get in trouble if he let me run away.

I realized that my older brother was just trying to protect himself!

So at twelve, I switched my belief from "the loving brother who didn't want me to leave" and created a new story that proclaimed my older brother didn't care about me at all.

As an adult, I saw how my belief changed the story about what happened. The fact was that my brother prevented me from going through the door; the rest I made up out of the assumptions I made as a twelve-year old.

11. **We create rituals for ourselves.** Many of us grew up feeling that there wasn't a lot we could count on as difficult events or situations may have arisen without any warning or preparation on our part. We often lived in a state of anxiety and fear. As adults, repeating the same satisfying activity over and over again, helps to provide a sense of needed reassurance.

    Rituals, such as taking a bath or a walk, are helpful to remind us that we do have control over some things in our lives today. This can provide us with comfort and enhance our sense of well-being. We are beginning to experience the benefits of our good choices with feelings of inner calm and greater peace of mind. We are grateful to begin to see the beneficial outcomes of our actions through rituals, **before we do them,** which helps to create a sense of security for us. We can become appreciative of the ordinariness in our lives and thankful to finally start to experience the changes we had been longing for. In this way we contribute toward our own restoration of sanity.

12. **We create a physical space for the objects which help us feel good or remind us of what we want to remember.** It can be a shelf, cabinet, box, or altar — anywhere we want to keep the material possessions which are sacred and meaningful to us. Many of us have a statue, picture, or small representation of something we relate to that helps us feel good. It might be a ceramic bear to increase our sense of inner strength or an angel for protection. One member keeps a card out in plain view that says, "I am a little piece of the Source."

    We are encouraged to create and provide whatever helps us connect to the truth of our being and helps bring balance into our lives. Many of us have a set of affirmation cards which we pull daily, or use when we want to. It is for each of us to discover what helps us connect to our good when it is most needed.

13. **We stop lying to ourselves.** Sometimes we tell ourselves things that we know just aren't true. We're afraid to admit that we know the truth or we say to ourselves that we can't do or handle something when we really can. We may not want to admit we can because we may not want to hold ourselves accountable for taking action. Or we may hear

ourselves say that we will do something when we really just don't know how to say "no" yet, such as taking over someone else's responsibilities when we already have a full schedule of our own.

Telling the truth opens the way for a Higher Power to work in us. We are learning how to be generous with ourselves and allow time for the benefits of working the 12 Steps to manifest.

14. **We create games for practicing what we want in our lives.** Being an adult abused as a child can be a heavy thing to deal with. We may perceive life as cumbersome, burdensome, or difficult. Looking at what we work toward as a game, lightens our experience of it.

Alberta plays this game:

When I write or type this year's date, I say to myself "I love myself. I love my body." Then I smile.

I created this game to remind myself of something that was very important to me. After that I found myself spontaneously saying "I love myself" with every mouthful of vitamins I took!

15. **We are specific as we remember and share about our abuse rather than generalize about it.** Being specific about each event allows us to be present with it in a different way than if we lump them all together. Focusing loosens its hold or grip on our emotions and minds. The

charge it has for us can be diminished by looking at each situation at a time.

All of the abuse events did not happen at the same time. Generalizing is not a powerful place for healing to occur.

16. **We practice self-awareness through being conscious of our inner self-talk.** We listen to what we say to ourselves as we go about our day. We discover if it is helpful or harmful to us on our healing journey. We create new inner dialogue if we notice it is not in our best interest. When we are scared, shocked, or make a mistake, it's an ideal time to "listen in" and see if what we are telling ourselves is supporting our healing.

17. **We look for beauty.** It brings us back to our true nature as humans. We see divinity in beauty. Sometimes life seems disappointing or despairing and we lose sight of the good before us. We may have lost a connection to what there is to be grateful for. Beauty is an expression of our Higher Power and reminds us that there is balance in our world.

18. **We focus on what we want.** Our brains will give us evidence for whatever we focus on. This evidence creates our experience of life. If we're looking for good, we see good. If we're looking for bad, we see bad. That's because it's all there, both within and without. So, we might as well look for what we want. We stoke our flames of aliveness and passion. We keep ourselves inspired through the Steps even before results show up.

Some say what we focus on **expands.** If we want to experience life as a gift, we can look for the blessings we already have. If we want peace of mind, we might focus on what brings us peace. We might go within to access the peace that already resides there. We might consider connecting with others with whom we feel peaceful and at ease. Noticing what shows up will reinforce that what we desire is available to us, that we're on the right track.

19. **We live in present time.** To make possible for healing from childhood abuse, it is necessary for us to remember that changes happen in present time only. As adults, it's imperative to want something for ourselves that we haven't been able to attain up until now. Since we want our future to be different in some way than our past, we must keep bringing ourselves back to this moment to actualize it.

    We may be afraid that what we want may never happen, because it hasn't happened yet. Whether we blame ourselves, other people, or outside circumstances for this lack of manifestation, we may lose hope that life could ever be different.

    The only way to make sure that our lives can shift and change is to keep our consciousness in today. We have no power or control over the past or the future. We can only make a difference toward having a different experience of life as we invest in today. We have faith in present time through our faith in our Higher Power.

20. **We have self-compassion.** We honor and acknowledge our emotional needs. As adults, we can learn how to nurture, respect, and love ourselves as we are today. This is the cornerstone of our healing. Self-kindness is being gentle with ourselves when we're feeling emotional pain or discomfort. We understand how scared or angry we might be. We remember all people feel pain. We remain aware and receptive to altering negative thoughts. We do not overidentify with those thoughts and feelings, nor do we deny them. Instead, we replace them with helpful ones which benefit our healing.

These suggestions are some helpful examples which facilitate our moving through the 12 Steps with support, greater ease, clarity, and self-honesty.

Notes

Notes

Meeting Information
for
ADULTS ABUSED
AS CHILDREN
ANONYMOUS

Note to the Reader

The following pages are a guideline for those of us who wish to start on **ADULTS ABUSED AS CHILDREN ANONYMOUS** meeting.

You may contact the author for information and support to facilitate the process. Contact information is at the beginning of the book.

Suggested Meeting Format for ADULTS ABUSED AS CHILDREN ANONYMOUS

Meeting Opening Statement

Read Aloud at Meeting

"We welcome you to the **ADULTS ABUSED AS CHILDREN ANONYMOUS** Meeting, and hope you will find in this fellowship the help and friendship we have been privileged to enjoy.

"We, who have lived with the problem of childhood abuse in our pasts, understand as perhaps few others can.

"We, too, were lonely and frustrated, but in **ADULTS ABUSED AS CHILDREN ANONYMOUS,** we discover that no situation is really hopeless and that it is possible for us to find contentment, and even happiness.

"We urge you to try our program. It has helped many of us find solutions that lead to serenity. So much depends on our own attitudes, and as we learn to place our problem in its true perspective, we find it loses its power to dominate our thoughts and our lives. Our situation is bound to improve as we apply these 12 Step ideas. Without such spiritual help, living with our past abuse issues is too much for most of us. Our thinking becomes distorted by trying to force solutions, and we become irritable and unreasonable without knowing it."

"**ADULTS ABUSED AS CHILDREN ANONYMOUS** program is based on our suggested 12 Steps, which we try, little by little, one day at a time, to apply to our lives. The loving interchange of help among members makes us ready to receive the priceless gift of serenity.

"Ours is an anonymous fellowship, everything that is said here, in the group meeting and member-to-member, must be held in confidence. Only in this way can we feel free to say what is on our minds and in our hearts, for this is how we help one another in **ADULTS ABUSED AS CHILDREN ANONYMOUS.**"

Meeting Guidelines

Read Aloud at Meeting

"These 12 Steps were not meant to be worked through by ourselves. Remember, we are not alone. It is not our job to heal ourselves. This is why it is suggested that we go to **ADULTS ABUSED AS CHILDREN ANONYMOUS** meetings and connect with others who have had similar pasts as our own. Everyone who walks into the meeting is considered a member if they wish to be.

"In the meetings, we are invited to share when we are ready. Many of us have faced difficult, life-long issues related to mistrust, betrayal, isolation, suppression, and poor boundary setting, to name a few. We are supported within the safety of this setting to tell our secrets. As a result we begin to experience the healing that accompanies working the 12 Steps. Through our shared experiences, we help each other feel hopeful and accepted as we are, and our lives change for the better."

Meeting Agreements

Read Aloud at Meeting

"As a group, we agree to the following **during all meetings:**

All sharing within the group will remain strictly confidential.

No one is to give advice. We are here to listen to each other.

No opinions are to be offered relating to what another has shared.

No asking questions of another member relating to what they have shared.

We share only from our own experience.

We don't make references to other 12 Step Fellowships, literature, or outside issues.

We are conscious of the lengths of our shares."

12 Steps of ADULTS ABUSED AS CHILDREN ANONYMOUS

Read Aloud at Meeting

Step 1:

We admitted we were powerless over the past abuse — that our lives had become unmanageable.

Step 2:

Came to believe that a Power greater than ourselves could restore us to sanity.

Step 3:

Made a decision to turn our will and our lives over to the care of God *as we understood Him.*

Step 4:

Made a searching and fearless moral inventory of ourselves.

Step 5:

Admitted to God, to ourselves, and to another human being the exact nature of our wrongs.

Step 6:

Were entirely ready to have God remove all these defects of character.

Step 7:

Humbly asked Him to remove our shortcomings.

Step 8:

Made a list of all persons we had harmed, and became willing to make amends to them all.

Step 9:

Made direct amends to such people whenever possible, except when to do so would injure them or others.

Step 10:

Continued to take personal inventory and when we were wrong and when we made progress, promptly admitted it.

Step 11:

Sought through prayer and meditation to improve our conscious contact with God, *as we understood* Him, praying only for knowledge of His will for us and the power to carry that out.

Step 12:

Having had a spiritual awakening as the result of these Steps, we carried this message to others, and practiced these principles in all our affairs.

Notes

The 12 Traditions of ADULTS ABUSED AS CHILDREN ANONYMOUS

Read Aloud at Meeting

Tradition 1:

Our common welfare should come first; personal progress for the greatest number depends upon **ADULTS ABUSED AS CHILDREN ANONYMOUS** unity.

Tradition 2:

For our group purpose there is but one ultimate authority—a loving God as He may express Himself in our group conscience. Our leaders are but trusted servants; they do not govern.

Tradition 3:

Adults abused as children, when gathered together for mutual aid, may call themselves an **ADULTS ABUSED AS CHILDREN ANONYMOUS** group, provided that, as a group, they have no other affiliation. The only requirement for **ADULTS ABUSED AS CHILDREN ANONYMOUS** membership is a desire to heal from the past abuse.

Tradition 4:

Each group should be autonomous, except in matters affecting another group or **ADULTS ABUSED AS CHILDREN ANONYMOUS** as a whole.

Tradition 5:

Each group has but one primary purpose — to carry its message to the adults abused as children who still suffer. We do this by practicing the 12 Steps of **ADULTS ABUSED AS CHILDREN ANONYMOUS** ourselves.

Tradition 6:

An **ADULTS ABUSED AS CHILDREN ANONYMOUS** group ought never endorse, finance, or lend our name to any outside enterprise, lest problems of money, property, and prestige divert us from our primary purpose.

Tradition 7:

Every **ADULTS ABUSED AS CHILDREN ANONYMOUS** group ought to be fully self-supporting, declining outside contributions.

Tradition 8:

ADULTS ABUSED AS CHILDREN ANONYMOUS should remain forever non-professional, but our service centers may employ special workers.

Tradition 9:

ADULTS ABUSED AS CHILDREN ANONYMOUS groups, as such, ought never be organized; but we may create service boards or committees directly responsible to those they serve.

Tradition 10:

ADULTS ABUSED AS CHILDREN ANONYMOUS has no opinion on outside issues; hence our name ought never be drawn into public controversy.

Tradition 11:

Our public relations policy is based on attraction rather than promotion; we need always maintain personal anonymity at the level of press, radio, TV, films, and other public media.

Tradition 12:

Anonymity is the spiritual foundation of all our Traditions, ever reminding us to place principles before personalities.

Introductions and Announcements

<u>Introductions by first name only:</u> Go around the room and each person who cares to can say their first name.

ADULTS ABUSED AS CHILDREN ANONYMOUS announcements: Ask if anyone has announcements related to our program or meeting.

Now You Are Ready to Hold the Meeting

Suggested Meeting Formats

Given the nature of why we attend, the group may decide that any member may share what is pressing in their lives, though it may not follow the theme of the meeting.

1. **Speaker/Discussion meeting** — a member shares without interruption for 10-20 minutes about their past abuse and/or their present life followed by others sharing about what came up for them from the speaker's share. There is no evaluating or discussing the speaker's life; each person speaks from their own experience.

2. **Read from program literature** — read the **ADULTS ABUSED AS CHILDREN ANONYMOUS** program literature and read aloud a passage, a Step, or a section and each member shares what it brings up for them.

3. **Discuss a specific theme** — members are asked what issue/theme they would like to hear discussed with one theme chosen by majority vote. Examples: surrender, fear, or forgiveness. Members take turns sharing on this topic.

4. **Write for five minutes if you are meeting in person** — each member writes for five minutes on whatever they choose, followed by sharing about what came up for them from the writing. They may choose to read aloud some or all of what they wrote.

Each group can rotate its format as often as desired or choose to follow only one, week after week. The length of the meeting is often between one and one and a half hours. A healthy meeting intends to begin and end on time.

Some meetings have tea or coffee and cookies available, if allowed where the meeting is held. Electronic meetings, Zoom, video, etc work just as well as in-person ones.

Sharing During the Meeting

We remember to speak only about our own lives, past or present. We do not comment on anyone else's share or their life experiences. We do not ask questions, give our opinions, advice, or suggestions to anyone during the meeting. We listen and do not interrupt.

If one member continually monopolizes the bulk of the time for the meeting in their sharing, the Secretary (or anyone present) may speak to this person either during or after the meeting and request that this person remembers to self-monitor the length of their share so others may have a chance to speak.

If someone is "out of order" during the meeting (giving advice, etc.) the Secretary (or anyone present) may gently remind that member to please share from their own life experience instead.

If someone requests emotional help during a meeting, someone can volunteer to escort that member outside of the room and be with them or contact them when the meeting is over.

Many challenges may arise which will require us to seek solutions in respectful and principled ways. We work our Program at the group level using the 12 Traditions to guide us.

Service Positions

The Secretary, Treasurer, and Literature persons commit to serving the group in the ways that the group has defined as their roles. The Secretary runs the meeting and maintains order during it. The Treasurer volunteers to handle paying rent for the room, to collect the money offered in the basket each week from the members, to maintain financial records, and to report the financial information back to the group on a regular basis.

Some groups may elect to have a bank account in its name. The Literature volunteer orders a supply of books that the group has decided it wants available. Ultimately, however, it is each group's responsibility to create and maintain a safe, effective, and orderly space for members to attend.

Monthly (or quarterly) business meetings, which can be held after the regular meeting, can address specific challenges that may arise in the regular meeting. Everyone in the fellowship is invited to attend the business meetings. The 12 Traditions are also helpful to groups as guidelines to follow in making decisions for the unity of the group.

After the Meeting — Closing Statement:

Read Aloud at Meeting

"In closing, we would like to say that the opinions expressed here are strictly those of the person who gave them. Take what you liked and leave the rest. The things you heard here were spoken in confidence. Keep them within the walls of this room and the confines of your mind. A few special words to those of you who haven't been with us long: whatever your problems, there are those among us who have had them too, and if you try to keep an open mind, you will find help. You will come to realize that there is no situation too difficult to be handled and no unhappiness too great to be lessened.

"We aren't perfect. The welcome we give you may not show the warmth we have in our hearts for you, but after a while, you'll discover that though you may not like all of us, you'll love us in a very special way, the same way we already love you. Talk to each other, reason things out with another human being, but let there be no gossip or criticism of one another. Instead, let the understanding, love, and peace of the program grow in you one day at a time."

Optional: Closing Prayer

If someone would like to share with the group, this is the time for a closing prayer.

Notes
___
___
___
___
___
___
___
___

Step 1
Through
Step 12

The Wording in the 12 Steps

"We" is the first word of each of the 12 Steps of **ADULTS ABUSED AS CHILDREN ANONYMOUS.** Even though it is only written out in Step 1, it is implied that "We" begins all the Steps.

We understand that the Steps are not designed to be gone through by ourselves. It is our relationship with a Power greater than ourselves that is paramount to help us create the changes in our lives that we have needed. It is this Power that guides, supports, and helps us through the Steps.

We are not alone. The idea and exploration of this greater Power is up to each of us as individuals. Even then, it is not uncommon for our understanding of this Power to change over time.

Some of the common references that people use to relate to this Power are:

- All That Is
- Beloved
- Breath
- Creator

- Divine Consciousness
- Divine Mind
- God/Goddess
- Great Mystery
- Higher Power
- Higher Self
- Love
- Nature
- Source
- Spirit
- Tao
- Universal Intelligence
- Universe

ADULTS ABUSED AS CHILDREN ANONYMOUS is a non-denominational program. We do not discuss religious views in the meetings.

The pronoun Him and the word God used in the 12 Steps of **ADULTS ABUSED AS CHILDREN ANONYMOUS** have been retained from the original 12 Steps of Alcoholics Anonymous written in 1939.

ADULTS ABUSED AS CHILDREN ANONYMOUS has no opinion on the gender of a Power greater than ourselves.

A sponsor is also a part of the "We," as are all members.

In addition to a Power greater than ourselves, we go through the Steps with other members of the **ADULTS ABUSED AS CHILDREN ANONYMOUS** program.

We are encouraged to ask a specific member to be our sponsor. A sponsor is a trusted member who guides or helps us as we progress through each Step. Ideally, they have been through the Steps themselves. (Some ask a therapist, clergy, mentor, or a trusted friend to be their sponsor, since confidentiality is paramount!)

We all share something in common in this 12 Step group...a childhood of abuse. We connect with others who understand and are "there" for us when we need them.

The Steps were not designed to be done in isolation. Sometimes we need another to hold the space for us to fall apart. However, some of us who do not have access to a meeting will successfully progress through the Steps with another trusted person.

Step 1

We admitted we were powerless over the past abuse – that our lives had become unmanageable.

Step 1

We admitted we were powerless over the past abuse – that our lives had become unmanageable.

Table of Contents

Introduction 73

The First Word Is "We" 75

Kinds of Abuse 76

Powerlessness 78

Admitting 79

Unmanageability 82

Step 1 Summary 88

Step 1 Affirmations 89

Step 1 Journal Questions 90

Step 1 Prayer 91

Note to the Reader

It is highly suggested that we read the Introduction (page 11) and Resources (page 23) to help us before beginning to read and work Step 1. This will help us understand and facilitate our use of the 12 Steps.

Step 1

We admitted we were powerless over the past abuse – that our lives had become unmanageable.

Introduction

The focus of Step 1 is to admit what really happened to us as children and to admit what our lives are like today as a result. If we don't see where the effects of our past are still showing up today, we will keep creating the same dynamic in current situations and be unable to create new experiences for ourselves for a better tomorrow. **It is important that we see the relationship between our past and our present as it relates to all areas of our lives.**

We learn to speak the truth without self-judgment and come to understand that there is no right or wrong about our part in the past. We must begin to recognize the critical voice that resides within us, otherwise we will end up making ourselves wrong. This critical part will hinder our ability to admit and say our truth. Therefore, we simply tell what really happened as we are learning and growing in our trust and acceptance of the truth.

In summary, the real work of Step 1 is to admit how we and our lives are evolving, and begin to share this with others as we become more comfortable speaking about it. We start to understand that we are no longer controlled by the power of others. We also begin to gain greater awareness of our abuse as a child from an **adult** perspective and are able to separate the facts from the stories we told ourselves as a child. These stories were created and believed by us then. However, as adults, it is beneficial to review them and see if they are still accurate.

Alicia's story:

When I was very young, my father abused me and I believed all men were scary. When I grew up and couldn't assert myself around them, I saw I was still living out of that story from my childhood even though the man I was with now treated me with respect.

When I realized I had chosen a safe man to be with and saw that my old story was no longer applicable in my present relationship, I changed the story I told myself about all men. Some men still feel scary, some men do not.

The First Word Is "We"

It is not our job to heal ourselves. It is important to remember that we are not alone in our healing. Ideally, these 12 Steps are not meant to be worked through by ourselves. We are meant to involve our Higher Power in every aspect of our healing through the 12 Steps. This power can assist us to discover new helpful aspects of ourselves and enlighten us toward new ways of handling our lives. We have only to ask or pray for help for this to occur.

It is suggested that we go to **ADULTS ABUSED AS CHILDREN ANONYMOUS** meetings and connect with others who have similar pasts as our own. When ready, we are invited to share our stories and our discoveries about ourselves during the meetings. We are also encouraged to listen to others as well, for this is how we learn. Many of us have faced life-long issues of mistrust, betrayal, isolation, and hardship with setting healthy boundaries. In the group, we can choose to tell our secrets and heartaches about the consequences of our abuse. It is when we explore and begin to understand how these "effects" from childhood shape us today, that we recognize and experience healing. We discover new ways of relating to ourselves and to the world around us. This is how our lives are changed for the better.

Kinds of Abuse

In the **ADULTS ABUSED AS CHILDREN ANONYMOUS** program, we do not distinguish one abuse as being greater or lesser than another. There are many different kinds of abuse and there is no one type of abuse more special or worse.

Our abuse may have included, but is not limited to, one or more of these:

- Abandonment
- Cults
- Emotional Abuse
- Mental Abuse
- Mind Control
- Narcissism
- Neglect
- Physical Abuse
- Psychological Abuse
- Religious Abuse
- Ritual Abuse
- Sexual Abuse
- Slavery
- Trafficking
- Witnessing Abuse
- Witnessing Domestic Violence

We may also have experienced other activities as abusive. It is important not to compare our past abuse with those of other adults abused as children. As adults, we discover that the effects of child abuse are more similar than not, regardless of the kind of abuse experienced. In the most basic ways, we see how alike we are. We have only our experience of abuse, our pain, our knowledge, and memories to draw from; we are the ones who decide whether or not we were abused.

Others in our lives, such as our parents, siblings, and caretakers, may have their own versions of what happened. We may discover that they have distorted views about it and about what happened to us. Sadly, our experience and the impact of our past abuse may not be believed, even by those who witnessed it. They may feel victimized themselves since the experience of witnessing abuse can be very traumatic. Consciously remembering it as it really happened may be too painful for them to admit, and therefore they deny it as real because they cannot remember it.

The confirmation and validation of our child abuse must come from us. We are the ones it happened to; it is sufficient to just admit what we know. Today we are eager to learn new ways of handling life from an updated perspective as an adult.

Powerlessness

The first admission to powerlessness is that we couldn't stop the abuse. What happened when we were helpless children couldn't have been avoided or lessened by us — we were children subjected to abuse by another.

We weren't weak, less than, wrong, or guilty! We were children, overcome in some way. We didn't have what it would have taken for us to stop the abuse or the ability to protect ourselves from it because we were young. Children are not expected to possess such power. We were overcome, overpowered, and overwhelmed; we were child victims then. It was our job to get through it as best we could, in the only ways we knew at the time. We were not responsible for the beginning or the ending of it.

Now, as adults we learn that we're still powerless over the past abuse. An opening to real adult power, however, will eventually appear after we admit our powerlessness over the past. We learn that we are not powerless over our attitudes and our actions in the present. We do not have to accept what is unacceptable anymore.

Admitting

Why do we need to admit that we're powerless over the past abuse?

If we do not admit powerlessness over the past abuse, we will spend our lives trying to control situations or trying to change other people in the present, hungry for experiencing some sense of power. We will never be successful in our attempts to change another person because it's out of our control to do so.

The only person we are able to change, or allow change in, is ourselves. This is why we have chosen to be on a 12 Step path which, if followed, offers us new ways of being and guides us in our healing from childhood abuse.

As children we were victims of abuse, but as adults, we are no longer victims. That is an important point to discern. Our lives will remain stagnant in the areas where we continue to believe we are still victims.

Blaming others or circumstances for our current unhappiness will only prolong the effects of the past abuse. Even as we understand that we are no longer victims, we may not yet know what to do to help ourselves.

When we admit the truth about our past abuse, we begin our journey of healing ourselves.

Many of us have avoided the pain, disappointments, rage, and other emotions that are common in child abuse, and instead we have focused on others and the outside world.

This action of avoiding our feelings has created a life of disconnection and has increased our sense of being alone with the abuse of our childhood. As we begin to tell our stories to one another, we remove ourselves from the isolation we have been living in.

It may be challenging for adults abused as children to admit that we are still powerless over our lives today because we felt so powerless when we were young.

As children, our sense of powerlessness was most likely created by mistaken feelings that may include blaming ourselves or feeling shame that we lacked the power, strength, or willpower to change what was happening to us. As a result, the vast majority of us have grown up being judgmental and critical of ourselves.

It takes a lot of courage to admit powerlessness, as it can conjure up fear, stress, confusion, anger, and many other emotions. We remember we are not alone as we do Step 1.

Unmanageability

Our lives had become unmanageable — what does unmanageability look like?

The next journey in Step 1 guides us to take a look at where our lives today are either out of control, out of balance, or creating misery for ourselves or others. This is what is meant by an unmanageable life in Step 1.

> **Loretta experiences unmanageability:**
>
> *One of the things I lived with as a child was my mother threatening to kill me. She told me how she would do it and threatened to kill herself too. She made it clear that when we died, it would be my fault. The fear of physical death was very real to me; it was so pervasive that talking about it would have been superfluous. It was simply the nature of my reality. I think of it as walking into a lit room, but not talking about the light being on in the room. It was just the way it was.*

Growing up in an abusive environment can lead to distorted views of reality and confusion about what are healthy and normal ways of relating. As a result, we might have had the mistaken belief that "love" is the absence of violence or "love" is attention of any kind given to us by another, whether healthy or harmful. In addition, we may still have trouble with authority figures, face issues of mistrust and fear others, or have difficulty maintaining relationships. Our unmanageable lives can appear in a variety of ways.

As adults, we may still live in a state of heightened anxiety, uncertainty, confusion, and fear, especially as we relate to new situations. Our increased state of vigilance and our mistrust of the world and others may lead us to tread as if we are walking on eggshells. We may be careful to a fault and limit our ability to relax and enjoy the present moment.

As children, many of us needed to be silent about what happened in order to survive. Thus, as adults, we may still be afraid of using our voices. Instead, we hide rather than risk being noticed. Being noticed may have been extremely dangerous when we were children.

Many of us grew up believing and experiencing that we didn't matter, that we were a burden or unwanted. We may feel that our feelings, needs, and words still don't matter today.

We may feel we are unlovable, that there must be something wrong with us. As children we became "good girls or good boys" trying to make up for our perceived shortcomings. As a result, we may be the adult today who needs to help when it's not necessary. We may be driven by feelings that we are not good enough, that we are damaged goods or unlovable unless we are pleasing others.

Healthy life experiences may have been missing, contributing to our lack of normal developmental growth. The area of our lives most impacted by this is our ability to form healthy, trusting, loving relationships.

We may discover we don't know how to show affection, or that we are terrified to love and be loved. We may not know how to nurture, show empathy, or compassion.

Lastly, we might have survived our childhood by being forced to serve another in an excessive manner. Thus we continue the role of caretaker today. We may not know how to really take care of ourselves or even give ourselves permission to do so. These are some of the effects that the past abuse have had on our lives, resulting in unmanageability today.

Gloria admits:

I had such low self-esteem that whatever I did, I had to do well just to prove that I was okay. I tried to be good at everything and to become perfect at it. I tried too hard to have some identity of my own, other than just serving others.

We are the cause of our changes

Without being willing, ready, and able to have a better life today, and to be truly in the moment, we will have no choice but to think and make decisions in our present lives similar to the ones we made in our past. If we continue, our future will look like our past. We will lead lives of frustration and angst trying to control people, places, and things outside of ourselves. We might force ourselves, others, or life events in a direction that is not for the highest good.

Our part in creating our new lives includes clearing up the past as adults, by telling the truth, and by creating possibilities for new experiences to appear. We do this through a change in attitude and openly growing and learning how to take "right actions" for our highest good.

Trying to control our lives or others' lives makes our lives unmanageable

The need to control our lives or others is often an attempt to cover up the real feelings that we have long avoided. Trying to control gives us a false sense of power, and up until now, we may have felt we had very little power. Given the experiences of our childhood and feeling so powerless then, we may cling to what we perceive as power today by trying to control or manipulate.

Looking at the unmanageability asks us to make an honest appraisal of our adults lives and behavior. For many of us, such honesty is new territory. In Step 1 we see and experience the need to begin admitting and open ourselves to the truths of our past and our present.

Angie offers:

In my family, there was so much violence with its accompanying noise and high volume, my mother screaming and shrieking, that the only option I had was silence. I felt I needed to maintain it, even though she increased her attacks on me to try to break my silence. It was the only way I could balance the chaos in my world. I felt so helpless and ineffective that I hid my opinions, my thoughts, even my personality, and tried to be what others wanted me to be.

I had spent a lifetime controlling, hiding, and silencing myself. As an adult, I have had to learn to have a voice, when to speak up, to surrender control, to tell the truth, and risk being seen.

Ryan learns:

It's taken me a long time to learn how to live with people who don't live the way I do. They either don't know how or don't want to embrace what's important in life to me. I've dealt with a lot of disappointment about this and am learning to accept life on life's terms. I need to take my focus off others and put it back on me. My only job is to be true to who I am and express it in my life.

Step 1 Summary

Wanting Something Better for Ourselves

There is one last requirement to begin our healing, and that is the need to want to feel better, to live a better or improved life in some way. We cannot skip over wanting something more for ourselves, such as: a desire for peace of mind, to become a true friend to ourselves, to improve our relationships with others, or to grow to trust life. We decide what it is we want.

Most of all, **we need to treat ourselves as if we count,** otherwise, change won't happen and our experience of life will remain the same. Our transformation comes through the door of self-compassion which helps shift our feelings, thoughts, and attitudes about ourselves, our lives, and the world we live in. Compassion is the kind and gentle willingness to accept ourselves as we are, unchanged.

Step 1 Affirmations

1. I am learning to trust others.
2. I admit with honesty what really happened.
3. I love myself as I am.
4. I am learning to appreciate my body as it is.
5. I am powerless over the past abuse.
6. I am courageous.
7. I am no longer silent.
8. I have what it takes to handle life today.
9. I am able to change.
10. I am not alone.
11. I am no longer a victim.
12. I am lovable.
13. I live in the present.

Step 1 Journal Questions

1. Notice where the past is still showing up in the present. Pick at least one thing that is happening in my life that isn't the way I want it to be. What action could I take that would help me change this area to be the way I would like it to be?

2. What secret is the hardest to admit? Why?

3. What progress am I experiencing as a result of shedding some light on an aspect of myself or my past that had been previously hidden or unclear?

4. Where am I no longer experiencing life as a victim today?

5. What am I doing today to try to get others to love me?

6. How am I creating safety for myself in my relationships? What healthy boundaries am I setting?

7. Which self-care strategy would be helpful today?

Step 1 Prayer

Dear Spirit,

You know how hard it's been for us living with the abuse that happened in our childhoods. We'll be going along just fine in our current lives and BAM some event occurs and the effects of the abuse are right inside or right in front of us in the present! We can become triggered and often surprised by the impact the past abuse has on us after so long a time.

Not only were we powerless in all ways while the abuse was happening, but even today, as adults, we're powerless over it coming up again! Our adult lives definitely can become unmanageable.

Pausing and assessing ourselves and the situation can help us get back into the present moment. We become curious about what we reacted to. We discern what we need to do to take care of ourselves.

We need a Power greater than we are, especially when our lives become unmanageable. Thank you, Higher Power, for being there for us.

And so it is.

Amen.

Notes

Notes

Step 2

Came to believe that a Power greater than ourselves could restore us to sanity.

Step 2

Came to believe that a Power greater than ourselves could restore us to sanity.

Table of Contents

Introduction 99

Beliefs 100

Came to Believe 105

What Is a Power Greater Than Ourselves? 107

Restoration 110

Restored to Sanity 112

Step 2 Summary 116

Step 2 Affirmations 118

Step 2 Journal Questions 119

Step 2 Prayer 120

Step 2

Came to believe that a Power greater than ourselves could restore us to sanity.

Introduction

In Step 1, we deepened our admission of being powerless and realized that our lives had become unmanageable as well. We have begun to see how our past beliefs affect our current lives and we are becoming more aware of how old patterns are often in the way of us living happy and fulfilled lives today.

We remember that healing is a process that takes time and are beginning to explore, believe, and trust in a Power greater than ourselves that can restore us to sanity. We may experience the presence of a Higher Power doing for us what we could not have managed to do for ourselves. Trusting helps to create the possibility for healing, hope, peace, and love to be truly available to us. This is the miracle that awaits us through the 12 Steps!

Beliefs

Step 2 leads us to hope and opens us to possibilities

The lesson in Step 2 is that healing cannot be found or achieved through our efforts alone, but through the belief in a Power greater than ourselves that can do it with us or for us.

As we begin to understand how unmanageable our lives have really become after we have completed Step 1, we don't want to stay in the misery or unhappiness that we admitted to in our present lives. We are awakening to the possibility that we can truly change. Yet, until now, we had not been able to effect the changes we desired. We have most likely discovered that our lives are quite depressing, discouraging, frightening, or just plain overwhelming. We have begun to openly explore them without self-criticism and judgment. Instead we have chosen to come from a place of self-honesty.

We need something "bigger" than we are to help us. What we really want is some relief from the effects of our child abuse, some options we hadn't been able to see or actualize on our own. It is for this very practical reason that we come to believe in something greater than ourselves so we can make peace with our past. Step 2 offers us that hope.

As Colleen states:

My childhood was sordid, a "bizarre" world. White seemed black and black seemed white, everything seemed backwards to me. Telling the truth didn't work, but lying did; when I risked telling the truth, bad things happened to me.

A belief is something we accept as true

Step 2 is a journey and an opportunity to end our old patterns, to examine our beliefs, and to begin to create new ones. **A belief is something we tell ourselves is so.** Changing our beliefs begins with us discovering and exploring what they actually are and learning or admitting how they impact us. When we make decisions, we check in with our belief systems because they formulate our values, our attitudes, and our opinions.

Jordan states:

I thought that in order for my life to be manageable, I had to change what was going on around me; I had to change all the violent people and change the violence itself. No matter how hard I tried, I couldn't eradicate all the violence I saw.

As an adult, going through the 12 Steps helped me see that I could live in a world with violence in it. I worked to discover and create skills and abilities to help me deal with a world I could not control. I learned how to be calm when others were upset; I saw I could develop patience, tolerance, and faith. I experienced my own bravery and began to see that my life could work even though the world outside of me had not been altered.

As I come to believe that I have what it takes to handle life as it is, it is easier for me to do the "will" of my Higher Power. Even though I'm powerless over the abuse of my past and the abusers themselves, I can still be sane today. I can have a sound body, mind, and emotions, and enjoy a balanced and harmonious life. That's what I mean by sanity.

When we were children we might have been told we were stupid, ugly, or lazy, and later we may have come to believe this as well. We notice how these thoughts governed our attitudes and actions. We may have held ourselves back from applying for a job or promotion, believing we were not smart enough. We may have created the belief that we were unlovable or undeserving of love because of the abuse itself.

In Step 2 we begin to explore how such thoughts led us to repeat the very same lies to ourselves. Now, when we recognize the power of what we say, we become more disciplined in our self-talk and more conscious of using statements which support the kind of person we want to become or discover that we already are.

We may have accepted thoughts or ideas as true which are not founded on current reality. It is very likely that we still hold beliefs from our childhood abuse that were created from the perspective of our young minds and, in turn, drew conclusions and made assumptions not based on fact.

As adults, we need to review our past and look for assumptions we are still holding on to that hold us back in unproductive ways. As we do this, we remember that changing our beliefs takes time.

As adults abused as children we may not have spent much time before this looking at our thoughts or examining how we feel about ourselves or even about life itself. Many of us have been conditioned to listen to and watch others, to follow their lead and not consider our own inner promptings.

In Step 2 we deepen our inner listening so we can discover whose beliefs and thoughts we are living out. Too often we repeat the very same lies, stories, and attitudes about ourselves that were told to us by others.

Fake it till you make it

In the **ADULTS ABUSED AS CHILDREN ANONYMOUS** 12 Step program, we often "fake it till we make it." In other words, if we've been telling ourselves we were stupid in the past, now we are beginning to tell ourselves we have what it takes to apply for that new job or promotion. At first, we don't have to really believe, we only have to pretend as if we do and take appropriate action. In time, we see we had more inner resources than we realized and were able to make decisions not based on past beliefs, but instead, on current possibilities.

Most often our old beliefs included ones such as:

- I am weak.
- If only I had…
- I am not lovable.
- I was bad.
- It was my fault.
- The world is not a safe place.

We have ample opportunity to change these beliefs. As we work the Steps and gain clarity, it will become more evident which beliefs need to be reassessed and which ones are still applicable.

Came to Believe

Step 2 does not say that "we believe" — it says that "we came to believe"

Coming to believe is a process, not an event. It may take some time for us to trust any Power greater than we are. As children we may have seen our abusers as Powers greater than we were, but now that we are adults we can begin to consider the idea of a benevolent greater Power.

We can take the time we need to come to believe in this benevolent Power. Some of us may see this Higher Power as being within us; some of us view it as outside of ourselves; some of us don't know where it is or yet what it is. **It does not matter how we envision this Higher Power as long as we know that we are not "it."** We come to a place of acceptance and willingness to simply believe that there is one that can restore us one day at a time.

This belief in restoration can lead us to questions such as:

- What are my beliefs and how do they impact my life?
- What is the power of believing?
- What is needed to believe?
- How long does it take to believe?
- What does a Power greater than ourselves have to do with child abuse?

- Where and how do we make this connection to a Higher Power?
- What does a Power greater than ourselves mean to us?
- How does a Power greater than ourselves relate to the 12 Steps?

These questions and many others help us grow and guide us toward a connection with a Higher Power, while deepening our discovery of what this Power is for us. We may decide to journal about what arises and share our thoughts with a sponsor or a trusted friend.

The Step 2 quest of "coming to believe" helps us begin to discover how this Higher Power helps in making our lives more manageable.

What Is a Power Greater Than Ourselves?

Some of the common terms that people use to relate to this Power are:

- All That Is
- Beloved
- Breath
- Creator
- Divine Consciousness
- Divine Mind
- God/Goddess
- Great Mystery
- Higher Power
- Higher Self
- Love
- Nature
- Source
- Spirit
- Tao
- Universal Intelligence
- Universe

If we don't have any sense of a Power greater than ourselves, it can be helpful to ask ourselves what we would **like** this Higher Power to be. We believe in that choice of a Higher Power until a new understanding emerges. We can have faith and receive help from a Higher Power even though we may not yet have figured out our sense of the source of that power.

In the **ADULTS ABUSED AS CHILDREN ANONYMOUS** program it is not uncommon for some of us to use the collective wisdom of the 12 Step group as a Power greater than we are. The idea and exploration of what a Power greater than ourselves means to us can change over time — many times. Remember this is a nondenominational program; we each decide for ourselves what a Higher Power is.

Why is the idea of "greater" necessary for our healing? We want our lives to change and we want to be more authentic in those lives. Up until now, we have not been fully successful accomplishing this on our own. Our personal efforts, though well-intentioned, are not enough to affect the kinds of changes we want.

For our transformation to occur, we need to expand our thinking and possibilities. We allow new ways to come forth as we begin our path. We may need to release our hold on the ways we've put "life" together. We may also need to release our hold on whom we think we should be or could have been. Who we thought we were, and who we wound up being, may need to be updated, as well.

We may need to let go of traits that are standing in our way. We want to manifest the changes that will benefit our lives. We need to let go of judgment, righteousness, and our critical nature. We are powerless over eradicating these on our own, or even coming to a place of balance. Often these traits are left over from our childhood abuse and can be healed.

When we allow connection with a Power greater than we are, our complete healing is possible. We learned that we take part in our healing by creating an inner consciousness of expansion where new "good" can show up. Our lives are not fixed. They are open to being created with the help of something greater than our human selves.

Restoration

A Power greater than ourselves does the restoration

Not only are we powerless over our past abuse, we are also powerless over restoring ourselves to a way of being and living that works for us and others in our lives. We have found it necessary to imagine our restoration being done by a Higher Power.

Working the 12 Steps allows the restoration to happen within us and can appear as inner peace, increased self-esteem, and healthy decision-making. We don't wait to go to our Higher Power until we are improved, changed, or "look better." We learn to trust that this Power accepts us as we are. It is our own lack of feeling lovable that would hold us back.

Restoration implies that we were once whole

Very few of us come into this program feeling good about ourselves. At first, the whole concept of being restored may be foreign to us. We may have no association with this experience of restoration or wholeness. However, it implies that we were "whole" at some point in our past, even if we can't remember when.

Step 2 tells us that we can be returned to that state. We used to believe that it was our responsibility to make ourselves whole. Now we are offered help to lead more balanced lives. In time, we go within and experience a sense of reassurance and comfort and begin to have some peace of mind in the good times and the tough times as well. **We start to discover and accept that we do have what it takes to handle our lives today.** We discover this through the restoration process that begins in Step 2.

Restored to Sanity

"A Power greater than ourselves can restore us to sanity." The term sanity in this Step is not a clinical definition as it relates to mental health. Sanity in Step 2 refers to the state of being where we respond appropriately to life from a place of wholeness, balance, or harmony. As adults, we can learn how to foster healthy thoughts, feelings, and actions and how to have them become a part of our daily lives.

> ### Jackie's Questions
>
> *One of the thoughts that comes up for me after I say that I can be restored to sanity is "I wasn't the insane one! They were. There's nothing the matter with me. My abusers were the ones who were cruel and unbalanced, so why do I need to be restored to sanity? What about them?"*

Being restored to sanity does not imply that we were insane as children, but rather that **our lives were lived in unnatural and unbalanced ways from the child abuse.** And still, as adults, our decision-making may not be in our best interest nor aligned with current reality. This is the insanity referred to in Step 2 as we begin to see where we have been affected by child abuse when we didn't even realize it. We didn't know there was a saner way to live, but now we have the 12 Steps and can begin to imagine some peace in our lives. We allow the restoration of our minds. We see our thinking needs to be aligned with choices for our highest good, and we learn to take action out of these new realizations.

Sane living is possible by remembering that we need to treat ourselves as if we count! We "come to believe" that we matter and treat ourselves as if we do. As we care about ourselves and our well-being, we are motivated to come to believe in a Higher Power. We invite restoration which will allow the healing that happens as a result of these new beliefs. We exercise faith in our ability to be part of the healing.

Restoration Can Be Like This for Bobbie

I'd been listening to my mental chatter and discovered that hundreds of times a day I had been saying to myself, "I don't care." Obviously it was a very old habit that I created to protect myself. "If I don't care, then I won't get hurt or feel pain."

I believed that caring involved pain and I wanted to avoid that. These days, when I hear myself say this old belief, I silently repeat a new phrase, "I do care and I won't necessarily get hurt."

Or for Charlie:

Abuse is insane. It's not the natural way of the universe and it's not natural for one person to treat another as if they are expendable, easily discarded, or discounted. It's an unsound and insane way to be heartless and cruel and any person who acts in this manner is abusive. From my father's perspective, I was expendable. My physical safety, mental sanity, and emotional stability were expendable to him. My life had no value in his world; he only valued himself and his needs.

The truth is, that he was no more valuable than I, and for me to believe otherwise would be unsound thinking on my part. There is no hierarchy of the value of individuals. It is not the natural order of things. Therefore, when I treat myself as less important than another, I call that unsound thinking (insanity) and need to remember that ultimately we're all created equal and treat myself as if I count too.

Step 2 reminds us that our Higher Power is the source of our restoration to sanity. We can go to our Higher Power when we're feeling insane and ask for help. It also helps us to distinguish when others are acting insanely. When they do, we choose not to participate with them while they are acting this way. Our healing helps us become centered, balanced, and able to maintain a state of clear thinking, not engaging in others' insanity.

Step 2 Summary

Hope and belief

Hope and belief are huge leaps in consciousness for adults abused as children. We have lived in unmanageability for so long we may not have known there was another way. Now we experience hope when we go to meetings or when we speak with other adults abused as children. We hear of their progress and witness their lives improving through working the 12 Steps. We begin to believe that the Steps can work for us too and we can be happy. This may be the first time we ever imagined "improvement" for ourselves and thus, through the process of restoration, we can imagine having more joy and fewer struggles in our lives.

Faith can help us discover we have choices

The experience of faith is one of awakening and realizing we have choices in deciding what to believe. We give ourselves permission to make conscious choices on our behalf, for our best interest and greatest good. It can be a monumental moment when we discover that we can and are supposed to make choices for our own betterment!

It is actually our responsibility as adults to help make our lives more manageable by updating our beliefs. We begin to uncover more about ourselves and live more authentically when we choose to release our false beliefs.

Faith is the path of free choice

Faith is the place where we exercise our will, where we make choices and decisions not based on facts, proof, or experience, but rather from that place of deep, inner knowing that a certain choice or way is right for us.

When it is challenging to have faith in ourselves, we can have faith in, and go to, a Power greater than ourselves until our faith in ourselves returns. Our journey of healing is not necessarily a straight path. It is more like a wave; our progress rises and falls as we continue.

We choose faith as part of our foundation of healing. We don't say our Higher Power will restore us to sanity, but that it **can** restore us. We have a part in our own recovery from the child abuse of our past as we allow emotional, physical, and spiritual help.

Step 2 Affirmations

1. I am restorable.
2. I give faith a chance.
3. My Higher Power has no limits.
4. My thoughts create my world.
5. I have what it takes to handle my life.
6. I am enough as I am.
7. I look for new possibilities in my life.
8. I leave abusive situations with ease.
9. I treat myself as if I count.
10. I protect myself from abusive people.
11. I am no longer a victim.
12. I let nature takes its course.
13. Restoration is a process.

Step 2 Journal Questions

1. Who or what do I think a Higher Power is?
   Who or what am I afraid it is?

2. Who or what would I like a Higher Power to be and why?

3. Do I believe my thoughts and feelings create my reality?
   Do I notice a dominant theme in my thinking?
   Is it helpful?

4. What do I believe I deserve?

5. What would I be like if I were restored?

6. What progress have I already made in being restored?

7. How do self-care and self-love help me to be renewed and allow my very nature to be transformed?

8. What would a sane life look like?

9. How are my needs being met by a Power greater than I am?

Step 2 Prayer

Higher Power,

We trust that you have a plan for each of us to discover and follow. When we are confused or lose our way, we trust you are there to guide us toward what is best for us and what we need to know. We have only to bring our attention to our minds or hearts to consciously connect with you.

In the quiet we are given direction, new ideas, inner strength, or the courage to move forward. All our needs are met. You are our hope for a fulfilled future. We are learning to trust your help, though sometimes we allow change very slowly.

Please be patient with us; we are doing our best. Our challenges seem very large to us. We become overwhelmed or despondent sometimes. We need you to be able to create new ways of handling life for us.

We know we are not alone. Please show us the way...Thank you.

And so it is.

Amen.

Notes

Step 3

Made a decision to turn our will and our lives over to the care of *God as we understood Him.*

Step 3

Made a decision to turn our will and our lives over to the care of *God as we understood Him.*

Table of Contents

Introduction 127

What Does It Mean to Turn Over Our Will? 129

Surrender 134

We Love Ourselves 141

Our Understanding of a Higher Power 144

Making a Decision —
We Discover that We Have Choices 146

Step 3 Summary 150

Step 3 Affirmations 151

Step 3 Journal Questions 152

Step 3 Prayer 153

Step 3

Made a decision to turn our will and our lives over to the care of *God as we understood Him.*

Introduction

As adults abused as children, we want the unmanageable parts of our lives to be transformed and bring us less strife. Through the journey of Steps 1 and 2, we discovered that we are connected in our humanity and share even more in common than we might have thought. We have opened to the discovery of powerlessness over our past abuse, and we have also begun to recognize that faith of some kind, if only in the Steps themselves, is possible for us. These levels of awareness did not require action, only acceptance. In Step 3 we begin to make decisions that will change our lives.

If we don't admit the unmanageability and come to believe we can be restored, we will remain stuck in our experience of unhappiness. Once again, Step 3 is motivated by wanting something better for ourselves. In this Step, our desires and our willingness are the doorways to our true power, power to choose the kinds of lives we want and power to be the kinds of people we want to be. These new desires motivate us and are the foundation of our strength to open to a Power greater than ourselves — "God *as we understood Him.*"

We sense that there is more "good" awaiting us and we want that "good." Why else would we make a decision to turn our lives and our will over to any concept of a Power greater than us? It is the desire and willingness to change that moves us forward.

This Step calls us to a decision. We must be willing to consider surrendering our will because it can block our opening to a Higher Power. We are eager to explore how we are able to let this Power in. Step 3 is our first real attempt to do this. The effectiveness of our journey through the 12 Steps will rest upon how well and earnestly we have tried to come to a decision to let go.

What Does It Mean to Turn Over Our Will?

Most often we recognize self-will as what we want, how we determined things should be. Our will is based on how we thought life should have turned out — our version, our vision, our way. When we release our hold, our will, on insisting that others or life be a certain way, and turn our will over to a Higher Power, we call this decision the act of surrender. Through acts of surrender our actions follow the most important key in this Step — a willingness to turn things over. Often, we will find ourselves remaking this decision and recommitting to this willingness on a daily basis.

As we begin to allow a Higher Power to be in charge of changing us and our lives in the ways we had hoped for, we deepen our faith. This helps open the way to a better understanding of this Power. This Step 3 decision changes us in ways we could not have imagined.

There are so many things we may want: to find or restore hope, to experience healing or peace of mind, to have more faith, or to discover how to live a different kind of life. It is the willingness to follow a path that leads us toward what we want. Surrendering to a greater Power helps us succeed. As we continue to practice this, our uncertainty and fears begin to fall away. They are replaced with a sense of the will this greater Power has for our lives and for us. This understanding of God's will does grow stronger over time. All we need to do is begin where we are.

Alice offers:

After I discover what I want, I turn it over to the care of my Higher Power because the truth is, I'm not sure that what I want is the best thing for me. In the past what I wanted was to feel good and I wasn't very selective as to how I accomplished fulfilling that desire. Now I realize that many of the ways were unhealthy, but they were all I knew. Being an adult abused as a child hadn't taught me healthy ways to feel good about myself.

To begin to experience turning our will and lives over to a Higher Power, it might be best to turn over some small matters first. An example of a small thing might be when our children call us on the telephone, we turn over our desire to complain out loud that it's been a long time since they called us. We might even ask our Higher Power to help us not bring the subject up at all. It's still challenging, but more doable. Even a small thing can appear big to us when we're feeling unsure about ourselves or judgmental of others.

It may be wise to wait until we're feeling stronger, more aligned with the will of a Higher Power before we take on larger issues. As we increase our admitting, our accepting, and our ability to surrender, we will discover new areas of our lives that need to be released. An example of a big thing can be: to stop hating your mother because she beat you as a child. The ability to release this hatred will be realized as we face our feelings and our fears honestly and become willing to surrender the hate to our Higher Power. This is the practice of Step 3. Willingness is what moves us along our path of healing from the effects of child abuse.

Why does turning our will over help to make our lives work?

As we align our minds and hearts with what's really possible for us, we become available and open to something greater than we are. Our needs are met in the present as we release our hold on the past. Alignment of heart and mind has many possible expressions: it can be the willingness to let go of our way, being open for change to happen, being accountable for our part in the present, or following the guidance of a Higher Power.

> **A Step 3 Share from Audrey:**
>
> *I'm being asked to align my will with that of my Higher Power. I have a will; everyone who has a life has a will. I see it as a little dynamo, a little engine inside. When I'm in alignment with God's will, I'm being as true to myself as I can be. I don't have to know what God's will is; I don't have to have that figured out. I only have to be willing to admit powerlessness and be willing to believe that there is a greater Power that can restore me to wholeness.*

When we don't wait for clarity or guidance from a Higher Power but instead take back control, it's still us determining what the help we receive should be. Unfortunately in doing so, we may block a far better response altogether. In those moments, our "insane" thinking has decided that we know more than the Higher Power does and we limit the possibility of something better coming into our lives. We need to find our own personal way to align our minds and hearts so that we can let go and turn again to that Power. We create the lives we want by allowing God to work in them.

We turn over that which we cannot do for ourselves

Step 3 reminds us that we, the more resourceful part of ourselves at least, can tell our minds what to focus on and not allow our fears or anger to determine our choices. Instead, we grow to trust that we can actually tell ourselves what we're going to choose. Then we turn over that which we cannot do for ourselves and ask for help from a greater Power. We give instructions to our minds, create intentions for ourselves, and follow them. We set our intention to be guided by this greater Power and remember there is no special way to surrender. We don't have to be **able** to turn anything over; we just need to make the decision to do so. We may believe that if we surrender "right," we'll get certain results. Again, that is us trying to get what we want. We can't control surrender.

The actions that lead us to true surrender are admitting we are powerless and counting on our faith to strengthen us. We turn our thoughts over to keep our minds open, since our old thinking can block us and keep us from receiving new possibilities from our Higher Power. Our footwork is to align our minds and hearts with the Higher Power's will for us and receive the results of releasing that which we cannot handle ourselves.

Surrender

How do we surrender? How do we turn over our will and our lives to a greater Power? We do this by "setting a policy" in our minds and giving our minds a direction to follow. Through our prayers and intentions, we ask to be able to surrender to a Power greater than ourselves and find healing. Surrender is a willingness to let go of our way of thinking and behaving. It unlocks keys that help us discover new and healthy ways of being.

Working Steps 1 and 2 has revealed to us more of who we "really" are and were meant to be. This is called being authentic. When we surrender, we are becoming more authentic. In the process of turning over the unmanageable parts (and even the manageable ones) new sides of ourselves are revealed and we surrender those as well. **Being authentic is all the Higher Power ever asks us to be.**

Being who we are is the highest gift we could give to ourselves, to others, or to life itself. We are meant to be honest about who we have become and accept it. Because of our past, some of us thought we had to get over being who we really are, but we learn all we have to do is to be true to ourselves and have faith in the Steps.

Being authentic helps to create manageability by helping us accept life and be honest with ourselves. We have been given all that we need to express our authenticity in the world. We turn over our wills one day at a time and use the power that our faith offers us.

Our willingness, our faith, and our trust are keys to surrendering so that the changes we want can show up.

What has our will been holding on to in an attempt to protect us from further hurt and harm? The answer is feelings, beliefs, attitudes, behaviors, and thought patterns that have made our lives unmanageable. It is important to know that feelings of doubt, shame, criticism, fear, rage, confusion, or judgment may arise as we surrender. We bring such feelings, our negative attitudes, unhealthy behaviors, and destructive patterns to our Higher Power. We ask for help, clarity, and guidance.

As we progress in Step 3, we will experience our own spiritual awakening in relationship to this Higher Power. It can be as simple as being deeply inspired to take quiet moments to reflect or pray and to make our wellness a focus through our willingness to surrender.

Shana learns:

I don't have to live an unmanageable life today because my parents were child abusers. That's what they did. Now I ask myself, what would I like my life to be about as an adult? My life can be about anything I want. The shift in focus is from what I don't want, to what I do want!

Turning our will over to a Power greater than ourselves is a process, not an event

There are many unmanageable aspects of our lives that we may need to turn over to a Power greater than ourselves. One such aspect may be a tendency to be unkind toward ourselves. In Step 3 we are encouraged to turn over our unkindness to a Higher Power. We set our intention to invite feelings of kindness within, to practice acting from kindness, and to notice when others are being kind. We don't have to have any idea how this will happen or to orchestrate it.

Eventually kindness will become more second nature to us! All we have to do is ask for help and be willing to allow the guidance of this Power to make it so in us. By having made the decision to surrender this aspect of ourselves, we are more able to follow our kind intentions from within.

The Higher Power will help our eyes to notice, our ears to hear, and our hearts to feel this kindness. All of this will strengthen that nature within us that has been waiting to be expressed. This is the restoration referred to in Step 2.

As we begin to sense the presence of our will and experience the letting go of its control, we open further to opportunities to heal. We become less resistant and feel our faith increase over time. We are able to start focusing on how we want to be and allow our Higher Power to make it possible for us to change.

As we practice Step 3, we sometimes find that our thoughts about this decision lead us to believe that we have to turn over our whole lives perfectly, right now. The truth is we do this one day at a time, and in many cases we turn over the same thing repeatedly.

When we begin Step 3, most of us have no idea what turning our lives and will over really means, feels like, looks like, or how to do it. We do not as yet know what it will come to mean in our lives. We learn that we can take small steps, breaking down the surrendering of our unmanageable areas into bite-sized pieces without our need to know the outcome. Through this process we develop greater trust and faith.

In Step 3, we can make our lives more manageable by focusing on each aspect of what we want or need to change as it arises. By exploring our physical lives, sexual lives, financial lives, and our emotional lives, we are reminded that surrender cannot be done all at once. It is truly a process and a day-by-day journey.

In Step 3, we keep it simple and workable as we willingly explore the abuse that happened to us, how we were affected as children, and how we are still affected today. We are asked to surrender each aspect of our past and our present to a Higher Power.

Charlotte thinks of it this way

I don't want my life today to be just about the torture of my past. Yes, it happened and even though it still affects me today, I am a lot more as an adult than the child who was abused. It's how I treat myself now that matters. I am creating a life based on what I want and not focused on what happened in the past.

We are all human beings — we all have a past — things happened to us

Some of us struggle with the knowledge that we didn't tell anyone about the abuse at the time. We may know of other children who did tell. Accepting that we did not may be difficult for us to admit. Many of us discover that we thought it was our responsibility to stop the abuse.

As adults, we remember we were just children and not telling may have been a matter of personal survival. This level of awareness and self-honesty may be challenging to deal with at first, but in time it becomes easier. We became much of who we are today as a result of our past experiences. We are the ones to whom the abuses happened. We are the ones having feelings and thoughts and possibly memories about our pasts.

As we accept and own what really happened and what it was like for us in the past, we open ourselves to experiencing peace of mind in the present and to feelings of greater self-love and self-kindness. This may be challenging for adults abused as children because we realize for our healing to happen, we will need to surrender thinking of ourselves as victims and create new identities for ourselves as adults.

One of the greatest gifts realized through the **12 Steps** for adults abused as children is a new way of looking at ourselves as we develop the ability to make decisions not based on our past, but empowered by acts of surrender, faith, and willingness. We learn new ways of being that we may never have thought possible. Some of us are afraid to admit when we are happy because if we are happy, what would that say about the abusers or the abuse itself? Would it say that the abuse wasn't "that bad?" Sadly, many of us have sacrificed our happiness as adults just to prove how horrible it was for us as children.

Maintaining "self" while turning over our will and our lives to a Higher Power

This can be confusing and scary for adults abused as children. We may feel that we are at risk of losing ourselves again to something bigger and more powerful than us. We are afraid that takes away our right to choose.

Up until now, mistrust has been such a big part of our lives. We grew up fearful of what was outside of us, afraid that it could or would harm us. With a history of abuse, letting go of control can be challenging, even though it is our way out of the old patterns that haven't worked for us.

We can't change by resisting the real world, we can only change by creating or allowing new ways to replace the old ones. Willingness is the key to our transformation.

In Step 3, we begin to explore where we fit into our own lives and how to create them. We begin to discover that, as adults, we make our own decisions. It is our right, responsibility, and need to choose. None of our adult choices is meant to be made for us by others anymore. As we come to have a deeper understanding of our relationship to a greater Power, we are assured that we will not lose ourselves, but instead discover and develop ourselves through the process. As a result, we will have more to offer ourselves and others as we expand and grow.

Recognizing the experience of turning over our will

- A sense of relief
- A lessening of life's stresses
- Peace of mind
- An increased sense of hope
- A sense of inner strength
- Clarity of purpose
- A sense of ease and well-being
- Solutions are realized

We Love Ourselves

As children, we may have assumed that it was our parents' job to love us. Now that we are adults, we learn that it is our job alone to love ourselves. It is not the responsibility of our spouse or partner, nor is it our children's job either. We are each accountable for loving ourselves. The love others give us is a gift, not their responsibility. They are not required to fulfill our expectations. In other words, they were not put on the face of this earth just to love us!

Since some of us did not feel loved as a child, as adults we still have the very strong longing to feel loved by another and think we need their love to be happy. However, it is good news for adults abused as children to find out that we can satisfy our longing to be loved by loving ourselves and allowing our Higher Power and others to love us naturally. **We see the experience of feeling loved is possible now because it is in our hands, not someone else's.** We make a lifelong decision to love ourselves no matter what! We are aware that this decision opens up a whole new world of possibilities for us. We are no longer trying to get love from someone else to feel good.

Many of us have developed attention-seeking skills to feel loved, but now we can surrender these old ways and just love ourselves as we are. We surrender being a "goody two shoes" so we'll be appreciated. We surrender telling others what they want to hear, whether we believe it or not. We let go of putting others' wants before our own, so they won't leave us. We release the need to maintain silence as we play small, so as not to take the focus off another. As we surrender one day at a time, we find we don't need to be anything other than who or what we are today to feel loved. We learn to give it to ourselves and are open to receiving it from a Higher Power.

Shari explains:

For me, the answer is self-love. It has become my spiritual practice. I remind myself often during my day that I love myself.

Our Understanding of a Higher Power

Step 3 is the first time the words, "God" and "Him" are referenced in the 12 Steps. God is any power we decide is greater than we are. God can be nature, breath, love, Goddess, universal intelligence, Source, the Great Mystery, Creator or a more traditional definition of God. For example, some believe in a "higher self" within, some in the river of life itself. As discussed in Step 2, the list is endless, including creating our own versions of a Higher Power. The **ADULTS ABUSED AS CHILDREN ANONYMOUS** 12 Step program is non-denominational. It does not focus on, nor support any religion, nor interpret any specific concept of God.

For the purpose of this group, we will reference "Him" as it relates to God, to honor the original 12 Steps written in 1939 in Alcoholics Anonymous. It does not mean that God has a male gender. There is no gender reference intended. It is solely to respect the initial drafting of the Steps that this reference will remain.

As we work the Steps for ourselves, we are welcome and encouraged to change words as we see fit in our own lives. However, at the group level, we agree to leave the 12 Steps as written.

Our Higher Power cares

Step 3 reminds us that a Higher Power cares about us in ways we may not have imagined before now. We will grow to discover that a Higher Power has always cared about us, even though as children, some of us were unable to experience that.

We may find it challenging to imagine a Higher Power caring about us today, especially if when we were children, the adults in our lives did not.

What Step 3 says is that our Higher Power cares about what we want, not that we're going to get everything, but it is part of our journey to surrender how we thought or believed things should be. In time, we will learn to see where the Higher Power has been helping us all along.

The only kind of Higher Power that we would turn our will and lives over to is one who cares about us.

Working Step 3 is an act of creation. It is about creating the possibility of change through our intentions and through the right use of our will. Through all the Steps, we need to remember to treat ourselves with gentleness, patience, and kindness.

Making a Decision — We Discover that We Have Choices

The first real decision of Step 3 is to turn our will over to a Power greater than ourselves. It may be difficult at first to understand the importance of making this decision to let go, and give our will and lives over to God.

The revelations found in the journey of Steps 2 and 3 are simple, yet profound. The further along we are in working the Steps, the more we discover the choices we have and the freedom and happiness that accompany them. Prior to this Step, we may not have had much experience making healthy decisions for ourselves, but in Step 3 we begin to gain confidence as we practice doing so.

In time, we discover the connection and importance of Steps 1, 2, and 3. The Steps build upon each other and are suggested to be worked in order. Step 2 is founded upon the discovery that we can and are being restored. However, for the restoration to happen, we must move on to Step 3 and release our attachment to doing it ourselves. This decision is an action that comes from within. With the help of a Higher Power, we are guided toward better and happier lives. We consciously use our will to choose the direction we desire and use our decision-making ability to surrender for our good.

When we do anything more than once, we call it practice. Repetition has value since it can help imprint new ways of being in us. It is part of the human condition to learn by doing things over and over again. Thus all the Steps are meant to be practiced and repeated over time.

When we turn our will and our lives over, we do it incrementally, one day at a time, one person at a time, and one situation at a time. It takes practice and is part of the process of growing. We should not expect ourselves to surrender all at once. We are moving forward and being guided by a Power greater than us toward what we want.

It is not uncommon to discover that turning our lives over can feel very overwhelming to begin with. We remember to examine areas of our lives instead of our whole lives at one time. We ask ourselves what is present right now that we want different...and turn that over. We begin to experience what it's like for us as we do this. We may feel hope, increased self-esteem, or new or renewed creativity as we get to see our true selves. We examine aspects and qualities of patience, acceptance, non-judgment, anger, and forgiveness through this self-discovery process. We turn over everything we uncover about ourselves. It is only after letting go that we can be restored to the possibility of wholeness that is always present for us.

The decision to surrender is a life-rewarding one. We are at a place where we want love, peace, and self-fulfillment. We are able to experience what we want as we release our grip on life, and receive guidance and clarity from a Higher Power. Our ability to create the kinds of lives we want is realized through the openness and willingness to surrender our will.

Beatrice shares about turning it over:

As a child I experienced a lot of abuse in tubs and showers, and as a result, I've experienced terror in those areas of the bathroom. My terror has affected my ability to care for my personal hygiene, having trouble getting into tubs and showers. I was powerless over my ability to bathe or shower and just couldn't make myself go there no matter how much I wanted to. My life had become unmanageable in my self-criticism, lack of hygiene, and in my own embarrassment. I was powerless over the unrealistic expectations I had of myself.

I had to turn over my feelings of shame, embarrassment, and self-betrayal, and I also had to surrender sadness, sorrow, and anger. What I really wanted was to be able to take good care of myself.

My expectations led me to believe that I should be able to get myself into a shower, but I couldn't, and what I ultimately wanted was to be clean. I had to begin with what was possible for me and take small steps toward what I knew I wanted. In my attempts to take care of my hygiene, I noticed where I was willing and able to begin to try and considered myself successful just doing one small act toward my goal.

In time I was able to bring myself to the edge of the tub but could not yet get in. I would fill the tub with water but not yet be able to enter it. This was another level of willingness and another success. It was the practice of each that made every new decision to try again easier.

Sometimes I did a sponge bath standing or sitting in the tub with no water in it. I was practicing getting ready to add water and was willing to believe that with the help of a Higher Power it would happen. This was a very big turning point in my life, as I broke the process down into very small attempts and acknowledged myself along the way with gratitude for my willingness. Eventually, I was able to bathe or shower on a daily basis. However, it was a one day at a time process that finally led to my success. The journey through the Steps led me on a path where I was able to admit how the past abuse still affected my life in unmanageable ways. My Higher Power did for me what I could not do for myself.

Step 3 Summary

"We" Made the Decision

The word "we" is understood to be the first word in every Step. It is suggested that we go to meetings if available and talk to others, as we learn through our sharing what it means to turn over our will. We begin to find what others say makes a difference to us and leads us toward better understanding, strengthens our willingness, and helps to guide us along our path. Most likely we will need the support of others as they offer understanding and extend compassion. By sharing, we will learn to be better, kinder friends to ourselves.

This is the time for us to focus on ourselves and let our lives be about us. As we get in touch with our own power, we discover we can channel and harness it. We use it to direct our will on our behalf! We experience the connection between what we want and our own personal will. We have already admitted that, up to this point, we have not succeeded in creating our happiness by using our own willpower by ourselves. Now we can succeed by allowing a Higher Power to work in us and for us.

Step 3 Affirmations

1. I am never alone.

2. I am patient with myself.

3. I believe I can be restored by surrendering.

4. I believe that my Higher Power cares about me.

5. I decide to align my will with the will of a Power greater than me.

6. I turn my life over to a Higher Power one day at a time.

7. I release my grip on problems.

8. I let go of control.

9. My Higher Power inspires me.

10. I discover I have many choices.

11. I let go and let a Higher Power lead me.

12. I love myself no matter what.

13. I step out in faith.

Step 3 Journal Questions

1. What are three of my most important values? Am I living them out in my life?

2. What does the right use of my will mean?

3. What preconceptions of a Higher Power have I relinquished?

4. When did I change my opinion or my mind about something? What did I learn from this?

5. In which area(s) of my life is my willpower in charge? Am I successful in getting what I want?

6. Where have I found it easier to decide to surrender, even if I didn't know what to do next?

7. What beliefs left over from childhood are standing in my way of being happy? Which ones would I consider changing?

8. What am I attached to that is keeping me from attaining my spiritual goals?

9. What pain am I afraid of facing and avoid it by using my self-will?

10. What measuring sticks do I use to make my decisions – integrity, respect, love, or fear and resentment? Am I satisfied with the results?

11. What do I fear by letting go?

Step 3 Prayer

Higher Power,

We know that your will is being made known to each one of us. We make ourselves receptive to your power by surrendering our will to you. We allow your power to flow though us, to manifest what is for our highest good. We know with you we can accomplish our greatest desires.

Our thoughts and actions can develop a new force of their own by aligning our will with yours. We are guided by your wisdom for right action in our best behalf. Free will is a gift from you, our Higher Power. A violation of the purpose of will brings harm to ourselves and others.

As we are guided by wisdom, we find fulfillment and happiness. We make up our minds to receive that which we need to evolve and grow. Help us to be active in our efforts to be authentic. We must never give up, our well-being depends on it. Thank you for caring for us.

And so it is.

Amen.

Notes

Notes

Dear past...

Step 4

Made a searching and fearless moral inventory of ourselves.

Step 4

Made a searching and fearless moral inventory of ourselves.

Table of Contents

Introduction 161

What Is an Inventory? 165

Why Do an Inventory? 167

We Assess Our Moral Inventory 170

Things to Note When Doing an Inventory 173

We Are Nonjudgmental 175

Ways of Writing an Inventory 177

We Inventory the Past and the Present 180

We Are Not Alone 184

We Are Fearless 186

Unmanageability Motivates Us 189

We Search Within 192

We Hide Who We Are 194

We Deny 196

Spiritual Principles 199

Feelings and Memories May Appear.................202

Self-Enhancing Character Traits...................207

Self-Diminishing Character Traits 209

Step 4 Summary...................................212

Step 4 Affirmations 214

Step 4 Journal Questions.........................215

Step 4 Prayer 217

Step 4

Made a searching and fearless moral inventory of ourselves.

Introduction

Steps 1, 2, and 3 The Foundation

The 12 Steps are written in a particular order because they are most effective this way.

In Step 1, we admitted we were powerless over the past abuse and our unmanageable lives.

In Step 2, we came to believe that we could be restored to some level of manageability by a Power greater than us.

In Step 3, we made a decision to turn our will and our lives over to that greater Power, as we understand it.

We made a decision and set a course to go through the Steps when we made a commitment to turn our lives and our will over to a Power greater than ourselves. In order to create the changes we desire, we have begun to believe in a Power that can restore us. We admitted we are powerless over our past abuse and have begun to believe, and possibly begun to experience, being restored to a new level of manageability.

In the first three Steps we have begun to investigate what is it to be authentic, to be who we truly are. In Step 4, we begin to look at ourselves honestly through a searching and fearless written moral inventory. We are asked to courageously discover who we are afraid we are, who we pretend to be, and who we have become. We may still be blaming current circumstances on our past abuse rather than accepting responsibility for the patterns and behaviors that make our lives unmanageable. As we uncover new realizations by completing our 4th Step inventory, we increase our ability to make progress and succeed in our healing.

In order to be restored to sane thinking and behavior, we need to understand what our thoughts, feelings, and attitudes are about our childhood abuse. We also need to consider how our views of the past still affect us today. We may have challenges with authority figures. We may have felt betrayed as children and presently have trust issues. We need a realistic foundation to help create, shift, and transform who we are. We need to know what we're working with, within ourselves. This foundation helps us shift our perspective, ideas, and behaviors. This ultimately changes our lives for the better.

Olivia admits:

As an adult abused as a child, I wasn't taught that it was okay or even safe to be myself. So, I've spent most of my life living as if I were bits and pieces of what others wanted me to be, wondering why my life wasn't working.

I learned I won't have the life that's possible for me if I go through life denying who I really am. I perpetuate my suffering this way. The first step in living my own life is to learn how to simply be who I am. This is being revealed as I write my inventory.

What is Step 4 asking of us?

It might seem odd for adults abused as children to look at **ourselves** through an inventory and not only at what our perpetrators did. We have probably spent much of our lives focused on them. As a result, many of us are intimately familiar with both the needs and desires, and fears and angers, of our abusers. Yet we may not have figured out these same aspects about ourselves.

We need to discover our own limitations, our own needs, and desires. We will look at the truth of our fears, resentments, and disappointments. How did our lives become what they are today? Step 4 is where we begin to take a deeper look from a place of great honesty.

We don't have the power to change someone else. Focusing on others doesn't give us the happy lives we want. We may perpetuate the lie that our lives will work if only others would be different or if only we could reverse the past abuse. Doing an inventory on someone else doesn't help **us** to have satisfying lives.

It is natural and healthy to want and need to talk about our past. This is how we heal. We share about our childhood abuse and also share how it is still affecting us. Secrecy is broken and healing begins. We find the courage this inventory requires to create inner peace and lasting change.

What Is an Inventory?

What does Step 4 mean by "made a searching and fearless moral inventory of ourselves?" It means that we begin to explore who we really are and who we have become as a result of our past. This is not done by looking only on the surface. This exploration can be both related and unrelated to our child abuse. We begin by acknowledging how old we were when the abuse happened and what it was like for us then. In addition to the child's perspective, if we are able, we write from an adult witness or an adult observer viewpoint, as if we were just watching. This witness can awaken us to truths not previously known or understood as children.

This exploration helps us discover decisions we made, patterns we developed, and beliefs about who we are. We learn more about how we relate to others and how we fit into the world. We see how our beliefs were created from the abuse we experienced as little children. What we learn can transform our adult lives and we become free in the process.

> **Sheldon shares:**
>
> Letting the world see who I really am on the inside is terrifying. I have many childhood memories of things going terribly wrong when I revealed myself to others.
>
> Today, I want a life where I can express my true self and explore my natural tendencies. Writing my inventory helped me discover myself at my core. Now I base my

*choices and decisions on who I **am**, rather than who I should be or who others want me to be. I feel more confident when I want to create new possibilities and take new risks.*

Taking an inventory of our adult selves is similar to owning a store and listing the contents found on the shelves. We take note of what we see and what is missing. That, in itself, is enough. For an adult abused as a child, the purpose of an inventory is to see what our character traits are, i.e., who we really are with no judgment.

Why Do an Inventory?

As we start a new way of life through the Steps, we want to release the struggles and burdens that have governed our lives and held us back from growing. Honest self-assessment is one of the keys to our healing. By recording our past and present lives on paper it is easier to see and harder to deny our true nature. Writing our inventory helps to resolve our shame, pain, guilt, anger, and other related emotions. The strength and insights we gain are invaluable to our healing.

As adults abused as children, we can be sure that emotions will arise. This is an ideal time to remember that our lives are in the hands of our Higher Power. With our Higher Power's help, we see the cause of our pain. Working through the 12 Steps we become willing and able to release our discomfort and suffering. We grow to trust our Higher Power and begin to overcome our fears.

Self-inquiry is the portal to personal freedom. We look at ourselves honestly instead of drowning in the past details. A written inventory unlocks parts of our minds that can remain hidden. Thus, just thinking or talking about it is not enough. The process of writing exposes our patterns and the recurring themes we created over time to help us cope with life.

Natalie states:

When I discover a quality that I don't like about myself and wish it were not part of me, I still admit it. I'm not going to get over being me, nor do I have to. I just write down what I see about myself. Knowing how and why I'm behaving in a certain way puts me in touch with reality. It's then that I learn what kind of a human I am being in the moment.

Doing a 4th Step inventory allows us to find out what characteristics are unique to us. It is easier to live without having unrealistic expectations of ourselves. We are no longer surprised at our reactions to certain triggers, as they match up with what we have learned about ourselves.

We become more comfortable admitting positive aspects and owning our skills and talents. Acknowledging these in an inventory clearly gives us a chance to create authentic lives and end living out what we thought we should be.

We Assess Our Moral Inventory

Morals are our principles or rules of right and wrong conduct. They help us to distinguish between right and wrong. As we do our inventory, some of us find it helpful to look at ourselves from the viewpoint of where we are "right on" in our thinking, perceptions, or conclusions and where we are "off the map" in our assessments.

> **Sharon shares an example of being "off the map":**
>
> *As an adult, I used to allow the part of me that thinks like a teenager to make driving decisions and drove my car like an immature 16-year-old might. I found myself taking risks that I would not have taken thinking like an adult driver. Without realizing it, I had handed the responsibility of driving over to my inner teen. I was "off the map" in allowing this to happen. While doing my moral inventory, I discovered that I believed that the laws didn't apply to me. This was a typical teenage way for me to look at life. Since I didn't think that the laws applied to me, my actions followed suit and were "off the mark" too. My life was definitely unmanageable.*

The issue of right and wrong in a 4th Step does not imply that **we** are right or wrong as people. Remember, before we began this inventory, we made the decision to be neutral and nonjudgmental. We are not being asked to assess whether we were good or bad as children or even today, as adults. Our critical selves, or inner judges, may want to have a voice, or the critical voices of others may want to be heard. If we allow judgment to occur, we cannot be truly fearless.

As children it may have been too dangerous to speak our truth; we may also have believed that we couldn't handle the truth. Some of us continued to lie to ourselves because we were too afraid of the truth. For our healing to occur, it is imperative that we revisit our version of the past abuse through our inventory.

> **Olivia offers:**
>
> *I lived in a world where evil was the ruling force and telling the truth was not only worthless, but actually dangerous to my well-being. I learned backward values as a child. Lying was safe; telling the truth put me in jeopardy of severe injury. In my twenties and thirties, I had to retrain myself to tell the truth. It was far too easy for me to lie. Now I understand why and have compassion for myself. This all became evident to me while writing my inventory.*

It is best that we look deeply into what moral means to us. The inventory can help us reflect upon the desired qualities and characteristics of our personality that work well in our lives. These might include kindness, patience, and generosity. We must also be equally honest to note those aspects which diminish us, such as gossip, jealousy, and envy. We may be pleased or even surprised to discover areas where we excel. We are reminded that our lives are balanced in these areas and draw our strength from those aspects. Other areas may still be weak, underdeveloped, or deficient altogether.

As we investigate our world, we see where our perspectives are skewed and appreciate how they make our lives unmanageable. Often, these jaded views are left over from our abusive childhoods. We will find that we need to update the views of ourselves and reassess who we have become. We will discover that moral values can be learned.

Things to Note When Doing an Inventory

The purpose of an inventory is to find out the truth of who we have become as it relates to our stories, beliefs, behaviors, and patterns formed along the way. It is our journey to discover how they impact our lives. Taking an inventory of ourselves does not in any way lessen the accountability of what the perpetrators or the abusers did! However, it is our turn to look at ourselves, **for** ourselves.

The inventory is not about changing or getting better at something. That part belongs to our Higher Power. Rather, the Steps are worked in stages, one Step at a time. As we progress, our ability to see the truth strengthens. Since we are always changing, an inventory we do today will most likely be different from an inventory we do 5 or 10 years from now. Our ability and willingness to search deep within will grow and mature. We can heal our past childhood abuse through self-reflection and self-discovery.

In the beginning of this process, we might not know how to be honest with ourselves. In addition, we might not know what to do with the feelings that come up when we are honest. First, we have to learn to deal with our fear of admitting that we don't know who we really are. **Our intentions and**

self-compassion are keys. What matters is our willingness to be as honest and fearless as we can be.

This moral inventory requires patience and understanding. Eventually, as we work the Steps, we will begin to feel a sense of peace and serenity that we may have never felt before. Some of us will experience relief early in the process; others may not begin to feel different until a later time. As we become more self-aware and self-accepting, we have the opportunity to learn better ways of dealing with life. This, in turn, reinforces and encourages our inner trust that we **can** have the kind of lives we have always wanted.

We Are Nonjudgmental

When we take a deep look inside, it is best to look at ourselves from a neutral or detached place. Some refer to this as the observer or witness point of view. Remember this is no time for blaming, shaming, judging, or criticizing ourselves or others. We need to be gentle as well as fearless. We examine our findings from a place of curiosity and self-love.

Being fearless requires courage and surrender to a Power greater than we are. Self-generosity and self-compassion are two of the best tools to use when doing our inventory. We cannot be fearless while looking over our shoulders with attacking attitudes, nor can we do it from places of condemnation.

> **Stephanie writes about nonjudgment:**
>
> *Surrender for me means being completely who I am and trusting a Power greater than I am. I have a habit of procrastination, yet it's not wrong to be a procrastinator; it's simply a fact. I don't have to come up with a plan of self-improvement or promise that I will never do it again. I don't have to do anything really. I just need to admit it. I don't have to rid myself of what I discover. Whatever ways I am going to change will be guided and supported by my Higher Power.*

When we make ourselves wrong for what we discover, we have turned against ourselves. This could block us from seeing perspectives we need to examine. We can't afford to allow these inner critics to have a voice while we're writing our inventory. It helps to be brave, even if in the past we have not had very courageous views of ourselves. Remember that we are adults now. We have a Power greater than ourselves to help us with this inventory.

We assess our frame of mind

It may help us to find out if we are in the right frame of mind before we sit down to write our inventory.

We can use an **assessment scale** to help us measure our readiness.

On a scale of 1 to 10, we ask ourselves how we feel. On the scale, #1 would indicate that we are feeling awful, and #10 indicates that we are feeling fantastic. If we are between #6-10 and feel good about ourselves, we proceed. If we are between #1-5, we don't work on the inventory at that time. Instead, we wait and recheck to see if we feel better later on. We cannot be searching and fearless when we're feeling bad about ourselves. Our perspectives will be jaded.

Ways of Writing an Inventory

It is suggested that we write down our inventory, however, this can take many forms. We can write it on a computer, in a journal, on scratch paper, 3 x 5 cards, or on post-it notes. The ways of recording our inventory have no limits. What is most important is to go deep and be as honest as we can be.

It is best not to compare our process with another's experience. We are meant to learn to trust our own individual ways. One member did it in cartoon form since she could not get herself to write it down with words. Later she met with her mentor and shared her inventory while explaining what she had drawn. Another member did her inventory three times in three different forms, one right after the other. She had heard how hard it was for others, and not finding it difficult for herself, thought she hadn't done it correctly; so she kept doing it over and over. Our experience of writing an inventory is unique to each of us.

Be deep and honest

There is neither a right nor wrong way of doing our fearless and moral inventory. What is important is to begin wherever we are at the present time. Some of us may be moved to write our inventory in a chronological manner, from birth to today. Some will begin right at the present moment. Others write only about major life events or about certain stages of life that they've been through. Please note, we will often repeat this particular Step through the years as more is revealed to us. The important thing is to start!

One way to explore ourselves is to discover our personality traits. What traits do we possess that help us create the kind of transformation in our lives that we want for ourselves? We can begin with a list of our positive traits that are working well for us. Starting with a positive inventory can be very healing and supportive. Later, we will need to move toward those characteristics that are more difficult to discover and admit. Remember we are looking deep within ourselves.

While there is **no fixed format** for our inventory and each of us must decide which method works best for us at the time, some suggested ways are offered here:

1. Chronological order – autobiographical, birth to present

2. Chronological order – autobiographical, beginning and ending at any time (example: teenage years)

3. Major life events – (example: confronting the abuser or telling a family member, career decision, graduating, enlisting, giving birth, getting married)

4. Stages of life

5. Child abuse years (from child perspective)

6. Child abuse years (from adult perspective)

7. Self-survey of present time

8. Self-enhancing character traits, past and present

9. Self-diminishing character traits, past and present

10. Where do I keep my word to myself and where am I out of integrity?

11. Where am I following spiritual principles and where am I not?

12. Self-survey of fears as a child

13. Self-survey of fears as an adult

14. Self-survey of angers as a child

15. Self-survey of angers as an adult

16. Self-survey of beliefs as a child

17. Self-survey of beliefs as an adult

18. Self-survey of assumptions and expectations as a child

19. Self-survey of assumptions and expectations as an adult

We Inventory the Past and the Present

We look at our past abuse from both our child's and our adult's perspectives. Both are necessary and valuable for a full picture of ourselves. Our child's version will most likely include what happened to us and what it was like in the past. The beliefs and assumptions we created at that time will also be noted.

In our adult's version, as we look back, we offer ourselves years of growth, experience, maturity, knowledge, and wisdom. They help us reconsider how accurate we are in our assessments of the past. We courageously review our lives both past and present.

Some questions we might ask ourselves in an honest inventory:

1. As a child, how did I feel and what thoughts did I have during or after the abuse? What thoughts and feelings does my adult have about my abused child today?

2. What did I think of the abuser when I was a child and how do I think and feel about the abuser now that I am an adult?

3. How do my childhood assumptions and beliefs about myself affect my life today? My beliefs about others? My beliefs about life? Were they accurate then? Are they accurate today?

4. Where am I still living out those inaccuracies and perpetuating a trend of thinking that was never accurate to begin with or no longer serves me well?

The purpose of a searching and fearless moral inventory is to help our inner child and adult selves see some new truths. In addition, it helps us have a larger picture of our childhood abuse.

We begin to look at what it was like to be abused, what actually happened, and what conclusions (beliefs and assumptions) we created at that time that we still hold on to today.

We distinguish fact from story

> *Claudia shares:*
>
> *When I was little and realized I was powerless over stopping the abuse, I decided that not only was I weak, but I was also **wrong** for being weak. In my 4th Step I saw that I wasn't really weak, I was just a little nine-year-old overpowered by people a lot bigger than I was. However, I lived as a child (and into my adult life) thinking and believing, "I am weak. I'm not enough..." as if it were the truth, even though it wasn't. That's why I call it a story.*

Our childhood stories tell what happened and what our lives were like for us then. **What happened from our point of view is our story.** The facts include what was done, what occurred, and what was said by whom. Our thoughts, feelings, assumptions, and opinions become a tremendous part of what forms our stories and beliefs.

> **Here is a good example of Melinda learning to distinguish the difference between fact and story:**
>
> These are the facts. I was 12 years old, naked in a ladies' locker room where my mother was throwing me against the metal lockers, beating me severely, and screaming at me. The women watching did nothing. My child's story included that obviously, it was my responsibility to take care of myself. I believed that I couldn't count on others, even others who are adults, and that I wasn't even worth rescuing.
>
> While writing my 4th Step, I realized even though the facts were accurate, the story I created around the event wasn't true. I still believed my story until I did my 4th Step. I was amazed at what I had made up and became interested in the question — if I'm not my story, who am I?

Writing an inventory can free us from our stories so we can discover who we really are! Our stories have deeply impacted our lives by significantly shaping our beliefs and assumptions and by defining us. As we search, we begin to discover that our stories are not necessarily true or based on reality. They are our interpretation of the facts. We think we **are** our stories, but we are not. We're unique human beings **with** stories. As adults abused as children, we learn to separate our stories from what actually happened.

Diana shares:

As a child, I made up a fantasy world about the future, not realizing it could never come true. It became my vision, my version of life as I expected life to turn out. I decided that what I needed to do was to stay alive until I could get out of my home and get away from the abusers.

Sadly, as an adult, I discovered that my version wasn't based in reality. I had created this fantasy as a child to balance the dark world I was living in at the time.

This fantasy life kept me alive as a kid. But as an adult, I saw that I would be dissatisfied forever if I expected life to meet the unrealistic expectations of my childhood fantasy.

While doing my 4th Step, I discovered my erroneous beliefs. I realized that I needed to release my fantasies, live in the real world, and rely on a Power greater than myself. Through the Steps, I'm learning that I do have what it takes to handle ***real*** *life. I no longer need to create a fantasy world to feel like I can survive!*

We Are Not Alone

We remember that the Steps are being done with the support, help, and guidance of a Power greater than ourselves. Step 4 is not meant to be done alone. We remember that this Power of our understanding, is always with us as we look within.

> **George shares:**
>
> *Given what happened to me as a child, I thought that responsible adults were supposed to be self-reliant. My thinking and belief systems were jaded. Even today, I slip into thinking that I am responsible for my own healing. I forget that I am limited as a human and that I am not in charge, my Higher Power is.*

The implied "We" in Step 4, shows that our inventory is meant to be done with a trusted other: a mentor, sponsor, clergy, friend, a fellow adult abused as a child, or a counselor. Because we know that we are not alone, it is possible to do the inventory in a searching and fearless manner.

David reveals:

When I heard that the rest of my life didn't have to be like it had been for the past 60 plus years, I wanted to find out what my part was to make those changes happen.

I understood that the answers had to come from a Power greater than me. Each day I asked to know what my footwork was. I tried to follow whatever guidance I could glean in the moment. I experienced many detours along the way while trying to discern my path.

After writing my inventory, my life changed as I changed. Having admitted who I had become as an adult, I felt more able to handle life. I have inner resources now I didn't have as a child.

I was willing to accept what I learned about myself. I have been able to make new decisions using this information. I practice allowing Spirit to guide me. I remember to take it one day at a time, and because of this, my life has changed for the better.

Today I enjoy less stress, more peace of mind, and improved relationships. These Steps provide the structure I need as an adult abused as a child. Now I can create the life I desire.

We Are Fearless

Two reasons why we adults abused as children may be afraid to look at ourselves

1. We may be afraid that we are empty, hollow shells, or even worse, imposters pretending to be someone we're not. Basically, we don't yet know who we are. We have lived in denial and hidden ourselves for a very long time. The belief that we are not enough is a real fear. It is a result of our childhood abuse. Many of us have lived with this fear our whole lives.

2. We are terrified that what we **do** see is going to be bad, that there is something basically wrong with us.

Adults who have been abused as children may develop many fears over time.

We may want to ask ourselves how these fears have affected who we have become.

1. How have our fears created our unhappiness, our loneliness, and our insecurities?
2. Because we're afraid, what are we putting off that we know we should do?
3. What are we doing to avoid looking at our fears?

4. What situations have we created from our fears?
5. Where are we afraid to say "no" in our lives?
6. How has fear dominated our decisions?

When we begin to look inside, it is a marvel for us to discover that indeed there is something good about us. Remember, this inventory is supported by our Higher Power and our willingness to surrender to that Power.

> **Reggie shares a thought:**
>
> *Fearlessness, for me, is not the same as bravery or courage. I am brave and I can muster courage from within, but fearlessness is not something I can accomplish by myself. I need to rely on my Higher Power to be fearless without experiencing any of my own terror.*

Being fearless is a practice of admitting something to ourselves in an honest manner. Fearlessness is made real in the presence of courage and our willingness to be brave. Ultimately, our experience of fearlessness deepens as we gain trust in the process and witness true healing through the 12 Steps.

As we learn more about ourselves, while searching through this deep and moral inventory, it is best not to make promises to ourselves that we will change. We do not have to come up with plans of self-improvement or know what we are going to do about something after we discover it.

Carolyn offers:

I am able to behave more fearlessly when I don't have the attitude that I need to be perfect and allow for mistakes. If I don't have to be a super being, then I can take risks and just be regular and be all right with that.

A Higher Power helps us through this Step. As we do our fearless and moral inventory, we can anticipate that feelings may arise. If our thoughts or feelings become out of control, unhealthy, or harmful to anyone, including ourselves, we must ask for help. Many of us seek support from a professional therapist or counselor, clergy, or spiritual mentor during times such as these. It is important to remember that we are not alone. Talk to someone else and use the support that is available. It helps!

Unmanageability Motivates Us

We have to decide for ourselves why we are doing this inventory. As adults abused as children, we may have a distorted view of ourselves. Most often, the pervasive thoughts and beliefs of today revolve around feelings that we are somehow flawed, bad, or not enough. We may think that the abuse was somehow our fault. The most profound belief that may still linger is the one that says that we should have been able to stop or prevent the abuse from happening altogether.

We may have learned how to blend with the needs and wants of others without taking the time to focus on ourselves. As adults, this is our opportunity to keep the focus on ourselves and less on others.

We were victims of abuse as children, and we may still experience feeling like victims in our lives today. If we strongly associate with the experience of being a victim, it may not be easy to see ourselves in a searching and fearless way.

In actuality we are no longer victims even though we can still feel trapped by our reactions to life's events. With the help of a Power greater than ourselves we can find the courage to admit that we feel like a victim.

We are not responsible for fixing the unmanageable areas of our lives. Our Higher Power has a plan of recovery for us.

We can trust that this Power supports us and is guiding us toward our healing.

> **Angelina contributes:**
>
> *I have always been self-conscious about my toenails; it was one of the things my mother used to ridicule me about. As a child, I was humiliated both in private and in public. She would engage strangers with references to my ugly toenails. She would start laughing and pointing at them, totally degrading me. I incorporated her attitude and need to remember that I'm powerless over being judgmental about my toenails. I am not powerless, though, over feeling compassion for me as the child who was made fun of. Having compassion for myself helps transform my feelings, thoughts, and attitudes. I have a gentle willingness to accept myself as I am today, unchanged, not perfect, yet still enough.*

To stay motivated through the Steps **we must want something that we don't already enjoy** — peace of mind, better relationships, or living authentic lives, for example. We must decide what is important to us, otherwise, the unmanageability will remain.

We Search Within

Searching implies that this is neither a surface nor cursory examination. We must be willing to go deep and become fully honest with ourselves. This is not a time to hold anything back, for what we hold back cannot be released and healed. Hiding the truth from ourselves will not allow us to move on and find peace. Our denial of reality and hiding how we feel may be how we survived our childhood abuse, but now is the time to come out of hiding so we can look through the veils of denial and tell the truth about ourselves.

Arlene checks her motives:

A friend baked me a special birthday cake that was not on my food plan. I didn't know if eating that cake would be an act of gratitude for her kindness or an act of diminishing me. I used the tool of checking my motives and asked myself these questions: "Why would I eat it? Am I hungry? Am I afraid of losing her affection, upsetting, or disappointing her? Am I putting her needs before my own, thinking she's more important than I am?"

*It was not as important to me whether I ate the cake or not, but rather looking into and discovering **why** I would eat it. I wanted to learn how to take care of my own well-being while acknowledging her generosity toward me. I had to find out what my motives were to make a healthy decision.*

Our fearlessness is a great aid in our searching efforts for our truths. Our willingness to be nonjudgmental makes deep inquiry possible. Our decision to surrender reminds us to trust the process of the 4th Step. Our Higher Power is always with us as we search.

We Hide Who We Are

Christy shares:

While writing my Step 4 inventory, I clearly saw that my seeming perfectionism covered up my inability to have closure or feel complete. The perfectionism masqueraded as a virtue, but I was really hiding behind it. I didn't have to face the fact that I hadn't progressed as far as I could have. Instead, I kept trying to do more and more with no beneficial results.

Being adults abused as children, we may hide our voices and protect ourselves from being seen. We often hide our opinions, what we want, and what we need. We hide our aspirations, our sexuality, and all too often, our dreams.

Hiding may have been how we kept ourselves safe as children. However, from a Step 4 perspective, hiding will not allow us to heal as adults. We do not deny the past, instead we live in the present. We need to be fearless and look honestly at the impact the past has had on our lives as adults. We cannot afford to hide any longer if we want to have satisfying lives today. Writing our inventory gives us a structure to look within. It provides safety for us to come out of hiding. After we reveal who we are in Step 4, Step 5 tells us what to do next. It is beneficial to remember to take as much time as is needed with Step 4 in order to be thorough.

For Amber, it looks like this:

*Whatever you liked, I liked and whatever you wanted, I wanted. My job was to make you happy. I had no value. I never let myself want anything because I figured I'd never get it. When I said that something wasn't important, what I felt was that **I** wasn't important. If I would say it didn't matter, what I was really saying was that **I** didn't matter. Today I have learned to listen to myself when I say something doesn't matter and make sure it is really how I feel.*

We Deny

Ruth discovers:

I tend to minimize how bad the abuse really was and how bad I felt. As a child, minimizing was a strategy that I developed. I was already feeling so little and the situation seemed so much larger than I was. I made what was happening to me smaller in my mind, so that as a little one, I felt I could handle it. Now, as an adult, I need to see if I'm just an older version of this small child or have I grown beyond that. My 4th Step inventory is helping me gain insights and see how I continue to make myself small as an adult. Sometimes I still hold myself back from taking a risk when I don't really need to anymore.

Denial, simply stated, is pretending that something doesn't exist or isn't important. Writing an inventory helps us break through our patterns of denial. We may not have known that we were in denial until we started looking at our past. Our denial may have begun when we were just children when the abuse occurred, back when we didn't understand that children were not responsible for the actions of adults.

For example, we may have forgotten (or dismissed the fact) that we were just 60 pounds or so, as a child, when a 200-pound adult abused us. It was physically impossible for us to stop them. Many of us believed that we should have been able to. As children it was just too scary to think about how powerless we felt and we lost sight of the facts. This is a form of denial.

We can begin by asking ourselves, "How do I even know that I'm in denial?" We all have blind spots, those things we cannot see. Some things we resist seeing altogether. Sharing with others helps us begin to explore this question. As we hear others speak about themselves, their inventory, or their awareness about powerlessness, we may have moments of revelation. This will help us discover where we have been in denial as we experience their honesty. We can also look at our areas of unmanageability and check to see if they have been impacted by our denial.

Nancy admits:

When I was a 17-year-old girl, I didn't know that I could say no to a boy. So, I didn't. I had no idea that I had a choice. I never had that choice while I was growing up with the abuser. The decision was made for me. I had no freedom to choose. Now that I am an adult, I need to be aware of when I am denying myself my rights. I see this old pattern clearly in my inventory.

Ann's denial looks like this:

I couldn't imagine that it was acceptable to be as lacking an adult as I knew me to be. So, I couldn't afford to admit who I really was even to myself. I had built a whole life style around being someone I thought I should be. Of course, I always came up short. It only confirmed, time and again, how lacking I really was! I thought by the time I was an adult I'd be beyond those things that still upset me. I denied myself self-acceptance and self-compassion, choosing self-condemnation instead.

Spiritual Principles

In the inventory process not only do we examine our past, we also inventory ourselves in the present. It may be helpful to observe and admit where we may or may not be following spiritual principles. Here is a list of some principles that we can live by and benefit from. As adults abused as children, we may not yet have incorporated some of these.

On the following page, after these growth-encouraging principles below, is a list of principles that impedes our spiritual growth. Becoming clear which ones we are following gives us the opportunity to choose those that enhance us and become the people we have longed to be.

Principles which encourage our growth

- acceptance
- authenticity
- balance
- being centered
- commitment
- focus
- forgiveness
- honesty
- honor
- humility
- integrity
- kindness
- love
- moderation
- patience
- present
- respect
- right actions, thoughts, words
- surrender
- thoughtfulness
- tolerance
- truthfulness

Principles which impede our growth

- abuse through actions, thoughts, or words
- arrogance
- bitterness
- conceit
- control
- cynicism
- deceitfulness
- deception
- denial
- diminishment of anyone
- disregard
- envy
- forcefulness
- hatefulness
- holding a grudge
- impatience
- inconsiderateness
- intolerance
- jealousy
- judgment
- lying
- manipulation
- neglectfulness
- omitting the truth
- prejudice
- procrastination
- resentment
- righteousness
- secretiveness
- self-centeredness
- stealing
- unwillingness

In a 4th Step inventory, we discover where we are following spiritual principles and where we are not. When we don't follow spiritual principles, what is the impact on our lives? Do they get us closer to being the people we want to be? Do they get us closer to leading the kinds of lives we want?

As adults, when we admit that we lack integrity concerning our spiritual principles, we learn that we may have developed these coping strategies as children. We may have thought they would protect us from harm, fear, and pain. However, now they make our lives unmanageable. These adult behaviors add to our suffering and decrease our ability to cope and heal.

Feelings and Memories May Appear

Feelings and memories may arise as we work through Step 4. There are endless possibilities of both comfortable and uncomfortable feelings that can manifest. As adults abused as children, it can be a welcomed relief, and not an uncommon experience, to feel a sense of restored hope, joy, validation, increased self-worth, and self-confidence.

Another welcomed experience for many of us is the well-deserved feeling of self-forgiveness. As our 4th Step inventory progresses, we may discover that we are in much better shape than we thought we were. It may be a relief to see that our foundations are stronger than we realized.

We may also experience uncomfortable or upsetting feelings such as:

- anger
- anxiety
- avoidance
- betrayal
- confusion
- denial
- depression
- despair
- helplessness
- hopelessness
- humiliation
- martyrdom
- oppression
- overwhelm
- pain
- powerlessness

- disappointment
- discouragement
- dismay
- doubt
- embarrassment
- fearfulness
- feeling wronged
- guilty
- regret
- remorsefulness
- resentment
- sadness
- shame
- uncertainty
- victimization

It is important to explore how we are feeling during this process. It is time to come home to ourselves and be honest. It is helpful for us to be prepared if a challenging emotion arises as it can cause upset and/or overwhelm. We need not be alarmed; it is not unusual. If it gets too difficult, press pause, walk away, close the journal, turn off the computer.

If we find ourselves triggered or overcome and are unable to help ourselves deal with an emotion to our satisfaction, we may want to call a therapist or another professional to help us. We can also call a trusted friend who can support us in our self-care efforts.

Brian shares:

I was taught and treated like a piece of dirt so I didn't believe that I had what it took to look at myself honestly. On my own, I have been too negative about myself. The only way I could do a fearless inventory was to do it with my Higher Power. Step 3 reminds me that my Higher Power will take care of me while I write my Step 4 inventory.

When dealing with stress, trauma, and crisis, it is crucial to remember to care for ourselves. New information, new ideas, or new realizations may appear. It is not uncommon to start remembering things that we hadn't before. Therefore, we need to know how to take care of ourselves if this happens. We need to take action on our own behalf. We seek the help we need and thus empower our choices and receive support.

Coping strategies

There are effective self-care strategies that are important for us to use while doing each of the 12 Steps and especially while writing our 4th Step inventory. One of the most beneficial of these is to review Steps 1 through 3. They are the foundation for all the other Steps.

When feelings or memories arise and we need support, we go back to Step 1 and say, "I am powerless over my feelings while I am doing my inventory, and my life has become unmanageable." We honor the need for self-reflection and simply acknowledge what we're feeling.

We return to Step 2 and remember that it says, "We came to believe that a Power greater than ourselves can restore our feelings to a level of manageability." Our Higher Power can help provide peace and calm while we write our inventory.

Lastly in Step 3, we are reminded that, "We made a decision to turn our will, our lives, and our feelings over to the care of our Higher Power." If we are having trouble coping while doing our 4th Step, we make this decision time and time again. It is helpful to say to ourselves, "I make the decision to turn my emotional life, my memories, and all my feelings or anxieties over to my Higher Power right now."

We use the previous Steps, 1, 2, and 3, as support through Step 4. This is how the Steps build upon each other and are intended to provide a foundation as we focus on each progressive Step.

In addition to the first three Steps, it is beneficial to know how we are going to take care of ourselves as we do our inventory. Having a self-care plan in advance is a good idea. Remember we have resources as adults that we didn't have as children. It will be helpful now to review the section found earlier in this book called "Resources to Help Us" on page 25. It includes a list of effective self-care strategies.

Anita explains:

I remember there are two things I'm not powerless over - my attitude and my actions. While I can't change the past, I can change my attitude about it. I can change the way I treat myself by adopting a spiritual discipline of self-love. Love was the missing link for me! How I was treated affected not only my perception of love itself, but also my being loved and my feeling of being lovable. I have compassion for my inner child who was love-starved. I experience transformation of my thoughts, feelings, and attitudes through self-compassion.

Self-Enhancing Character Traits

What character traits do we possess that help us create the transformation in our lives that we want for ourselves? Which ones hinder us?

One way to deepen self-reflection and introspection through our inventory process is to explore the traits of our personality. We can begin by making a list of positive character traits that are working well for us. Starting with a positive inventory of traits can be very comforting, healing, and supportive.

☑ We list our gifts, talents, abilities, skills, and aptitudes.

☑ We ask ourselves what (who) leaves us feeling more expansive and self-confident?

☑ We feel good about ourselves when _____? (Fill in)

☑ What helps us be more genuine?

☑ What do trusted others tell us they admire about us?

Some **self-enhancing traits** we may have:

- accountable
- adventurous
- authentic
- calm
- caring
- centered
- honest
- hopeful
- humble
- kind
- loving
- loyal

- committed
- compassionate
- courageous/brave
- creative
- devoted
- faithful
- generous
- nonjudgmental
- open
- patient
- thoughtful
- trusting
- trustworthy
- willing

Self-Diminishing Character Traits

We need to discover those characteristics and traits as adults that are more difficult to admit. Remember, this is a fearless and moral inventory. It requires us to look with utmost honesty. Self-diminishing character traits keep us from being truly authentic and can prevent us from being all we can be and from having the kinds of lives we want.

Some **self-diminishing character traits:**

- avoiding
- belittling
- blaming
- bullying
- complaining
- controlling
- cowardice
- criticizing
- dishonesty
- dishonoring
- envy
- fearing
- gossiping
- hiding self
- jealousy
- lying
- manipulating
- minimizing
- resisting
- rigid
- self-abusing
- self-denying
- self-hating
- self-judging
- shaming
- sneaking
- stealing
- unforgiving

As adults abused as children, we tend to over-inflate our negative traits and minimize our positive ones. We may be surprised at the helpful aspects we find when we examine ourselves as adults and as children. We will discover that we have past and present characteristics that work for us, help us, and support us.

Penny applauds herself:

When I did my Step 4 inventory, I realized that when I was 7 years old, I protected the younger ones in the group who were going to suffer abuse in the next few moments. I believed that they were less prepared for the abuse than I was. I saw that my 7-year-old cared about them and became their protector. By doing my 4th Step, I had to admit and applaud my 7-year-old self for risking more pain to protect other children. I had never quite realized or gave myself credit for being that kind of a little one before!

*I had only focused on what I was powerless over and neglected to see and acknowledge where I wasn't solely powerless, but in fact, determined, courageous, and selfless. I had never thought about looking at who I **was** as a child. Instead, I saw only the negative at who I **wasn't**. I found out more about myself than I knew and it was profoundly positive!*

The purpose of taking an inventory is not to change ourselves. The purpose is to assess and be willing to be responsible for who we have become and what our lives are like. We can make healthier and happier choices based on what we discover.

We heal through changes in our beliefs, attitudes, and actions. The inventory is not about figuring out what is the matter with us and then coming up with a plan of self-improvement. Step 4 is about self-responsibility, self-awareness, self-acceptance, self-love, and self-knowledge... all made possible through our ability to be totally honest.

Step 4 Summary

The power of Step 4 becomes evident when we gain clarity about who we have become, why we behave the way we do, and what roles we play in our relationships today. It can be exciting to learn why we pick our partners or certain types of friends and why we treat our children the way we do. As we grow through the Steps, we have the opportunity to choose differently, if we wish.

In Step 4, we are accepting what it is like to be human. This takes courage and willingness. We discover it is the misery of the unmanageability of our lives which motivates us. As adults abused as children, we care enough about ourselves to want something better than what we already have! Self-care has become a strong motivating factor as well.

As we discover who we truly are, the possibility of self-advocacy emerges. It is the ability to speak up for ourselves, make our own decisions, and take actions on our own behalf. We need to understand ourselves, realize our needs, and know how to get them met. The skills to communicate our needs can be learned.

Our Step 4 inventory is an invaluable tool for us to become aware of our strengths and challenges. This information is useful to know what we want and what is possible to expect. As we advocate for ourselves, we need to know our rights and responsibilities as well as our thoughts, feelings, and beliefs. Self-honesty and self-awareness are essential.

Self-advocacy helps create self-confidence, independence, and empowers us to find solutions to problems. We become able to make choices and decisions that benefit our lives. We explore our assets and liabilities highlighted for us in our Step 4 inventory. The strongest self-advocates are those who feel best about themselves. We do this by knowing who we are at our core.

By unlocking the power within us, we learn we have everything we need to create lives of joy, have peace of mind, and contribute to others in our communities. Our inner attitudes of appreciation of ourselves support our shifts toward greater self-acceptance. We begin to connect with our humanity and our inspiring qualities already apparent to us. This is what makes all the difference in our success in our healing from childhood abuse.

Step 4 Affirmations

1. By releasing the past, I am creating space for new possibilities today.//
2. I find peace of mind as my life becomes more manageable.
3. I choose to trust the process of doing my inventory.
4. I align my mind, attitude, and actions with the truth of my being.
5. I am healing through the 12 Steps.
6. I have ample opportunity for enjoyment today.
7. I have what it takes to handle real life.
8. My Higher Power cares about me.
9. With courage, fearlessness is made real with my Higher Power.
10. Self-love creates a life that is worth living.
11. Being authentic feels good.
12. I am coming out of hiding and revealing who I am.
13. Just for today, I accept what is and what is not.
14. I am enough.

Step 4 Journal Questions

1. How is my distorted thinking still affecting my life?

2. Am I aware that avoiding pain makes my life unmanageable? When is this most evident?

3. What strengths do I see in myself that were revealed in my inventory?

4. In what areas of my life do I demonstrate balance?

5. Who is part of my support system?
   How do I express my trust in them?

6. List some ways I have asserted myself recently.

7. How do I still treat myself as if I don't count?
   How does it feel when I do this?
   How does it feel when I treat myself as if I matter?

8. Do I notice areas of excess in my life?
   What are they?
   Have I considered surrendering them to a Higher Power?

9. Where have I taken responsibility for things that were not my fault?

10. What was it like for me the last time I said "No" and meant it?

11. Where do unrealistic expectations of me still trigger my need to be perfect?

12. Do I ask for what I need? Is it becoming easier?

13. List some "mistakes" I have made recently. What positive changes did I make as a result?

Step 4 Prayer

As an adult abused as a child, I realize how important it is to discover the part I play in my own life. I seek to know and understand why I react to certain people and circumstances in the unhealthy ways I do. I ask for help to uncover what is triggering me. I want to learn what is it about me that gets upset or scared.

As I find out these answers and more, I remember to turn them over to my Higher Power and ask for guidance and clarity. I pray that I'll have the inner strength to direct my will to follow these promptings.

I am grateful for whatever courage I can muster. I trust that I do have what it takes to create a new life for myself with my Higher Power's help. I begin with self-honesty. That is enough for today.

Thank you, God.

And so it is.

AMEN

Notes

Notes

Step 5

Admitted to God,
to ourselves, and to
another human being
the exact nature
of our wrongs.

Step 5

Admitted to God, to ourselves, and to another human being the exact nature of our wrongs.

Table of Contents

Introduction 225

Wrongs 230

Exact Nature 235

Structure for Admitting 238

How to Do a 5th Step 240

Admit from an Adult Perspective 241

Admit to God and to Ourselves 245

Admit to Another Human Being 249

Sponsorship 252

Service 254

Step 5 Summary 256

Step 5 Affirmations 260

Step 5 Journal Questions 261

Step 5 Prayer 263

Step 5

Admitted to God, to ourselves, and to another human being the exact nature of our wrongs.

Introduction

Step 4 asks us to do a searching and fearless moral inventory of who we are **as adults.** We strive for an honest and raw examination of ourselves as we look at how our past abuse has shaped our beliefs, actions, and attitudes.

As we study ourselves, it becomes evident where our lives have become unmanageable and have caused harm to ourselves or another.

Emily shares:

When I first read Step 5, I thought it was asking me to admit that what I did as a child was wrong. I didn't understand what I had done to cause or allow the abuse, so I didn't know what to admit. Then I learned that what I'm admitting is my "off the mark" **adult reactions** to my childhood abuse, not what I did as a child. I had believed certain negative things about myself which turned out to be false. I also had expectations of life which were unattainable. Since I was so young when the abuse started, I got confused about my part in my life. I was ruled by my skewed child-like perceptions resulting from the abuse.

Romy adds:

What was required of me as a child was to serve my mother unreservedly. I was her slave. I was her companion, her confidante. She treated me like I was her friend in the sense that she would tell me private, inappropriate things that a mother shouldn't tell a child. My life revolved around her moods, her physical needs, and wants. I was told that I was only alive to fulfill her requirements; she determined my life. She beat and attacked me regularly. At home, there was no room for me to have an emotional or physical life of my own. It's been challenging ever since to learn how to develop a life, apart from others.

Step 4 has guided us toward a deeper understanding of what it truly means to be authentic. As a result, we have created a written list and prepared our personal inventory. This wasn't easy. It took a great deal of courage for us to have come this far. Step 5 is asking us to continue upon our courageous path of transformation.

If our inventory or self-examination is done with great honesty, we are apt to find a lot more to admit as we continue with the Steps. Step 4 is a worthy endeavor to revisit, if necessary, as it helps guide us to be thorough and fearless. Often during Step 5 we become aware of more items to add to our inventory as we gain greater clarity and understanding of ourselves.

As adults abused as children we need to explore where our misguided assumptions originated in our past. We investigate where we still have errors in our thinking, or poor attitudes toward ourselves and others. We discovered these patterns when we wrote our 4th Step inventory.

It is common for us to read the whole inventory to another person as we work Step 5. We continue to make healthy changes and follow what Step 5 asks of us. Through the act of admitting to God and another human being, we deepen our faith. We gain greater humility, self-respect, and self-honesty as we continue to grow spiritually.

Step 5 provides us with the opportunity to begin to mature spiritually, mentally, and emotionally. We begin to accept true accountability and responsibility for our adult actions, our beliefs, and our lives. It provides us an opening to unload the burdens of our past.

> **Arnold contributes:**
>
> *Sometimes I'm as honest as I can be, but I haven't a clue what to do after that! I've noticed that my self-honesty is usually focused on an aspect of myself that is not pleasing to me and is challenging in some way. I know honesty is in my best interest, so I'll continue, even if I don't have answers or solutions for myself for what to do after I'm honest and admit it.*

Doing the Step 4 inventory can be a very solitary endeavor. In Step 5 the issues are so huge that we create a means of sharing to allow us to change. Why do we want to change? Because we want something better for ourselves than what we have now! Why else would we admit the exact nature of our wrongs? We do so because we want to release the past that lingers in the shadows. It has been weighing us down, has been held in secrecy, and has caused us so much anguish, fear, and pain.

Barbara explains:

In sharing my 5th Step, I became aware of what I call my "left-over thoughts" from the past. These thoughts seem to appear out of nowhere. Sometimes they're triggered by a situation in the present that is still bothering me from the past. If I recognize that these scary thoughts are negative or harmful, I remind myself that my life has changed and I don't have to be so afraid or angry anymore. There are no dangers in my current life to cause these "left-over thoughts." Often, I will remember to reorient myself to present time by taking deep breaths.

This journey takes all the courage we have. We may not believe that we have enough courage, because we mistakenly concluded that if we had had enough courage, we would have done something to make the abuse stop. That is how a child may have interpreted courage then. Now, as adults, we know that it takes courage to tell someone else about how helpless we were as children and about whom we have become today.

Wrongs

To discover the exact nature of our wrongs, we ask ourselves to be willing to explore the causes and issues that have created our unmanageable adult lives. We admit where we have gone amiss or are out of alignment with what's happening in our lives today.

> **Michael fears:**
>
> *I'm afraid that my current wife will cheat on me like my first wife did, even though she shows no inkling of being that kind of a woman. She's aghast that I would even think those kinds of things about her with no provocation on her part.*

What actions have we taken that are not morally right or good? Where have we acted out of incorrect judgment? We must explore these areas with openness and honesty or we will get lost in the drama of the past. It is the drama that forever ties us to the stories of our abuse. The drama mercilessly holds the reins to our suffering from the past, as well as the suffering we create today.

Maddie uncovers this while doing her 5th Step:

When I was cut off on the road by another driver, I became triggered from feeling controlled by someone else's abuse of power. I used to react with rage and became uncontrolled myself. I acted out and created unsafe conditions for the other drivers in the vicinity.

This is a fact-finding and fact-facing process that challenges the lies we hid behind to cover our true selves. Much of what we will uncover and reveal has been hidden from us as well. The point of Step 4 is to begin to detach from "the story" we created about ourselves and about the world in which we live. Now we are being asked in Step 5 to strip the story down even more.

Step 5 is the point when we admit how our childhood abuse has affected our lives today and the lives of those around us.

Adults abused as children most often live in a world filled with denial. It may have been difficult for us to admit how bad the abuse really was. We may have denied the extent of the damage that was created. Some of us weren't ready or willing to see the impact.

Our denial was not necessarily a conscious decision. It could have been something that we hadn't realized yet. Once we have admitted these wrongs to God, to ourselves, and to another, we are unable to go back to our old ways with a clear conscience. **We are not the same people;** we carry a conscious awareness that strives to create better lives for ourselves.

It is understandable why an adult abused as a child might try to skip this Step due to the fear that surrounds our lives, our suffering, and our stories. It is a heavy price to pay, to not share our "wrongs." The decision to **not admit** is to stay entangled with our past, our suffering, and the unmanageability of our lives. Step 5 is paramount in our journey toward the creation of the lives we have always wanted and toward the healing we have longed for.

Let's look a little more deeply into the nature of our wrongs. Stealing and being a thief, is wrong, but what is the exact nature of the wrong in this action? It could be a lack of trust that there is enough of something for us. It could be a lack of respect for another. It could be a sense of entitlement, justifying our actions. Looking at our wrongs is looking at our beliefs, assumptions, misconceptions, and our misguided actions... these are our wrongs.

As adults abused as children, we may have done things from uninformed, misinformed, obsolete, or misguided places. We have been closed-minded or closed-hearted, with erroneous beliefs and actions that didn't match up with our best selves.

What is meant by wrong is where we did not value ourselves or others. It is also where we see lack or where we make erroneous assumptions.

Fran realizes:

In giving my 4th Step inventory away, I saw that I still have shame for how I sat on my father's lap until I was 12 years old. It was inappropriate to sit facing him with my legs around his waist, but I did not know that at the time. Now that I'm an adult I see that my shame is misplaced. I was so love-starved and fearful that I would have done almost anything, and did, to get the love I craved. I was just a child. My father was one of my perpetrators.

In relationships many of us have lived with expectations about what we want or how we think others should be. We don't see how skewed our relationships with ourselves, others, or with the world are.

In Step 5 we are searching for the beliefs that limit our growth and interactions. We explore those beliefs that tell us others don't love us, understand us, or accept us. We share where we still feel dirty, or where we think there is something wrong with us. We explore why we are still afraid, resentful, bitter, ashamed, blaming, or angry.

We have been incorrect in some of our assessments, our actions, and beliefs. We tell God, ourselves, and another human being about our unmanageable lives. We see where we have been misunderstanding or misjudging the world around us. In the action of admitting, we create better lives for ourselves. It helps us release a tremendous burden of guilt and shame.

> **Fay contributes:**
>
> *The human condition is not at all what I thought it was. I thought the goal of being human was to be pure and good. I learned that we are not pure; we're human and imperfect. As a child, my decision to be pure was wanting to be what my abusive parents weren't. In order to have a different experience of life, I thought I must be the opposite of them. They were impure, so I must be pure. They were hurtful, so I must be blameless. The 12 Steps have given me a different goal: to find out and be who I am. I say "yes" to my Higher Power and develop a relationship with this Power.*

Exact Nature

We notice that the only time in the 12 Steps the word "exact" appears is in Step 5. The intention of the word "exact" is that we offer our personal best to this process. We are specific as we carefully look at the nature of our wrongs. We seek to know what lies under our motives. We are not bound by the concept of perfection or doing the Step 100% right. We are being asked to be as detailed as possible, to go beyond our story, pull the curtains back and truly discover ourselves.

The guiding principle of being "exact" reminds us to focus on what is really driving us. We look upon our wrongs, as we have listed them through our 4th Step inventory. We strive to be as exact as we can and admit them honestly.

Examples of the exact nature of wrongs as adults

- Disrespecting or dishonoring another person
- Experiencing feelings of superiority
- Experiencing unfounded feelings of inferiority
- Gossiping
- Insisting on having our own way
- Lying
- Misusing power
- Physically harming self or another person
- Refusing to grow up and act maturely

- Righteousness
- Scarcity thinking
- Self-hating or blaming self
- Taking on too much responsibility that is not ours
- Thinking we know what's best for another person
- Unwillingness

We made decisions based on errored thinking and incorrect conclusions. Sometimes the nature of our wrongs led to the actions we took. We want to become aware of the ways we sabotage ourselves and others.

The table on the following page is one way of looking at what happened and the progressive results of one particular abusive experience. We can see where we may have had false beliefs and reached erroneous conclusions.

Process for looking at our wrongs

	What Happened?	Results for the Child
1	**Abuse Experience**	Often not allowed to eat food at home as a child.
2	Reaction to the Pain of It	Shock, despair, stress, forced into survival mode, eating always felt like an emergency.
3	Issues or Problem Areas	Fear of starvation. Obsessed with food. Forced to cook, but not allowed to eat. Stole and hid food.
4	Conclusions or Assumptions	Up to me to stay alive and feed myself. Can't count on others for my needs and survival.
5	Beliefs	I am not important enough to feed. I'm not valued, wanted, or loved.
6	Thoughts	Heightened awareness of food for survival. I knew stealing food was wrong, but I was in survival mode. Confusion about right and wrong. My parents are wrong.
7	Feelings	Fear of starvation. Afraid to make waves. Being alone with the problem.
8	Attitudes	Fear ruled my life. If I don't take it, I won't have it. I must not count. General confusion about life.
9	Choices/Decisions	Need to get through this time until I can leave home. Got used to living in overwhelm. Powerless over others.
10	Actions	Stole food from refrigerator and hid it.
11	Impact	Mastered cleverness, slyness, sneaking, hiding, and stealing food. I survived. Food addict as an adult.
12	Adult Desires for Health Today	Inner peace and enjoying food. Eating moderately. Surrender food to my Higher Power. Honor and be grateful for my body. Bless my body.

Structure for Admitting

Admitting our wrongs uses the principles from the first four Steps:

- The process of admitting uses the principle of powerlessness as practiced in Step 1. We create connection and break isolation.

- We are accessing the faith we have developed and experienced in Step 2 as well as looking more intently at our beliefs.

- We are willing to surrender what we want and turn our lives over to a Power greater than ourselves as called for in Step 3. We are building trust and a belief that we will continue to be taken care of.

- We are drawing upon the principle of self-honesty, developed and revealed through Step 4. We tell the truth and understand what our part is in those unmanageable areas. We see the impact of our choices on our adult lives.

Now that we have developed these principles, we are at a point in Step 5 where we are learning to trust ourselves, a Higher Power, and another human being by honestly sharing the exact nature of our wrongs.

Alice writes:

There's nothing wrong with me as a person. I have aspects of myself, like impatience, that make my life difficult. I wish they weren't there, but they are. I choose to accept these characteristics because it's **me** I'm talking about. Who else will love me as I am? My Higher Power.

As I admit who I really am today, I see how I am both unique and the same as everybody else. I feel compassion for myself as I resist accepting the things I don't like about myself. What I like, I call good. What I don't, I call bad.

My rights as a child were denied me. My interpretation of this at the time was that I was not valuable like other children. Today, as a senior, I've challenged that conclusion and have made great progress in treating myself well. I don't know what I would do if I didn't have a Higher Power. I am grateful every day that my Higher Power is teaching and helping me create the best life I can have.

How to Do a 5th Step

The answer to how to do a 5th Step is quite simple. We can do it any way that works for us. The focus of this Step is our 4th Step inventory. We can read it aloud to another human being, all at one time, or over a period of time, taking days or weeks.

It can be shared in person, over the phone, in a park, anywhere where we feel comfortable. It is ideal to choose a place where there is privacy with as few interruptions as possible. It is helpful to remember to turn off phones and other electronic equipment.

Some of us make copies of our inventories for the other person so that they can read along with us as we share. It can be sent electronically or through the mail service. This process of sharing can take as little time or as long as we want.

There is no right way to do the 5th Step! If our admitting is not working to our satisfaction, we can change how we are doing it. Many of us will do more than one 4th Step inventory as we change, and thus we will do more than one 5th Step sharing. We will often discover that as we learn, heal, and transform, we experience consistent growth. We change as our understanding of ourselves increases.

Admit from an Adult Perspective

Admitting in Step 5, comes from sharing our Step 4 inventory with God, ourselves, and another human being. It is done by looking at our inventory through the exact nature of our wrongs. **The exact nature of our wrongs in Step 5 does not mean what we did wrong as children,** how we felt wrong, or were made wrong by others.

The type of wrong that is being addressed here is this: as adults we come to understand that as children, we may have assumed certain things incorrectly. We may have arrived at erroneous conclusions, mainly about ourselves, but also about others or life itself. We were not wrong as children; we were just children, thinking and acting like children.

Too often we think that what happened was our fault and we are to blame, or at least we should have been able to stop it. Many of us will discover that we are heavily burdened with shame and guilt, thus character assassination of ourselves has been easy for us.

In Step 4, we discovered that we were "wrong" for following self-destructive beliefs. The impact upon our adult lives from these beliefs will help us see how we may have taken responsibility for certain issues that were not ours to claim.

Laura shares:

All my life I've had great shame about my personal hygiene. I didn't keep myself as clean as I thought I should. While doing my 5th Step and reading my inventory aloud to a trusted friend, I realized that the effect of the trauma of my sexual abuse in the bath tub and shower prevented me from getting into them. It had nothing to do with my not caring about myself or not being a clean person. I became triggered and powerless in the shower and tub. My beliefs about myself were incorrect or "wrong."

We may believe that we are unlovable, not worthy of good things in life and thus deny or shy away from opportunities for real happiness. We may also be wrong about the assumptions we made about the perpetrators, our family, or those who knew about the abuse and did nothing to stop it.

We are not saying that they were right or that we are condoning it, but there were circumstances that those involved were experiencing that we could not have understood as children. We can now begin to understand as adults.

Complexities surrounded the circumstances of our childhood abuse, making it difficult to reveal the "secrets" we have been carrying for so long. Denial, withholding, and misguided beliefs were deployed by us when we were young to protect us from further harm. Step 5 helps us unburden ourselves by admitting and telling of our wrong thinking.

> **Nick admits:**
>
> I was sexually abused as a child by my older sister. When I grew up, I had an insatiable desire for sex. I looked for it everywhere. I would never admit this secret. It consumed my life.
>
> I tried to hide it from my wife. The lies got out of control. One night I told her I was going out to get milk and instead, went to a local bar that had a lingerie show. My life fell apart.
>
> It was only when my dark secret was exposed in my 5th Step that I began to feel some self-compassion. I no longer felt like I was a horrible person for the actions of my past. I realized that I had been traumatized as a child and needed healing as an adult.

We don't need to know or understand all the events or situations that happened to us as children or as adults. As we take the focus off the ones who knew about it, and most importantly the perpetrators, Step 5 guides us to bring our focus back to ourselves.

Admit to God and to Ourselves

The action of admitting to God, to ourselves, and to another human being allows our past to become more real as it becomes "history." In time, it loses its control over our lives. We don't get to keep the newfound information that we learned from our Step 4 inventory, only to ourselves. By sharing we are revealing the false truths, the misconceptions, and the limiting attitudes which have been driving us. The benefit of Step 5 is the experience of knowing that we are beginning to rebuild our lives based on integrity, truth, honesty, and our continued growth through greater self-love and self-respect.

The 5th Step says "admitted" which reminds us that there's nothing else to do, but admit. Most of the time, we're telling what we already learned about ourselves from completing Step 4. Yes, new things may come to light, but for the most part we already know what we're going to say when we share our inventory. We've already written it down; we just hadn't told anyone else yet. Sometimes we may not even have let ourselves know what we know.

> **Tracy discovers:**
>
> *I tend to keep things from myself – secrets and other information. In the past I didn't trust myself to admit that I knew who I really was. I didn't want to be accountable because I wasn't ready or willing to accept myself. I also*

feared I might use the self-knowledge against myself. I feared I was too fragile, that I didn't have what it took to handle the truth.

I discovered I knew things in my heart and body a long time before I let myself acknowledge them in my conscious mind. Part of the importance of Step 5 is telling myself the truth and seeing that I won't perish from the imagined pain of it.

When we do a written inventory, it becomes part of the admitting process. It demonstrates to us that we have a measure of trust in ourselves. We experience that we **do** have what it takes to look at reality. Writing it makes it real. It's not just a memory or information that moves through our minds and never settles anywhere.

We speak in depth and at length about many issues in our lives. Through working Steps 4 and 5, we have the opportunity to examine the many times we've dealt with these same issues. Repetitive patterns and ways of being emerge for us to review within the structure of these Steps. We are able to look back and assess our lives in a systematic way. We may find ourselves viewing things over a long period of time, not just as isolated occurrences.

Delores writes:

One of the ways I did an inventory was to write an autobiography of my first 21 years, when the abuse stopped. I had never actually paused and thought about 21 years of my life all at one time. It was overwhelming. I was able to see patterns which enlightened me. The scope and depth of the inventory gave me a perspective I did not have access to before.

I could not have looked at 21 years of my life in a short period of time. It took me a couple of months to complete the autobiography. I'm grateful I didn't rush the process.

Just as the 12 Steps themselves are worked in a specific order for us to work them best, the process outlined in Step 5 is also ordered. Our first admission of our wrongs is to God **as we understand God,** then to ourselves after that. It's not that our Higher Power doesn't already know our wrongs, but we hadn't trusted this Power enough to admit them. We may not have believed that there was a Higher Power. Sharing our inventory strengthens our faith. We see we are not punished for telling the truth. We experience the care of our Higher Power as it states in Step 3.

This conversation with a greater Power helps us open to what needs to be revealed. Once we have mustered the courage and the integrity to become honest with God and ourselves, we experience our willingness and desire to be transformed. After that, becoming honest with another human being becomes easier!

In Step 4 we listed both our assets and our liabilities. We are not responsible for what others do. However, as adults, we are responsible for how we react to what others do. Through the help and caring of a Higher Power we can adjust our behavior.

Humility is part of our healing process. Up until now, we may have been running away from a Higher Power as well as from our inner selves. We see where we have gone off track and are eager to develop a new relationship with this Power so we can get back on course. We find ourselves open to guidance as we take responsibility for our actions. We experience acceptance and forgiveness from a Power greater than ourselves. Then we are able to accept and forgive ourselves.

> **Marty shares:**
>
> The scars that I bear are not erasable by force of will, but with the tools that I have learned, my Higher Power transforms my life one day at a time.

Admit to Another Human Being

In Step 5 we are asked for the first time to share with another person. The first four Steps are all done with a Power greater than ourselves, but this Step demands that we include another person as well.

After we admitted our wrongs, many of us who have taken Step 5 experience our relationship with a Higher Power in a new way. We feel the caring of this Power through another person who knows the "worst" about us. When we are honest with another human being, it confirms we have been honest with ourselves and with God.

Admitting to God and to ourselves is difficult enough, but telling someone else the exact nature of our wrongs can be frightening. As adults abused as children, we have been keeping secrets, by hiding our faults and shortcomings. We hid what we believed was wrong with us. Now we are being asked to openly share our wrongs with another human being. This is a leap of faith, a deepening act of surrender, and a monumental act of trust.

Fear can get in the way of our sharing. Eventually we realize that it is time to move on; it is time to reveal all. We can't sit with our wrongs forever. It is not healthy for our mental, physical, emotional, or spiritual lives to carry such a burden. When we admit our wrongs to God, we are essentially asking for forgiveness. Once we know that our Higher Power has forgiven us, we will be able to focus solely on our healing without the guilt of the past. Forgiveness becomes a turning point in our lives. This sharing is the beginning of a spiritual awakening. We feel understood, accepted, and enjoy a sense of belonging. Wanting to heal gives us courage.

As children, our abuse led most of us to believe that we were unlovable and our ability to trust others was greatly affected. Today trusting that another human being believes us, is nonjudgmental, and loves us as we are is a huge step. It is certainly one that needs to be commended.

We remember to appreciate our courage, strength, and honesty as we are in the act of admission. It is critical that we release any self-shaming or self-criticism, making ourselves wrong. Once we share our hidden world with another, the whole dynamic of our lives can change.

How do we decide who we share our inventory with? It is helpful to remember that what is most important is our willingness to trust and choose someone appropriate for us. It could be another person in the program, a counselor, a mentor, a therapist, a spiritual friend, a member of the clergy.

Trust is the key. If we choose someone to hear our 4th Step inventory who understands the process we are engaged in, often they will be honored to share something which is so important to us. Since we are sincere in our efforts we will usually be met with great respect.

We choose an understanding listener, one we trust who will maintain confidentiality. We are taking advantage of an opportunity to enhance our emotional health and spiritual well-being.

Lenore admits:

I thought I would never tell anyone that I slept with another man thirty years ago when I was pregnant and married. I shared this with my confidante, though I was filled with shame and embarrassment. She was not shocked by my admittance. Later I felt peaceful and free. I was not judged.

Sometimes the mistakes from our past seem huge and unforgivable since we have kept them to ourselves for so long. When we share them, we can finally lay them to rest. It's human nature to make mistakes but through our faith in a Higher Power and through the support of others, we allow the healing that follows admitting those mistakes. We remember we are not alone and begin to feel free to be who we are and begin anew. Step 5 offers us an opportunity to heal our childhood abuse and get a fresh perspective for our future.

Sponsorship

We learn that there is a tool for adults abused as children called a sponsor. A sponsor may be someone who is actively going to meetings of ADULTS ABUSED AS CHILDREN ANONYMOUS and is working the 12 Steps themselves.

This is a good time to remember that everything shared in the meetings, member to member or at the group level, is confidential. Nothing is taken out of these meetings or private conversations to be discussed by others at a later time.

Being entrusted with what another member has shared, including their written inventory, is sacred and held in the strictest confidence. A sponsor is the person we choose to help us go through the 12 Steps. Ideally, it is best to choose a sponsor when we start to work Step 1.

We agree to sponsor another, knowing that this is done from a place of sheer willingness to support each other. We share what is or is not working in our lives: our progress, successes, difficulties, struggles, and frustrations.

Remember if our sponsor does not seem right for us, we can change sponsors at any time. This is our healing. We don't have to ensure that our sponsor understands why it's time for us to change. There is no need to apologize, we simply thank our recent sponsor and ask another to sponsor us and move on. As we are changed by the Steps, the need to change sponsors might be appropriate.

"We" is the first word that is implied at the beginning of every Step. We are not meant to work the Steps by ourselves. We can try to do the other Steps in isolation, but Step 5 cannot be done alone; it requires us to tell another. Since we respect the intention of this Step, we must now involve someone else in our healing.

As we stated in the ADULTS ABUSED AS CHILDREN ANONYMOUS program, our sponsor is another member who is actively working the Steps themselves. What do we do if we're ready to do a 5th Step with someone but we're not in a program and don't go to meetings? We choose a trusted other to listen to and witness our Step 4 inventory from a nonjudgmental and confidential place. As previously mentioned, a mentor, clergy, friend, or counselor will serve us just fine.

Feedback, counseling, and advice-giving are not necessarily parts of the Step 5 process. The other person can act more as a witness. You and your sponsor can decide what your sponsor's role will be. Our job is to simply admit what we discovered about ourselves from writing our Step 4 inventory and share that.

Service

Sponsorship, at the personal level, is a way of doing important service in the ADULTS ABUSED AS CHILDREN ANONYMOUS program. Service is an act of providing and fulfilling a need for another. It begins with our willingness to be part of someone else's healing.

At the group level, service may look like getting the meeting room ready, setting up chairs, turning the heater or lights on, putting out the **ADULTS ABUSED AS CHILDREN ANONYMOUS** literature. In addition, there are other group service positions that need to be filled:

- running the meeting by being the secretary, keeping order
- being the treasurer
- helping make tea or coffee
- greeting, welcoming newcomers and all other members
- handling the program literature
- being the Zoom host

Positions are usually rotated within the group as we take turns doing service. Service is seen as an important tool for our recovery. It is powerful to discover and experience how we are benefited by the service we do while making a difference in someone else's life. By becoming truly invested in helping others through service, we help ourselves.

We are encouraged to call or meet with one another in good times and bad, to admit our wrongs or to share our progress. The person we connect with is being of service to us. Often at the end of these conversations, we experience being filled with appreciation for the other who was there for us. In addition, the other person will often tell us how much they got from the conversation as well. In reality, we are being of service to each other.

By working the Steps with a sponsor, both parties benefit. We bring new wisdom and consciousness forward together.

Adelia shares:

As others were ready to work their 5th Step, I was asked to hear the 4th Step inventory from other adults abused as children who were not well known to me. They had heard of me from another member of the group and asked if I would hear their sharing. I learned who we share our inventory with, is up to us. From a place of service, I witnessed their admitting. I was not their sponsor, but they chose to share it with me anyway. It worked well for them.

Step 5 Summary

Step 5 is a major step in self-responsibility while Step 4 is a powerful guide toward greater self-discovery. Through the journey of the 12 Steps, we learn to love ourselves using the tools of self-acceptance, honesty, and right action. Love takes many forms. When directed toward ourselves it may present itself as self-discipline, self-care, or self-generosity. When offered to someone else it may be shown through being present, attentive, or listening without interruption.

> **Joy writes:**
> For most of my life I have had contempt for my body. Now I can approach my physical body with willingness to accept it as it is. Spiritually, I observe myself as a creation of my Higher Power, made to be loved and accepted.
>
> While doing Step 5, I had a fundamental shift in my attitude and now I see my body as a gift. Instead of focusing on shape, I focus on function. I can be thankful for the health I enjoy and take charge of how I treat my body today.
>
> My past cannot be erased; however, I acknowledge that I'm powerless over what happened to it. As an adult I have the willingness and ability to choose to love my body. Therein lays the solution to powerlessness.

For adults abused as children, one of our greatest wrongs is to believe that we are unlovable. We have been waiting our whole lives to be loved. Our instinctual needs, desires, and expectations as children were to be loved. If the perpetrator was a family member, and especially if they were our parents, it makes it that much more challenging for us to feel lovable as adults.

Today many of us still have the expectation and belief that it is someone else's job to love us. When we were children, we assumed that it was our parents' job. **Only as an adult can we learn and experience that it is our job to love ourselves.**

Betty says:

I realized I tended to be possessive with the people I love. I became controlling and wanted to manage their lives. I think this came from a lonely and unloved child place within me. I really want to be able to trust others' love for me.

I am willing to release the responsibility for others to make me happy. I want to be able to express my adult love toward those I previously wanted to possess or keep close so I could feel secure. I need to set them free of being responsible for meeting my needs.

We still long for love; most everyone does. Thus, one of the largest illuminations in Step 5 is to discover that it is our job to love ourselves. We do this through self-honesty, accountability, acceptance, transparency, and sharing. Our list will continue to grow as we journey through the Steps, especially Steps 4 and 5.

Loving ourselves is paramount to our healing and the creation of the lives we have longed for. What awaits us is a greater sense of self-fulfillment, peace, and understanding ourselves.

Self-love helps create and maintain an experience of life that's worth living. It sets the standard for how we allow others to treat us, and of course, how we treat ourselves. We have an opportunity to be something more than what happened to us as children. We choose new paths that serve us now.

We will continue to make errors in judgment because we are human. That does not make us wrong, weak, or stupid. We are coming to know the exact nature of our wrongs. We will have areas in our lives where we won't see clearly or may not have found understanding yet. As our nature becomes more evident to us, we become willing to be accountable for our part in our adult lives and experience a sense of healthy personal power.

Susie shares a similar sentiment:

I used to put a lot of energy into looking for love. I wanted my friends to tell me I mattered so I would feel worthy. I wanted to feel like I belonged somewhere. When I did my 5th Step and read my inventory to another person, it became obvious I was using others to make me feel whole.

Step 5 Affirmations

1. I accept my own worthiness.
2. Gratitude helps me accept.
3. I live as if I have value.
4. I honor myself.
5. There's nothing wrong with me.
6. I live as if my body matters.
7. Insecurity is a feeling. I let it pass through me.
8. I accept my past one day at a time.
9. I love myself no matter what.
10. I honor my courage as an adult.

Step 5 Journal Questions

1. Where have I put my life on hold waiting for something to change on its own?

2. Do I still think I am what I do and how well I do it?

3. What decisions do I make when I lose faith in my goodness?

4. What decisions do I make using my free will poorly?

5. What false ideas have I believed that I need to relinquish?

6. In my practice of self-awareness where is my self-talk still harmful?

7. Where am I letting circumstances direct my life instead of taking right action from the cues within me?

8. Do I get upset when someone else is upset with me? Who does or doesn't this happen with?

9. Where and when do I treat myself as if I don't count? Where do I see progress?

10. Where do I see myself as not enough?

11. Where do I think I have the right to make decisions for others because I know better?

12. How have I used Step 5 as a path to personal freedom?

13. What obstacles do I need to overcome to achieve peace of mind?

14. Where do I give unwarranted power to my fears and anxieties?

15. What decisions did I make as a child that are no longer appropriate or necessary as an adult?

16. Where do I try to play the Higher Power to get some control over something or someone?

17. In which areas of my life do I come from a victim mentality? What part of my nature is being revealed?

18. What do I want to create or work toward in my life?

19. When did I have the courage to say something difficult lately?

Step 5 Prayer

As I discover where I've erred in my thinking or my actions, I simply acknowledge it. I am willing to be responsible for where I was off base and the impact that has had on my life. I pray to treat myself as if I matter, especially when I make mistakes or make errors in judgment. I am no longer afraid to reveal to another what it's like to be an adult abused as a child.

I have faith in the power of healing through these 12 Steps. I intend to reap the benefits as I work them. I am grateful to my Higher Power for the help I receive with every effort I make. I direct my attention to my Higher Power's care of me and release any anxiety that may appear and watch it dissipate. I remain calm and trusting as I reflect and share.

Since I do this journey with my Higher Power, I enjoy a sense of peace. I share myself from a place of nonjudgment. I am learning to accept myself and love myself as I am today. I experience a sense of well-being, for which I am grateful.

Thank you, God.

And so it is.

AMEN

Notes

Notes

Step 6

Were entirely ready to have God remove all these defects of character.

Step 6

Were entirely ready to have God remove all these defects of character.

Table of Contents

Introduction.................................. 271

The Principle of Readiness..................... 274

Becoming Ready 277

Let Go. Let God............................... 279

God Removes Defects........................... 282

We Allow Removal 288

Our Defects of Character 291

List of Some Character Defects 294

List of Some Character Assets 296

Step 6 Summary................................ 298

Affirmations for New Behaviors................ 301

Step 6 Affirmations 303

Step 6 Journal Questions...................... 304

Step 6 Prayer 306

Step 6

Were entirely ready to have God remove all these defects of character.

Introduction

The active word in Step 6 is "God." God, or whatever we call our Higher Power, does the work of removing. As adults abused as children, we allow ourselves to be renewed and transformed. We are preparing for these actions from our Higher Power. We choose what to believe a Higher Power can do, provided we are willing to let go of what's not working in our lives. We follow the guidance we receive to move our healing forward.

At this point we have come to terms with admitting our character defects. We have also admitted that we, alone, have failed to reform ourselves in the ways we wanted. We have not shown up in life as we would have liked to. As long as we cling to the illusion that **we** can eliminate our character defects, we are not ready. As long as we hesitate to depend on a Power greater than ourselves, we are not ready. However, with Step 6, we are reminded to accept ourselves how we are, and become ready!

> **Michael reveals:**
>
> Contemplating a Power greater than I am gives me hope. I can hope for change even if it's only my attitude that's willing to let go of a character defect. Sometimes I have an attitude of willingness on one hand and holding onto the defect with the other. It would naturally take a Power greater than me to remove the defect. Now I understand why the intended first word of every Step is "we." It is not possible for me to do this Step on my own.

Eventually, we admit we need our Higher Power to help us. We become open for this Power to replace our flaws that stand in our way of being all we can be, with all that we need. We want to be authentic and do what is ours to do. We have most likely discovered that our past abuse may influence us more than we ever imagined. What can we really do when our best efforts have not been successful? We hold on to what we desire for ourselves and ask for help from a Power greater than ourselves...the God of our understanding.

As children, we developed character defects (coping strategies) as patterns to protect us from harm, pain, and fear, but these strategies are ineffective as adults. Time after time they lead us away from our spiritual integrity in attempts to help us cope with our anxieties. They create lives of unmanageability for us and for others. Unless these traits are healed, they will continue to add to our suffering and our inability to cope.

Sylvia contributes:

As a child growing up with abuse, I had severe low self-esteem. It felt very risky for me to admit that there was anything wrong with me. Being a person of extremes, I believed that I was either blameless or responsible for everything. I became a workaholic to fix my feelings of inadequacy. I chose others before myself. None of this worked.

I resisted change and continued to be miserable and ineffective. My need to be right (the nature of my wrong) showed up as stubbornness (the trait). I forgot to place my trust in God, instead I felt separate from Him and completely out of control. I disappointed myself again and again.

Today, I work my 12 Step program of healing and readiness, as best I can. So far, the results are better than anything I could have come up with on my own. I am grateful.

The Principle of Readiness

As adults abused as children, Step 6 gives us hope for even greater healing and transformation through the 12 Steps. Step 6 requires our faith and acceptance in a Power greater than ourselves to allow for the removal of all our character defects. Our defects of character are the traits and characteristics that get in our way of being all we can be and prevent us from having the kind of lives we want.

Our journey through the previous Steps has given us an ability to believe in the possibility of surrendering our will to a greater Power. Now we are offered the opportunity, through readiness, to have God remove all of our character defects that we explored and identified in Step 4, and admitted to in Step 5. The wrongs we discovered in Step 5 are manifested in the character traits we explored in Step 6. Gratefully, we are being prepared and given the hope that a Power greater than ourselves can remove all these defects when we are ready.

The key principle of Step 6 is **readiness**. The goal of being **entirely** ready, if taken literally, can feel out of the question. We also risk creating unrealistic expectations and pressure on ourselves to have our Higher Power remove "all" our defects of character. For some of us, we could be waiting a long time for all of them to be removed. The gift of Step 6 asks us **only to be ready.** It is a good time to remember to take life one day at a time, and become ready one day at a time as we move through Step 6.

Rachel shares:

I need to remember that there's no place to get to by "becoming" ready. It's not a goal to reach, which challenges the perfectionist and over-achiever in me. I still think I need to be different or better than I am.

David offers:

Entirely, to me, means to the best of my ability when I make an honest effort. I'm a human being willing to do something entirely, not a robot, computer, or machine. I don't want to prevent myself from moving forward in my healing and working the Steps by fearing that I don't have what it takes to release a defect. Otherwise, I might as well not even start. Doing Step 6 in increments stops me from procrastinating.

Some of us may not yet be ready to let a few character defects go. They have become part of our identities, our personalities, and they are comfortable and familiar to us. Our character defects may have become protectors or allies.

We believed we required them for our survival. For example, we may have remained silent when we wanted to speak, but were afraid to rock the boat. We thought silence protected us from harm. We will know our true time of readiness, as we continue to build trust from experiences gained through the continuation of our journey within the 12 Steps. **We take Step 6 one defect at a time.**

It is enough to do our personal best today. We can support ourselves with loving kindness by first accepting, and then offering these character defects to our Higher Power for removal. It is worth restating that we are being made ready for God to remove the character defects that stand in the way of our self-realization and self-fulfillment. This is why Step 6 is worth our time, commitment, and personal investment of energy.

Becoming Ready

How do we become ready? Understanding this question and discovering the answers will help us to prepare and gather clues that guide us and show us how to proceed. Readiness in Step 6 is made possible through the aid, awareness, and support of the previous Steps.

Step 1 helps to remind us to admit that we are powerless over our character defects. We admit they have created unmanageable aspects in our lives. This level of self-awareness and our growing self-acceptance helps us as we admit the impact of the unmanageability.

With the aid of Step 2, we are able to look more deeply at our beliefs. We renew or deepen our trust in a Power greater than ourselves to help us in our readiness. Step 2 is the place we go to regain our trust, strengthen our faith, and be restored to sanity

Step 3 asks us to turn our lives and our will over to the care of a Power greater than ourselves. We need to trust, allow, and have faith that God is able and will remove all of our character defects as we are ready. We allow this Power to take care of our lives, our will, and us.

Fortunately, Steps 4 and 5 have helped to deepen our readiness. This happened through the actions of discovering who we were, sharing, and trusting another person and a Higher Power. Through Step 5, the act of telling God helps us to become even more ready to trust God in Step 6. We deepen our trust through the acts of deep surrender, humility, and courage gained and strengthened in the prior Steps.

Heidi looks at it this way:

As an adult abused as a child, if I'm having a day like today, where I don't feel very together, the idea of becoming ready gives me assurance that I'm not always going to be feeling this way. It also reminds me that who I really am and my perception of who I think I am, are still far apart. I need a better perspective about myself to know which defects need to be removed and which don't.

Barbara's thoughts:

Making myself available to be ready is a clear message to my Higher Power that I'm asking for help. Otherwise, I wouldn't have done the work of being honest about my defects of character. I see where they prevent me from being available to my Higher Power and I want them removed.

Before Step 6, I wouldn't speak of my character as defective, since I had no solid foundation of self-love from which to examine myself. My feelings of unworthiness would not allow me to take a leap of faith and release my character defects until I was grounded in a relationship with a caring Higher Power.

Let Go. Let God.

What do we do while we're waiting for God to remove our defects? We **practice** what we would like to be like. We **practice** how we would like to treat others. We **practice** changing some of our viewpoints or our thinking. We remember to be willing to release what is not in our best interest, or not for our highest good. We **practice** letting go and letting God.

We seek support and encouragement from others who care about us. We reach out, connect with them, and ask for help when needed. We pray for guidance and inner strength from our Higher Power to keep on keeping on while we wait. We maintain hope that God is doing for us what we could not do for ourselves. We allow change.

Sue learned:

I've been holding onto beliefs and dreams that will never come true, fantasies that will never happen, and versions of how my past should have been. Now I am becoming ready to let go of my tight grip on them. I started with the willingness to consider the possibility that there might be another version of life, another way to get through the day, other than the ways I've come up with. I admit I don't always know what's best for me. I am ready to examine my analysis of life, which might be too limited.

When we make an earnest effort, and regularly affirm the outcome we wish, the journey toward readiness eventually gets easier. We just try our very best one day at a time. It helps to realize that in letting go and allowing our Higher Power to remove our character defects, we are not giving something desirable up, but rather we are learning to think and behave differently in ways that better serve us.

From Henry:

I am ready to let go of the pain around my childhood experiences and my fear of feeling pain at all. I feel comforted that as most human beings, I let go and then grasp again, let go and then hold on again, over and over. That's how I become ready, through practice. This gives me permission to do well sometimes and other times, not be able to do it at all. Sometimes I waffle back and forth on the same issue, on the same day.

Matthew contributes:

Becoming ready for me is about letting go of control. If I am still manipulating, that's not becoming ready to let go of anything. I need to be willing to look at new ways of relating without knowing how my new behavior will be received. These are the facets of becoming ready and letting go of control that I'm focusing on now.

Step 6 takes tremendous courage, trust, and faith in a Power greater than us. When we begin this Step, we may not know what will be needed for us to become ready, or how long it will take.

What is certain is that it takes time! It requires our patience to be open and allow ourselves all the time that is needed. It is relevant to remember that transformation can take longer than we thought. Insights gained through conversations and sharing with others will help us to prepare.

We remember to be kind, nonjudgmental, compassionate, and gentle with ourselves through this Step.

God Removes Defects

We have to release our hold on the traits we think are necessary for our survival. It can be humbling to notice that we have immature tendencies and haven't developed beyond that state yet.

We search for what we might be protecting by maintaining this defect of immaturity. We might find it's the way we rebel. We might find that we're afraid of rejection, or we get attention by acting immaturely. Our defect could be caused by any number of things. Even if we don't know the cause, we can create a space in our minds and hearts for what will naturally offset our defect. We could ask God for the willingness to take a risk or be counted on. We want to receive whatever guidance would balance our immaturity.

Norma offers:

Most of my life I chose men whom I allowed to make important decisions for me. I didn't think that I had what it took (lack of self-confidence) for me to make the decisions myself. I deferred to the men.

Beneath my deference was the fear of abandonment from displeasing them with my decisions. I didn't trust them. I didn't trust me. I stayed in the relationships by being what made me feel secure. I gave myself away, seeing no other choice at the time.

When I did my 6th Step, I discovered my defect of character was a lack of trust in people, especially myself. As an adult abused as a child, I hadn't yet believed that I could handle life by myself without relying on someone else to survive. After my previous husband died, I realized I would need to make some new choices about maintaining myself as a whole woman. Since I wanted to feel equal, I decided I would risk revealing myself in any future serious relationship I might have.

*I started to trust my Higher Power in new ways. Even though I tended to isolate, when I did get out, I experimented with initiating conversations, dancing by myself in a crowd, or going home when I was ready. Eventually, I met a man who actually fell in love with me **because** I was who I was. (He said he was attracted to my energy!) We're married and learning how to be partners in our relationship. I see my progress in trusting myself through trusting God.*

In another example, we trust that we are **enough** (or have enough) to neutralize jealousy or envy. In that space we focus on believing that we are okay as we are. As we believe, we mentally release jealousy and practice trust in its place. We can fake it till we make it, or pretend as if we believe we're enough, until we do. We may need to be mindful and practice refocusing many times until the life and the way we desire to be takes hold. Eventually we notice jealousy no longer has as strong a grip on us as it previously did, and sometimes we are completely free of it!

As we become ready to have these characteristics removed, we find some may disappear and some may not. Even if we think otherwise, some may not need to be removed and some may be removed at a later time. We also have character defects that will be transformed into character assets, like stubbornness becoming stamina! Our Higher Power may decide to remove a trait we were not even aware of yet. We allow God to look at us and decide what is to be removed. We are not responsible for figuring out what God wants.

Rita thinks of it this way:

Often the changes my Higher Power makes are very subtle and I can't see that I'm changing. I think I'm the same because I can't see progress. Sometimes it's only in looking back, that I get a sense of being transformed.

Vivian shares her thoughts:

Often, I feel ready to allow my Higher Power to remove a defect, but something inside me is standing in the way of allowing a replacement attitude or action. Obviously, I am resisting change and resisting letting go. I decide to go back and consider Step 2. I remember I am being restored, not by my doing, but by a Power greater than myself. I have learned from working previous Steps that when I reach an impasse, to look at my part in the Step, see what is mine to do, and do it to the best of my ability. I let go of the outcome and trust my Higher Power is helping me overcome my resistance. The fear of trusting God is the defect I'm releasing. I consider it a character defect because the fear of trusting keeps me playing smaller in life than I really am. Playing small or minimizing myself is a dishonest way for me to live, and I don't want to live dishonestly any longer. I admit I'm powerless over my resistance and I surrender the fear and Step 6 to my Higher Power.

We need to be willing to turn away from old habits. Sometimes we become attached to them because they are familiar and make us feel more secure. When we try something new, feelings of uncertainty can arise. Though this can be very uncomfortable, we have decided to let our Higher Power manage our lives and follow the guidance we receive.

Step 6 requires that we be willing to stop clinging to our self-destructive habits and patterns. Lastly, we choose to actively cooperate and participate with our Higher Power to help guide our lives to be changed for the better. Our Higher Power is in charge and we are grateful.

Candace sees it this way:

I want to put myself in an environment where I'm available to my Higher Power. I picture myself holding an open umbrella above my head, and there's help coming from my Higher Power. But my umbrella, which is open, is deflecting the help so I'm not feeling it. The help is not touching me and I'm not receiving it with an open umbrella. This is not an environment where I'm available to my Higher Power.

If I close the umbrella, the help that is coming can reach me. I witness my putting up and taking down the umbrella regularly. In Step 6, I ask God to take the umbrella away as my desire for readiness increases.

We Allow Removal

Here are some suggestions for allowing our defects to be removed. These suggestions will make a difference in our lives by enhancing our sense of self and our well-being.

- We consciously choose to be willing to let go of old habits.

- We take educated risks with trust and courage.

- We anticipate a positive outcome.

- We affirm desired ways of being through our words and actions.

- We have a mindset of humility by admitting we need help from our Higher Power.

- We have a desire for new ways of being and thinking and welcome them.

- We are open and grateful to a Power greater than ourselves for helping to clean up our lives.

- We learn discernment by choosing what to keep and what to let go of.

- We become conscious of our excuses and rationale for acting in unhealthy ways.

- We have clarity of mind that helps us create transformation.

- We create our thoughts with conscious intention toward the lives we desire. The use of conscious intention helps us to direct our actions. New neural pathways in our brains are created which open the door to possibilities we hadn't yet imagined.

As adults abused as children, we assumed our sanity, and at times our survival, depended on ourselves. Step 6 reinforces that we learn it is not our responsibility to find solutions, to improve ourselves, or even know what to do next. That is our Higher Power's job.

Diana feels like this:

When I think about the fact that it's not my responsibility to change myself, I catch myself thinking that's too lackadaisical for me. It seems too wimpy. I've turned my will and my life over to a Power greater than I am, I've asked others for help, I've told them my secrets. I've surrendered a lot. This is so opposite of the way I needed to be as a child to get through the abuse. I still resist letting God be in charge sometimes.

Many years of my life were spent figuring out solutions to problems, yet I felt miserable much of the time. I repeatedly tried the same solutions, telling myself that this time I'd do it better, more often, more creatively – and that would work, right? There must be **something** *I can do to make my life better. I tried to thread needles* with hammers. I finally saw that my way wasn't working. I realized this could continue for the rest of my life and nothing would change. I was failing to give myself the chance to have the kind of life I truly wanted. I was clear I wasn't happy.

Ruth sees it this way:

I was shocked when I first discovered that I didn't have the power to remove what I didn't like about myself. I'd always expected that I had to do the removing. When I realized that my best was not good enough to do that, I thought there was something the matter with me. I can't make myself better? What a failure I was, I told myself.

Now I know the difference between me and my Creator. My Higher Power is the greater Power, a Power beyond my capacity of understanding, a Power that loves me unconditionally and wants the best for me. I am learning what my responsibility is and what it isn't. I remember the Serenity Prayer at times like these:

> **God, grant me the serenity to accept the things I cannot change.**
>
> **To change the things I can.**
>
> **And the wisdom to know the difference.**

Our Defects of Character

As adults abused as children, we experienced life through the character defects of our abusers. We were not able to separate their character defects from the individuals themselves.

Our early life experiences were not congruent with healthy, normal lives. Our childhoods were marred by abuse. The abuse we experienced became the foundation that our beliefs about ourselves and the world were built upon. The word defect can be very challenging for adults abused as children. It may imply what some of us already feel: that there is something very wrong with us and our place in the world. Our defects of character, as seen from a Step 6 perspective, can give us a new and more helpful understanding of them.

Ann shares:

I was forced to do many inappropriate and unfair things, impossible things; I came out looking bad, like a failure. I was asked to do things I couldn't do. I was asked to be someone I wasn't and to play a role that wasn't mine. I had no idea how to deal with all of that. But I did get used to having impossible things asked of me. Later I asked impossible things of myself.

Tania contributes:

As an adult abused as a child, I have felt defective from the day I was born. It is difficult for me, even today, to admit that I have a defect of anything. I didn't know I could afford to admit how defective I already felt. I felt so wrong about who I was at my core, that in doing Step 6, I had difficulty letting go of even the defects, afraid that without them, I would disappear.

It is helpful to realize that what have been termed character defects may also be life-sustaining instincts. These instincts are related, but not limited to, eating, sleeping, security, relationships, communication etc. Those are all supportive and healthy until they spiral out of control. At that point they become part of, and contribute to, our unmanageable lives.

When our instincts become regrettable behaviors that drive us toward unhealthy relations with self and others, it is then that they become character defects. For instance, if overeating is ruining our health or our sense of well-being because we are seeking food for comfort to fill a sense of emptiness, then overeating has become a character defect that we might like to replace with a life-affirming activity.

Character defects can be seen as imperfections, flaws, deficiencies, weaknesses, inadequacies, limits, failings, or incompletions. Any of these meanings or interpretations can prevent us from being people of merit or from being effective in life.

An important part of Step 6 is defining what our character defects actually are. Fortunately, after having worked Step 4, most of us are beginning to have an understanding of them. It can be helpful to re-read your Step 4 inventory. **Look for adult patterns of unwanted, undesirable behaviors. These traits, which show up in our behaviors, are known as character defects.** Some of these patterns of behavior that create unhealthy lifestyles are listed next.

List of Some Character Defects

arrogance
bigotry
bitterness
codependency
complacency
control
criticism
depression
dishonesty
disloyalty
envy
fear
gluttony
gossip
grandiosity
greed
hatred
impatience
intolerance
jealousy
judgmental

justification
laziness
lust
lying
manipulation
minimization
perfectionism
pessimism
prejudice
procrastination
rageful
rationalization
resentfulness
resignation
rigid thinking
self-centeredness
self-pity
slothfulness
thievery
victimization
willfulness

As we review our inventories from Step 4, it can be a helpful exercise to write down each individual character defect as we notice them. This way we are able to see which character defects have a larger impact upon our lives than others.

Once we have compiled our lists, write next to each character defect the desired behavior or trait that we'd like to replace it with. For instance, if we identify lust as a character defect, we could choose marital fidelity as something we aspire to. If lying is one of our character defects, we could choose honesty and transparency as traits to affirm in our lives. We let our lists be as long or short as they need to be. There is no rule that says we only do Step 6 once. Remember doing the Steps takes time.

List of Some Character Assets

In addition to our character defects it is helpful to note our character assets as revealed in Step 4.

accountability	helpfulness
authenticity	honesty
awareness	humility
care	humor
confidence	independence
courage	integrity
creativity	kindness
curiosity	love
dependability	loyalty
devotion	open-minded
diligence	patience
efficiency	surrender
equality	tolerance
equanimity	transparency
focused	trustworthiness
forgiveness	vulnerability
generosity	willingness
gratitude	wittiness

For adults abused as children, the true nature of our character is a combination of character assets and defects, qualities distinctive to each of us. Step 6 is the only Step that addresses the issue of our moral character. It gives us a chance to rebuild our character into traits that are healthy, likable, and lovable.

Building healthy and desirable traits will lead us toward the lives that we have been hoping for. It is possible for us to create the changes we have long desired. This is one of the most joyous outcomes of the journey through Step 6.

Step 6 Summary

Step 6 is the turning point, a golden opportunity to be created anew. Our unmanageable lives are becoming more manageable. We're becoming more familiar with who we really are.

As we discover what stands in our way of being satisfied and feeling fulfilled, we release these ineffective patterns and choose new ways of being. We let our Higher Power deal with these obstacles and help us shape the course of our lives.

After we let go of a detrimental characteristic, it's like we have a blank slate on which we can create something new. We choose to place on that slate what we want. Choice is essential as it relates to the human ability to create.

Our ability, need, and right to choose are uniquely human. We use this power of choice on our behalf and everyone benefits from it. We become the author of our own lives. We take responsibility as we align our will with the will of our Higher Power. Our daily lives become easier to deal with as we become more authentic and more effective.

After the childhood abuse we endured, today we experience the lives we had hoped were possible. As adults, we can let go of these self-destructive patterns that diminish our joy and happiness. We are lessening our pain and moving toward healing. It is a process we engage in every day.

Janice expresses it creatively this way:

I think of my Higher Power as a spot remover that is put on something soiled. It lifts the dirt out; I vacuum it and whisk the spot away. If that has any corollary to how God does it, God must somehow penetrate my being and change my composition to allow a release. Then God comes by and sweeps my dirt away.

Could a defect of character be a spot on my emotional, physical, or spiritual being? Looking at my spots is what I did in Steps 4 and 5. My own cleaning fluid didn't work. I didn't hide it or cover it up, though. Instead, I exposed it enough to allow the spot to be removed.

This is my part in Step 6. I cooperate with my Higher Power (the spot remover) to lift it out for me. It becomes lighter, smaller, or removed completely. I have not caused this progress but allowed the change to happen. My desire for transformation was noticed and respected by God. First, though, I had to be aware that I needed some transformation. The earlier Steps showed that quite evidently to me. I progressed from awareness to desire and willingness.

Once we turn our will and our lives over to a Power greater than ourselves, how and when our defects are removed is not up to us. Step 6 gets us ready to follow our inner guidance.

We do our best to determine and humbly surrender to our Higher Power's will. We become willing and able to identify our self-sabotaging behaviors when they appear and then let go of them. We are seeking progress as we continue the process of healing. **There is too much at stake for us to pass up a chance to heal.** Courage is not optional when our future depends on it; courage is essential. It's time to dedicate ourselves and pursue what's important to us. We use the power of a surrendered will to rise to a level of success we have never before been able to reach on our own.

We remember, it's not a character defect to have character defects. It's human!

Affirmations for New Behaviors

We can take each character defect and write a few positive affirmations, i.e., statements that help us affirm and create our newly desired behaviors. Creating affirmations can be a very helpful tool. As we write and review our positive statements, we are affirming how to live healthier and happier lives.

Affirmations empower our choices and guide us toward the lives we want to create for ourselves. Through the use of affirmations, we are focusing on ourselves and better defining the changes we truly seek.

It is up to us to affirm and help in the creation of our desired life changes. We affirm that which will fill what has been removed.

It is best to write our affirmations as if we've already achieved the desired behavior. For instance, if our character defect is overeating, we might write:

- I choose healthy foods that nourish me deeply.

- I no longer overeat; I am able to choose portions that are healthy for me.

- I choose to allow my eating habits to change and I do so successfully.

- I ignore false messages of hunger and eat only when appropriate.

- I forgive myself for eating in unhealthy ways in the past.

- I love my life and am immune to the temptation of eating foods that are not good for me.

At the beginning and end of each meal, repeating these affirmations quietly or aloud is an effective way to affirm that letting go of character defects will open the opportunity for a better relationship with food. This realization helps to create the willingness, awareness, and the motivation needed for readiness in Step 6.

The doors are now opening for creating ourselves newly as we shift our relationship with ourselves. We become people we can be proud of and feel gratitude and respect for. We are able to love unconditionally and be tender and compassionate with ourselves.

As we let go of doubt and receive the benefits of Step 6, we are filled with the reassurance that when we are ready, our lives will most certainly change for the better. We are the ones with a Power greater than ourselves, the Power that is making these changes possible!

Step 6 Affirmations

1. I give myself time to mature.//
2. Difficulty is not a sign of failure.
3. I release fear and choose faith.
4. I openly welcome something better that what I have now.
5. I let nature take its course.
6. I shift my beliefs to a more positive point of view.
7. As I release, my inner light reveals what once appeared in the shadows.
8. My ability to make wise choices increases.
9. I am filled with the expectation of good.
10. I offer compassion to myself as I am healing.
11. I am a healthy, whole, and productive person.
12. I am grateful for the Higher Power of my understanding
13. It's becoming easier to express my true nature.

Step 6 Journal Questions

1. Which of my traits do I find challenging to let God remove?
2. Who would I be and what would I look like after God removes my defects?
3. Which traits diminish who I am or limit me in some way?
4. What traits expand or enhance who I am naturally?
5. In what areas of my life am I still living from my fears or anger?
6. What do I want to create in my life?
7. What decisions did I make as a child about who I should be that are no longer appropriate?
8. What do I want to shift now that has stopped me before?
9. What would I find inside myself if I slowed down?
10. What am I committed to?
11. What could I do that would be an expression of my commitment?
12. What help do I need today?
13. Where in my life am I aligned with my Higher Power? Where am I not?
14. Where have I fallen short in thought, word, or action?

15. What past behaviors, thoughts, or feelings make me feel guilty or ashamed?

16. What effect has insecurity or low self-esteem had on my life?

Step 6 Prayer

I offer to my Higher Power what I have learned about myself by working these Steps. I come from a place of humility and self-love. I am patient with myself as I grow. I practice willingness to be transformed by keeping myself available to God; I remain open and vulnerable as a human being.

My imperfections are not an indication of anything wrong with me. They are merely manifestations of my humanity showing up as traits or characteristics. I remember that I have an eternal connection to Source – my Creator. I turn to that Source for guidance, trusting what I receive.

When I stop thinking about my problems and focus my attention inward, I move beyond my thoughts to a place of stillness. In quiet communion with my Higher Power, I am able and ready to receive the guidance I am seeking one day at a time.

Thank you, God.

And so it is.

AMEN

Notes

Step 7

Humbly asked Him to remove our shortcomings.

Step 7

Humbly asked Him to remove our shortcomings.

Table of Contents

Introduction 313

Humility 316

Our Relationship with God 321

Ask for Help 323

Remove Shortcomings 330

Step 7 Summary 336

Step 7 Affirmations 339

Step 7 Journal Questions 340

Step 7 Prayer 341

Step 7

Humbly asked Him to remove our shortcomings

Introduction

As we progress in our healing, we recognize that the path through the Steps has required a tremendous amount of honesty, faith, courage, willingness, and trust to advance to this point. Step 7 is better than halfway through the journey to our desired creation of the kinds of lives we want for ourselves.

 In review, Step 1 helped us admit we are powerless over our character defects that have created unmanageable aspects of our lives. This level of self-awareness helped us bring **honesty and acceptance** to the fore.

 With the support of Step 2, we were able to look at our beliefs and renew or deepen our trust in a Power greater than ourselves, the God of **our** understanding. Step 2 is the place we go to regain our **hope** that a Higher Power can restore us to sanity through our readiness to have our character defects and shortcomings removed.

Step 3 asked us to turn our lives and our will over to the care of this greater Power to be restored to sanity. We need to trust, allow, and have **faith** that God can remove all of our character defects when we are ready.

Step 4 asked us to do a searching and fearless moral inventory of who we are today. With **courage** we looked at how our childhood abuse impacted our beliefs, actions, and attitudes in ways that our adult lives have become unmanageable. Step 4 is an invitation to **courageously** explore and discover what it means to be truly authentic. We were willing to admit how our unmanageable lives caused harm to ourselves and others.

Step 5 asked us to continue upon our courageous path of transformation and healing through the act of admitting our wrongs to God, ourselves, and another human being. The nature of the admitting in Step 5 is done from a place of tremendous moral **integrity**. We need to depend on trust and honesty to admit our character defects. The act of telling God helped us become even more ready to trust God to remove our defects.

Step 6 helped us have **willingness** and become ready to have a Higher Power remove all of our character defects and shortcomings. When we recognize the humility we have gained and the courage we have expressed as a result of working the prior Steps, there is no reason not to trust God.

Step 7 is asking us to be **humbly** open for our Higher Power to remove our shortcomings.

It is about asking for help! The reminder here is that we cannot heal ourselves, nor are we expected to do so. This

Step can be an ideal time to share our thoughts about our shortcomings with a trusted confidant. We can't see our shortcomings without stripping away our ego and defensive pride which takes tremendous courage and allows us to develop a humble attitude. Step 7 empowers and embodies the miracle of transformation as we turn our shortcomings over to God.

Shirley contributes:

It's useful for me to observe that my resistance to ask for help is not outside of me. It's not another person I'm battling... It gives me comfort to know that when I can trust, life is not as hard as I thought it would be.

Freedom comes from turning our will, our lives, our character defects, and our shortcomings over to God, allowing what is standing in the way of our healing to be removed. We become free to be all that we are and all that we wish to be.

We use the word Him in this Step as a show of acknowledgment of the original 12 Steps of Alcoholics Anonymous which still uses this word. **We** have no opinion on how the Higher Power is viewed. Each of us determines for ourselves how we express our beliefs.

Humility

Step 7 says we "Humbly asked Him to remove our shortcomings." The first aspect of this Step is to explore and understand what it means to be **humble**, to come from a true recognition of our humanness. In order to allow a Power greater than ourselves to remove our shortcomings, we must be humble enough to ask this Power to do so.

The willingness to ask for help is an act of humility itself. After having admitted that we are powerless to remove our shortcomings ourselves, we are very grateful that our Higher Power can and does! Let's explore how we have gained **humility** through the 12 Steps.

Humility is achieved through the Steps through:

1. **Honesty:** Admitting that we need healing, that we are powerless, and that our lives are unmanageable takes **great humility.** This action requires vulnerability and honesty.

2. **Hope:** Believing that a Power greater than ourselves can restore us to sanity takes **resolute humility.**

3. **Faith:** Deciding to turn our will and our lives over to the care of God requires **unwavering humility.** We are worthy of being helped by God.

4. **Courage:** Doing a searching and fearless moral inventory of ourselves requires soul-searching and introspection as we open to the severity of our character defects. As adults abused as children, we tend to deny and minimize the pain

our character defects inflict. Therefore, as we try to assess them, unless we take a very humble approach, we may underestimate their power. To be willing to look at our character defects takes **profound humility.**

5. **Integrity:** *We surrender our pride and become truly authentic by admitting our character defects openly to ourselves, to God, and to another, This act of admitting takes* **tremendous humility.**

6. **Willingness:** *Opening in readiness for God to remove our defects of character requires* **true humility** *as we surrender our will and trust our Higher Power.*

We gain humility and appreciation for the enormity of God's power to transform our lives through the journey of the 12 Steps. Not only do we **have** a path, we take actual Steps **on** that path. For this, we are accountable.

The word humility has the same root as the word human. The Latin derivative of human is *earth*. We are of the Earth on the physical plane. We are, in our physical essence, human earthly beings, not heavenly beings. Being human is not lowly, bad, weak, or small. Remembering our relationship with a Higher Power can quickly bring us home to our highest human selves! That in itself is very humbling.

Miranda shares her thoughts on humility:

It is humbling to be in a relationship. It entails two beings, me and my Higher Power, in this case. When I think of humility here, there's a "me," and there's an "other." The other is a Power greater than I am. I wasn't created to be the greater Power. However, I am learning and growing to be a better **human being** *by accepting my humanness and not expecting me to be all powerful.*

Humility is about accepting our humanity. It is about recognizing our limitations as humility deepens each day that we give our will over to God and live in faith and trust that we are cared for.

Humility is **not** humiliating. There is no humiliation in being human or our willingness to admit powerlessness. It is not meant to be humiliating to admit our shortcomings or to be willing to have a Higher Power restore us to sanity. There is nothing shameful about asking for help to accomplish what we do not have the power to do by ourselves. There is a tremendous distinction between humility, asking humbly, and feeling humiliated. If we forget our humanness, then we may feel humiliated when we need to ask for help.

Child abuse could not exist without deception. We were forced to participate in hiding the truth. **We have lived lies.** We felt anger, fear, and hatred and may have had to hide it all to protect ourselves. We had to submit to the perpetrators and felt powerless. As children, we may have loved the abusers and were confused. We protected the abusers with our silence. We may even have deceived ourselves. Child abuse could not exist without deception.

As adults, getting honest with ourselves may be quite challenging, yet the Steps require us to be honest. Using the tool of humility can help us deal with our child abuse. We may crave the power that was taken from us when we were children. We may still experience issues of control and being right.

Step 7 is a perfect place for us to practice acceptance and experience some peace of mind. Honesty helps us learn how to live life more fully and depend on a Higher Power. Humility, not self-will, makes our healing possible.

As adults abused as children, we may have learned that it was safest to rely on ourselves. It was difficult and scary to rely on others because our trust was impacted by our past abuse. The previous Steps have helped restore our trust in our adult selves and in a Power greater than us. That is why it is suggested to work the Steps in order, so we would be ready to ask God for help to remove our shortcomings.

Our shortcomings can be obstacles to our healing or may even prevent it. We can use our shortcomings to remind us that we need a Power greater than we are. Owning and admitting them open the door to opportunities to increase our availability to be restored and transformed.

David thinks of Step 7 in this way:

When I look at my shortcomings and see where I'm lacking, I see them more as opportunities to invent new ways of being or doing something. I don't look at myself as a failure, or that I'm wrong and need to fix something inside of me. If I need to, I humbly ask for help from my Higher Power and don't get stuck in my feelings of disappointment about how I think I should be.

Our Relationship with God

Step 7 is asking us to be in a relationship with our Higher Power. This Step refers to this as Him. However, we remember that each of us decides for ourselves what our Higher Power is. We ask for help, not knowing what the help will look like or when it will come, but knowing that it **will** indeed come. As we connect with our Higher Power, we develop an inner knowing and trust that aid us in riding the waves of life, instead of habitually responding with fear or anger.

Carol shares a moving story:

I asked myself, is my lack of faith a problem? To me, it underlies many of my actions or inactions that I observed and included in Steps 4 and 5. Then in Step 6, I was gladly reminded that God does the removing of my defects and shortcomings. God is the one who decides if I could use more faith. It appears to me that my lack of faith keeps me from being all I can be, as well as doing what I came here to do in life. In Step 7, I am able to ask for clarity and help with that need. Since we are human, I remember everyone has shortcomings. This helps me remain humble and nonjudgmental.

We remember that we are all created by a Power greater than ourselves, and that Power is God, or whatever name we choose to give to this Source, if we give it a name at all.

We are the human beings and God is the creator. God is in charge of our restoration process. We are provided with the inner strength we need to lessen our grip on our shortcomings. As they are being removed, we notice our peace of mind increasing as a result of seeking to know God's will for our lives and following it to the best of our ability.

Sally shares:

Through the power of surrendering my will, I can reset my focus and blaze new trails that will show me new possibilities for myself. The past cannot hold me back nor the future intimidate me. I can choose to live consciously in the present and go forward with trust in my Higher Power.

Ask for Help

As adults abused as children, we may not have considered having any Power greater than ourselves to go to for help. We may have thought we were our **own** Higher Power.

We counted on ourselves for survival. Many of us didn't know there was a Power greater than ourselves that we could count on.

We may once have confused our perpetrators as Powers greater than ourselves, and sadly, for good reason. We certainly couldn't ask them for help! We may not have had **anybody** we could go to. As adults, asking for help may still not come easily for us. However, it is something that can be learned - and that is encouraging.

Asking for help implies **allowing** it. If we don't ask for help, we are getting in our own way of healing. When we remember we are human and when we feel humble, it seems only natural to ask. Our job in Step 7 is to learn that asking is expected of us. It is like a baby learning to walk. Naturally, they reach out for someone's hand or hold onto a solid object to support them in their learning. We would not expect them to teach themselves to walk, just as we are not expected to complete our own restoration.

We may think powerlessness is a weakness. Any admission of need may seem like a weakness. We may be too independent, headstrong, or self-important to ask for help. We may feel there is too much "stuff" in our way: low self-worth, not deserving, or lack of self-acceptance.

> **Jay explores this thought:**
>
> I remember I don't need a plan of action or a plan of improvement, and it's truly fine if my progress through the Steps is slow. It's all right that I still question my worthiness. I ask myself, "Shouldn't I have already shown more progress? How can I go to my Higher Power when I have discovered that I'm not even the kind of person I **thought** I was?"
>
> The difficulty on my part is to connect with my Higher Power when I judge myself. "How is it possible that God will feel differently? How is it possible for God to accept me with all my faults?" Though I see, time after time, God does.

We may prevent our readiness out of our fear of failing to have our shortcomings removed. We may not yet believe that our Higher Power is capable of doing this on our behalf. We may be fearful since we don't know what will fill the place of our shortcomings. We may even believe that our shortcomings protect us from further trauma.

We learn that we deserve and need help throughout our lives. It is the natural design of life to need and ask for help. It is the way human nature was created to bring ease of learning and growth. We were not born comprehending the complexities of this world.

Humility is the precondition to our healing. As we admit our powerlessness, we remember that humility opens the door to make asking possible.

Gary adds:

It seems to me when I humbly ask for help, I trust there is help available to me. Then I act on that belief. Step 7 doesn't say I demanded, begged, pleaded, or bargained. All I need to do is ask. This Step is the first Step I actually ask for something. I walk in faith and expect to receive help from my Higher Power.

We don't have to be good to be deserving of our Higher Power's help. Sometimes the best God can do for us is help us press *pause*. It may not yet be time for the outcome we believe we want or expect. Change is found in allowing and accepting that things happen in their own right time. The no or not yet is not an absolute, but a reminder that there is time enough for the removal. We surrender to our Higher Power's timing.

Having our shortcomings removed is an ongoing process. We need only trust, ask, and be open. Asking God implies a dialogue. When we ask, we leave ourselves available for a response. Do we expect to be given what we want without having to ask for it? When we get tired of beating our heads against the stone walls of our character defects, we ask God to get them out of our way.

One of the main ways we learn and form the foundation of our lives is from others. For us, adults abused as children, our original foundations were shaky. Now we have tremendous support to relearn, recreate, and rethink our lives as we journey through the 12 Steps. The kind of help we're asking for is what we need to be the kinds of people we want to be and have the kinds of lives we know we want to enjoy.

At this point, we have spent a great deal of time with the Steps, raising our awareness and gaining insight into the nature of our character defects and shortcomings. In Step 6, we have been made ready to have our defects removed. Now all we have to do is ask, right? Not exactly! There's more to Step 7 than humbly asking for help, waiting for a response, and watching for the desired changes to happen all on their own. There's spiritual preparation, a spiritual readiness, and a commitment that we must engage in on this journey.

Ann shares:

When I approached Step 7 and started looking at what may be lacking in my character as an adult, I discovered that I was not as grateful as I thought I could be.

I wasn't judging myself, but saw it as a missing piece from a spiritual perspective. I wasn't grateful enough for what was good in my life. I was stuck in being disappointed about what **didn't** show up the way I thought it would. Not just in a relationship or a job - but in life itself!

I realized that I needed to give my disappointment in life over to the care of my Higher Power. In the meantime, I started focusing on what **was working** in life and began a practice of gratitude. It's not that I hadn't **seen** the good, I just got stuck in my own human disappointment, so the good didn't mean as much to me.

I asked for help from my Higher Power and eventually, I felt more accepting of how life turned out by trusting. In addition, my own personal power seemed to grow when I altered my focus.

We need to become familiar with the spiritual principles of each Step. These principles will replace our character defects, yet it takes time and commitment to grow a deeper understanding and integration of them into our lives. Trust, faith, courage, and humility are central to Step 7. We focus on the actions **we** must take: humbly asking, practicing spiritual principles, getting out of our Higher Power's way, and taking inspired, right actions.

We want to fully develop ourselves so that healing from our childhood abuse becomes a reality. In Step 6 we spent as much time as we needed to become ready to ask our Higher Power to remove that which was preventing us from enjoying the best lives we could have.

As we work Step 7, we align ourselves with our Higher Power and enjoy increased freedom from the burdens of our defects and shortcomings. We begin to live in harmony with our true inner selves and release our demands of the outer world. From harmony, we find peace.

Remove Shortcomings

A true Step 7 story recounted by Ruth:

A 50-year-old woman and her sister were in a concentration camp in World War II. She witnessed her sister being tortured by an SS Guard. Her sister died soon after that, not having a strong constitution.

After the war, the woman became a missionary. At one of her speaking engagements in Germany, she encountered that same SS Guard. He wheeled himself up in front of her in a wheelchair, having lost limbs himself. There were tears in his eyes. He looked at her and stretched out his hand for her to take. She recognized him at once and froze. She was not able to lift her arm up at all to take his outstretched hand in hers!

In that moment, she prayed and asked to be able to forgive him in her heart. After long moments, her trembling hand was out in front of her and he took it in his.

This is what I want for myself – forgiveness in my heart.

When we stay in the present, we are more able to remain open and vulnerable as we wait for help from our Higher Power. As we release the pain of our childhood abuse, it becomes easier to deal with our adult lives today. From our life experiences, we have access to aspects of ourselves now, such as wisdom and maturity, which were not available to us in the past.

The 12 Steps provide a path to freedom from the hold the past has had on us and opportunities to begin anew. This is the continued promise and outcome of working the 12 Steps.

As adults abused as children, we have lived with a tremendous amount of suffering, anger, guilt, pain, and fear throughout our lives. We welcome the relief we are discovering on this journey. By being open to humility, we have been brought closer to our Higher Power. We don't have to improve ourselves to be worthy of letting go and letting God.

We simply communicate what we see about ourselves. Then we open to trust and have faith that our Higher Power will help us. Faith is the ability to believe in something that doesn't have to be proven. It is with willingness and acceptance that we remember and are granted love and care. Willingness is our ability to say yes to what is being asked of us or given to us. We remember that the experiences of limitation are natural parts of all human lives.

Shortcomings imply a lack of something, areas where we come up short. We may have a sense of scarcity, needs not being met, incompleteness, or not meeting a certain standard.

We may look at our bank account and see less than we need. That means we need to increase money in the account. What can we do if we come up short of patience? We can focus on and have an intention to allow an increase in patience. **Anything we focus on, increases!** If we come up short of faith, we can increase our faith. Sometimes it's easier to increase something that we want **more** of, than it is to decrease something we want less of. Our Higher Power is the filler of the lack; we are the receivers.

How do we allow an increase of a characteristic or trait, like tolerance? We see and admit the lack, deficiency, or need. We ask for help from our Higher Power and create a new practice or mindset for ourselves. For example, we may have a jealous or suspicious nature left over from a previous relationship where our partner was unfaithful.

We remember our Higher Power is handling the increase of trust, when the opportunity appears, we find we have easier access to trust, as God removes our obstacles to peace. We can now take a new step or action, allowing this increase of trust. We watch for the results and are grateful for them.

Beverly offers this:

I think intolerance is one of my shortcomings. When I start to focus on having intolerance removed, it's very difficult for me. It feels like I'm focusing on something negative, and it seems almost impossible. For some reason, it just feels easier for me to focus on increasing tolerance

> than trying to decrease intolerance. I have spent many years trying to remove the parts of me that I didn't think were ok.
>
> I thought I needed to eradicate the unwanted parts. I didn't think I could possibly be all right the way I was, defects and all. I couldn't be lovable until all those bad parts were gone. I tried and failed many times to remove the traits I didn't want.
>
> It helped me think of a recipe where it tasted too bitter. How do I remove bitterness? I add more sweetener. This approach leaves me more hopeful, replenished, and more mindful of the life experiences that I want for myself.
>
> It's easier to focus on what's ok about me while my Higher Power is helping to remove the shortcomings. I have faith and trust that it will unfold as it needs to over time.

Without attending to the work of the previous Steps, Step 7 would be difficult to do. As adults abused as children, working through Steps 4 and 5 brought us to grips with our pasts as we have come to better understand the exact nature of our wrongs as **adults**. This helped us be ready and able to humbly realize what we are asking of our Higher Power. We are letting go and letting God with humility.

Linda shares her thoughts while working Step 7:

I tended to sell myself out in order to get my needs met by other people. I found I minimized what was important to me in deference to what others wanted. I was afraid to choose myself and lose their affection. I waited to act lovingly toward myself, until I took care of other people. I realized my confusion and lack of understanding about my responsibility to love myself while doing Step 7.

I asked for guidance and clarity from my Higher Power so I could learn how to take care of myself. I'm practicing taking risks with people as I'm learning to trust. I know my Higher Power is helping me release this old pattern.

Some of us may discover we have a lack of trust or faith in our Higher Power. Or we may discover it's about our lack of self-esteem and trust in ourselves and in others. Our shortcomings may be holding us back from taking risks or being honest. Our part is to look at ourselves, admit what we find, and prepare ourselves to allow our Higher Power to remove each shortcoming.

Shortcomings can change over time. Sometimes they come and go. As humans, we should not be surprised if a shortcoming returns after a long period of absence. It can happen to anyone. We repeat the process of Step 7 once more and witness the removal again. Some defects may not disappear entirely, though the potential may remain. However, they can remain inactive as long as we are focused on letting a Higher Power be in control of our lives. We are open for our Higher Power to do for us what our self-will cannot accomplish.

Everyone has shortcomings, but the only ones we ask our Higher Power to remove are our own. We focus on learning how to change **our** adult thinking and behavior as we've seen that we are powerless to change other people.

We admit our tendencies and reactions to life that hold us back from our healing and are willing to release the ones that harm us or others. We find that it's part of our character to fail to meet certain standards. We see these as specific traits that could use some adjustment as we focus on character **building** through Step 7.

Our sanity and healing do not depend on external circumstances or past events being how we wanted them to be, but rather on us following our Higher Power's will today.

Step 7 Summary

We are actually asking for change to occur. This is the beginning of our new lives. We have gone through Steps 1 through 6. It took courage, willingness, faith, and awareness. We have deepened that awareness through our 4th and 5th Steps. We looked not only at our liabilities, but also at our assets.

Asking for change, for a fundamental shift in our beings, can be scary. As adults abused as children, we need to know what there is about us that we can count on. What can we hold on to while our Higher Power is changing us? This is where the inventory of our assets in Step 4 is most helpful.

It is also a time to reflect on the experience in Step 5 of someone loving us, having compassion for us, witnessing, and listening to us as we shared. We are encouraged onward and can count on the fact that we are not alone.

Being entirely ready to change comes in handy here. Our attitudes about having our shortcomings removed mean we have become willing to be changed. Willingness is the key. Our healing builds on itself; our development is progressive.

We owe ourselves the opportunities to live our adult lives focused on what is possible in the present. We no longer try to cope with our shortcomings in our previous headstrong ways. We become teachable and learn new coping mechanisms. We focus on character building as our Higher Power guides us to be the best we can be.

We remember once again that the implied first word of every Step is "we." It can be useful to include our trusted confidants to review our lists of shortcomings. Their feedback will give us another's perspective.

Sometimes what we think of as shortcomings can be demonstrated as assets. Perhaps stubbornness could be seen as perseverance to align our will with our Higher Power's; it depends on how we apply the trait. Especially being adults abused as children, our perceptions of ourselves may be jaded, with gaps between our views of ourselves and how others see us.

Alice offers:

For me, making a written list of what I perceived my shortcomings to be was important. How could I ask my Higher Power for help without knowing precisely what I thought was needed?

As our shortcomings are being removed, we may find ourselves less self-centered and more useful to our Higher Power and others. We might allow our selfish behaviors to be changed into selfless acts. We can say to God, "You know who I am. I have told you all my secrets. Please take away what I need to release so I'll be more useful to you and my fellow human beings. I want to be and do the best I can!"

We turn to a loving Higher Power and rely on it for our needs. God may not remove our pain but instead gives us the strength to deal with it successfully. We can experience freedom and develop our potential to heal from our childhood abuse one day at a time. Happiness comes as a byproduct of seeking to know and follow our Higher Power's will. We put God in charge of our renovation and reap the rewards!

Step 7 Affirmations

1. I trust my Higher Power and allow changes in me.
2. I have courage.
3. My life is unfolding in wondrous ways.
4. All my needs are met.
5. I want to be all I can be.
6. I am healing.
7. Peace fills my heart and mind.
8. I release that which no longer serves me.
9. Listening connects me to this present moment.
10. I am loved as I am.
11. I make life-affirming choices.
12. I have compassion for myself.
13. Wholeness is my true nature.
14. I am worthy of releasing my family's perceptions of me.
15. I release my demands of the outer world.

Step 7 Journal Questions

1. Where in my life do I still try to get control over something I can't?
2. What qualities do I have that contribute to my success in an important area of my life?
3. Where do I assign unwarranted power to my fears?
4. When I get upset what could I do that would help me?
5. What possibilities do I see for myself today that I hadn't seen before?
6. Where do I experience a lack of compassion for myself?
7. What is the nature of my Higher Power?
8. Is my life going in the direction I want it to go? If not, why not?
9. Am I quick to be angry?
10. If I tend to fabricate the truth, how do I rationalize it to myself? Does it relate to any fears I may have?
11. What is it like to live inside of me these days?

Step 7 Prayer

Each time I ask for help from my Higher Power, I am placing my trust in it. By choosing to take this Step, I am open to receive. I go directly to the source of help.

I know answers and guidance are available to me; my healing path is being made clear. I confidently allow new ideas to be expressed by me as they assist in planning my new future.

I step out in faith as I anchor these opportunities with action. The place to begin is always with my Higher Power as I move in the direction of the guidance I receive. My concerns fall away, and I am peaceful.

Thank you, God.

And so it is.

AMEN

Notes

Notes

Step 8

Made a list of all persons
we had harmed,
and became willing
to make amends
to them all.

Step 8

Made a list of all persons we had harmed, and became willing to make amends to them all.

Table of Contents

Introduction 349

Make a List 352

Harm 360

Harm to Ourselves 362

Self-care 368

Harm to Others 371

Became Willing 375

Make Amends 380

Forgiveness 388

Self-forgiveness 390

All Persons We Harmed 393

Step 8 Summary 397

Step 8 Affirmations 401

Step 8 Journal Questions 402

Step 8 Prayer 403

Step 8

Made a list of all persons we had harmed, and became willing to make amends to them all.

Introduction

We are not implying that when we were children, that we inflicted harm on others. However, some of our adult character traits may be harmful and can impact the ways in which we behave.

What does Step 8 mean by **our causing harm** to ourselves or another? Simply put, what we did hurt someone. Gossip, theft, verbal character assassination, physical assault, and bigotry are examples of harm. It does not mean that we are intentionally hurtful people.

When we begin Step 8, it might be challenging for us to admit that **we** had harmed anyone. After all, we were the ones who were abused; we were the victims. We were overcome, overwhelmed, and overpowered. The idea that we have done anyone else harm may be brand new to us.

We might have felt, and still believe, that we are helpless and powerless. Many of us think we are weak. How could we harm someone else?

False childhood beliefs, and our actions stemming from them, can be explored now. When we admit our part in our own adult lives, we can shift into powerful places of ownership...not criticism! Accountability, yes. There is no blame in Step 8.

There are two things to do in Step 8: (1) make a list and (2) become willing. That's it. We write down whom we harmed and what the harm was - what we **did**. Step 8 is the beginning and preparation for our personal journeys toward clearing our sides of the street.

Alice offers:

A woman who had dated my husband before we met, sent him a Christmas card addressed only to him though she knew we had married and knew my name. I was indignant! What poor manners she had! I felt like I didn't count at all. I was devastated.

About eight months later I had the opportunity to share with her what receiving that card was like for me. In my extreme insecurity, I thought she was feeling about me the same way I felt about myself, that I didn't matter.

I didn't realize any of this before I did my 8th Step. The harm that I had done to her was to judge her actions before I had communicated with her and gathered all the facts.

We have reference points to help us begin to make our lists. We might choose people from our inventory in Step 4. It revealed our human limitations and those who were impacted by them.

Step 8 is not easy. It demands a new kind of honesty and forgiveness. It is in this Step that we consider self-forgiveness, forgiveness of others, and being forgiven. With our Higher Power's help, our willingness to create new kinds of lives for ourselves opens the pathways for us.

Lastly, it is essential to separate Step 8 from Step 9. Step 9 will come naturally when we are willing, able, and ready – **after** completing Step 8. It is best not to project ahead to making the actual amends. Engaging in that exercise could become a stumbling block and distract us. At this point, we do not focus on how, when, and where the amends will be made. To receive the most benefit, we have experienced the wisdom of following the Steps in the order in which they were created.

Make a List

Step 8 is an opportunity to rebuild our relationships. We took our moral inventory in Step 4. We expand this journey now by making a list of those we hurt and how we hurt them as adults. We are becoming ready to make actual amends to them all.

Some long-forgotten emotional wounds stemming from our childhood may be reopened. If making our lists appears to overwhelm us, we ask our Higher Power for help and support.

The previous Steps have helped us gain insight into the importance and experience of willingness. This is an ideal time to pray for willingness. Remembering our decision in Step 3, we turn to our Higher Power. We do not have to make our lists on our own.

There may be pockets of emotions filled with guilt, blame, or pain. Fear, resentments, and deep sadness may have been stored inside us, stuck to the shameful aspects of our past deeds that have caused us and others harm. We reach out to those who care about us, share our feelings, and ask for support. Connections can be vital in Step 8 for our healing and release.

We may have regrets when we took actions that were not in alignment with our personal values. We are not bad or worthless because of our behavior. We admit our mistakes and our burdens can be lifted. This way, we can prevent regrets in our future, while providing healing in the present.

In reality, sometimes we're right on and sometimes we're off the mark.

Some of us make our lists by drawing three vertical lines on a piece of paper creating three columns. At the top of the first column, we write "Who Was Harmed." The second column is titled "Harm I Caused." We may choose to include our character defects and/or shortcomings in column two. The third is "Choices of Amends." We leave space for us to complete the third column when we do Step 9.

See "Sample Step 8 Amends List" on the following page.

Sample Step 8 Amends List

	Who Was Harmed?	Harm I Caused	Choice of Amends (to be completed in Step 9)
1	Me	Belittled myself in public *Shortcoming:* lack of self-love *Character defect:* self-abandonment	
2	Older sibling (one of the abusers)	Maliciously gossiped *Shortcoming:* immaturity and diminishment of another *Character defect:* revengeful and bitter	
3	Employer	Stole money from cash register, loss of income *Shortcoming:* lack of honesty *Character defect:* self-centered	

	Who Was Harmed?	Harm I Caused	Choice of Amends (to be completed in Step 9)
4	Me	Stole money from employer's cash register *Shortcoming: lack of integrity* *Character defect: untrustworthy*	
5	People of a different ethnic background	Verbally diminished a whole group of people *Shortcoming: lack of respect* *Character defect: arrogance and bigotry*	
6	Neighbor's barking dog	Kicked the dog causing pain and suffering *Shortcoming: lack of caring and control* *Character defect: meanness and immaturity*	

My Step 8 Amends List

	Who Was Harmed?	Harm I Caused	Choice of Amends (to be completed in Step 9)
1			
2			
3			

	Who Was Harmed?	Harm I Caused	Choice of Amends (to be completed in Step 9)
4			
5			
6			

We can make our lists with the help of a confidant for a much-needed reality check. It is our intention to be as inclusive on our lists as possible. However, with childhood abuse in our pasts, we adults may have distorted views of our impact on others as well as on ourselves. It's not uncommon for us to think we have either done no harm at all, or believe that everything is our fault. We might lose sight of the middle ground.

We put names on the lists from a mindset of no blame, no shame, and no guilt. We come from willingness, readiness, and humility. These states of mind and heart will help us be as objective as possible. Our Step 8 lists will grow as we grow. A revised Step 8 list is an option as we become more understanding of who we are and the harms we have caused. We remember to have compassion for ourselves and embrace our humanity.

> **Abby reveals:**
>
> *As a child, my value was determined by others. I became driven to justify being alive at all. I was afraid if I couldn't prove myself worthy, my life was in danger. Even when I did everything I was told to do, I lived in fear of being attacked. As an adult, I have had to learn that I'm valuable*

just being me. I've been discovering how brave I can be in the face of opposition. Putting myself on my amends list helped me see how poorly I had been treating myself and the price I had paid for living out old beliefs.

Before we can rebuild relationships, we must identify those who were harmed by our adult character defects and the unmanageability of our lives. As adults abused as children, many of us will find that our lists also include those who have harmed us in some way, as well. Listing these individuals is not easy; it can bring up long-standing resentments.

We might wonder why **we** need to make amends when they harmed us too! We remember this is our opportunity to get on with **our** lives. We identify our feelings and ask our Higher Power for help.

Our lists may include those we are asking forgiveness from, as well as those we need to forgive. Some names may appear in both columns, to forgive and be forgiven. As children with abuse in our pasts, we may have gotten caught in a never-ending spiral of hurting another and being hurt. We can break this cycle of mutual resentments as we make our amends.

The length of our lists is not the most important aspect here. What impacts our success is our willingness to be honest. Our growth and our healing give us the confidence to make amends as we deepen our understanding of our adult selves.

Harm

Let us think about the harm that we've caused. What does it mean to harm one's self or cause another harm? The definition of **"harm"** found in the *Merriam/Webster Dictionary* is:

- To do or cause physical or mental damage or injury
- Moral injury, evil; wrong
- To be the cause of someone's hurt, their brokenness, being made less valuable or less successful
- To harm one's reputation

Harm to self or another can result in emotional pain, physical injury, mental anguish, or loss/damage of personal property. **Harm is the creation of some type of misfortune for another or ourselves.**

Step 8 helps us acknowledge where our adult beliefs and behaviors have caused harm. This practice strengthens our ability to focus on the lives we want for ourselves now and be accountable for our past. We are on this journey through the Steps to actualize the health and well-being that we have wanted. We begin by healing our relationships with ourselves and those we have harmed.

Sharon admits:

When I was growing up in an abusive household, I was not allowed any privacy. My mother demanded that even my bedroom and bathroom doors were always open. I was not allowed to claim any private space of my own. She interrogated me by asking questions that left me with no boundaries. Her interrogations were demeaning, intrusive, and controlling. I was not allowed to keep any part of my life, just to myself.

As a young adult, I developed a habit of questioning others as a way to keep them talking to me. I had decided early on they weren't really interested in me. Afraid of being alone, I took them hostage with my questions. My lack of social skills was evident, as was my lack of self-worth.

When I did Step 8, it became obvious to me how manipulative I had become, asking lots of questions. I had matured enough to be genuinely interested in people and needed to find more respectful ways to communicate. Constant questioning had become a habit that I wanted to break. I asked my Higher Power to help me learn to risk trusting and being vulnerable, being who I was. I hoped that would be enough for others to be interested in me.

Harm to Ourselves

In Step 8 we discover how we have caused harm not only to others but also to ourselves. Many of us put ourselves at the top of our amends lists! As adults abused as children, **self-neglect, self-denial, and self-abandonment** may be common issues. Some of us have a hard time feeling deserving and worthy of self-love and self-acceptance.

> **Renee admits:**
>
> *I have harmed myself physically by smashing my head against a wall and pounding my thighs until they were black and blue. Out of anger, I have hit my fists against steel railings and door jams until blood vessels broke. Step 8 helped me recognize that there was a part of me that was self-destructive and self-hating. It was time to look at my violence toward myself. As an adult, I had already learned that I didn't have to let other people abuse me verbally or physically. I realized that I couldn't let me abuse myself either.*
>
> *I learned early on through the Steps that I needed to set limits not only with others, but also with myself. I forbid myself to hurt my body on purpose, ever again. I made a commitment to myself, and I've been successful in my commitment, one day at a time.*

We can bring harm to ourselves in numerous ways. Some of us will pick at fingernails or toenails until they bleed. We may have an eating disorder. Undereating is as harmful to our bodies as overeating. Over-exercising can cause physical harm. Abusing drugs or alcohol are other avenues of harm. Anything we do in a compulsive or addictive manner can cause harm to our beings in some way.

Those of us who have been abused as children may not have developed a relationship with ourselves that included self-care. Not taking care of ourselves is an **abandonment** of our bodies.

We may neglect ourselves by not brushing our teeth regularly or not maintaining our personal hygiene. We can be **self-abandoning, self-diminishing, or self-destructive.** We may think that we don't count or are not important. We may feel that we are not worthy of self-consideration, self-respect, and self-love.

These underlying beliefs, left over from our pasts, influence our attitudes and actions toward ourselves. Shifting these outdated beliefs may be all we need to do to make amends to ourselves in Step 8.

Continual worry is also a form of self-harm since it is so stressful on our bodies and minds. For example, stress can lead to insomnia, loss of mental clarity, or even cause high blood pressure.

Not feeling safe enough in our bodies, we may not have fully inhabited or become aware of our physical beings. Thus, we can be unconscious of our surroundings and find ourselves bumping into things and causing accidents to our physical bodies.

Self-abandonment has a significant impact on how we feel about ourselves. It leads to deep-seated beliefs that we are unloved and unlovable. These feelings are profoundly self-harming.

Dani remembers:

One of my unmanageable behaviors was to treat my body as an object. I used it to get love, especially sexually. I would lose weight to gain acceptance. I thought if I had a nice physical appearance then people would like me, accept me, or feel positive toward me.

When I did Step 8, I saw how I was harming myself. Because the truth is, my body is not an object or a thing; it's a part of who I am. Stemming from my early experience of it being used inappropriately by so many others, I believed that my body was a thing to be used and abused. I used it to get things and manipulate people. I finally realized the harm I had caused myself and others and became willing to cease my harmful behaviors.

We can learn to stand up for ourselves by setting healthy limits. For adults abused as children, this may be challenging. With the fear of others rejecting or abandoning us, we abandon ourselves and our healthy boundaries. We fear the loss of connection with others. As a result, we go along just to get along, to stay connected. We are afraid to say no or truly share what we need; thus, we self-abandon. We may need to press pause and admit that we don't yet know how to set limits for ourselves. We remember we are human and respect our humanity. We ask our Higher Power and our support systems for help. We can learn.

The ways we acted that caused self-harm may have been unconscious until now. It could be our past training, old hidden patterns, and beliefs left over from our childhoods. These old patterns are part of what make our adult lives unmanageable. Step 8 continues to aid us in revealing our shortcomings and character defects. We want to discover the ones that create harm and become willing to make amends for them.

This is a good time to remember that the only two things we can change are our attitudes and our actions. We can become conscious of them as they help us become the people we want to be and the lives we want to enjoy.

John reflects:

For me, it was too painful to have a body on a physical or on emotional level. I also separated myself mentally from it. On an emotional level, my body was not really part of my conscious awareness for most of my life. The journey through the 12 Steps has helped me reconnect to and appreciate my body. I am beginning to take care of it now.

Sylvia adds:

It's taken me many years to be willing to care for my body. Having a body in my past was dangerous. As a child, when others acknowledged that I had a body, bad things happened to it – that was clear as day! Why would I want a body after that? Consequently, I rejected it. Now I realize that physically denying that I had a body, was harmful to me. By thinking like a perpetual victim, I became my own perpetrator. That's what I did out of having such a painful relationship with my body.

Self-care

The opposite of self-harm is self-care. It can feel unusual, frightening, or confusing as we begin to focus on taking care of ourselves. As adults abused as children, we can learn to be open, willing, and able to have healthy relationships with our bodies, minds, and spirits. We continue to discover ways to care for and about ourselves as we end the patterns of harm we have caused. The Steps are opening us to healthier ways of treating ourselves and others.

Bernie's thoughts:

I find when I take good care of myself, it strengthens my internal harmony with the world while increasing my ability to care for others.

Sharon shares:

Very often, when I think I've harmed someone, what I've actually done, is taken care of myself. I didn't know that I was allowed to take care of myself if it meant that someone else would feel bad. I never wanted another to be hurt, having been so hurt by others myself. Sometimes I have difficulty with this concept of self-care and choosing self before another.

As adults abused as children, we begin to learn how to care for our little inner children, the ones within us who were there when we were young. We nourish and nurture them by speaking kindly and acting lovingly toward our child-selves who were wounded.

If we find it challenging to care for our adult-selves, we can begin to practice caring for our child-selves. If we don't take care of ourselves now, we accept the harmful messages that we don't matter, don't count, and are not important. We will have difficulty changing our lives if these messages continue.

We can stop the harm that did not end after our childhood abuse ended! We are waking up to discover our own abusive patterns as adults, bringing an end to self-abuse. We see the impact that our character traits have had on our lives and on the lives of others.

Today we want to be accountable for our deeds and right the harms we have caused. Making amends gives us the chance to live happier, more honorable lives.

Adelia reveals:

When I made my list, I was really scared; it was hard for me to look within. So, what I did to help myself was to imagine a little wicker basket in front of me. I mentally took the harm I had done, put it in the basket, and pictured it there instead of inside of me. It made the examination of myself more objective and helped remove my judgment about myself that arose with this rigorous, honest self-evaluation.

Harm to Others

Step 8 is guiding us to understand how we do harm to others and its effects on our lives. As children, we were victims of abuse. We need to heal those aspects of ourselves that would turn our pain from the past onto others. Otherwise, the chances of becoming perpetrators ourselves are alarmingly high. Child abuse often occurs over generations. However, through the 12 Steps, we have opportunities to end the patterns of abuse and harm in our lives and those who follow after us.

> **Adele shares:**
>
> I was a young mother who was abused as a child. When I married, I turned our children against their father by blaming everything that was wrong in our family on him. I taught them that he was lacking as a husband and a father. I constantly put him down. I humiliated him in front of our children. As they grew up, they started treating him as poorly as I did.
>
> After more than a decade, when we got divorced, I was so insecure that I made them choose to be loyal to either him or me. I thought I needed their love to live; I had to possess it all. I could not imagine the idea that they could

love both of us. The children and I made the divorce his fault. Another decade has gone by and they still treat him poorly.

Fortunately, while compiling my Step 8 list, the harm I had done to us all became crystal clear to me, and I sobbed. Our family still needs a lot of healing. Many years ago, I started us on a destructive path that I am now willing to make amends for. I have no idea where to begin. I'll ask my Higher Power to show me.

We may be the ones who are perpetuating child abuse, spousal abuse, or partner abuse. Abuse crosses all lines, including gender, intellectual ability, education, economic status, race, and age. If we know that we harm others, we must get help immediately! It is our responsibility to tell someone that we need help. We might strongly consider involving a professional for our healing.

Lastly, when Step 8 says to make a list of all persons we have harmed, it is not limited to an individual. Harm can be done toward groups of people, such as ethnic or religious ones. We can harm groups with our biases, prejudices, political ideologies, bigotry, judgments, intolerances, and lack of acceptance of our differences. It can be harm done to a business, institution, or organization.

Examples of harm to others

- Imposing our reality
- Creating some type of misfortune
- Causing diminishment
- Withholding love, compassion, or understanding
- Being overly critical or judgmental
- Taking advantage
- Physically or verbally causing hurt, injury, or pain
- Causing grief
- Manipulating others or circumstances to our advantage
- Being prejudiced
- Being self-righteous
- Making another wrong
- Denying others' feelings and sense of reality
- Lying
- Stealing
- Being possessive, manipulating to get our needs met
- Objectifying our bodies or using sex to buy love

It is human nature to do what's familiar, rather than take risks and develop new attitudes, behaviors, and beliefs. When it comes to harming others, those of us who were harmed as children, could turn to how we were trained or treated as an option for ourselves. We might cause harm without even realizing it.

As we journey through the Steps, we expand our knowledge, empower our choices, and release old patterns and beliefs from our childhoods. We are replacing them with healthier ones.

We may or may not have caused harm to ourselves or others when our childhood abuse occurred. As we experienced what happened to us as children, however, we made decisions and created beliefs out of those early experiences.

As adults, we discover some of those beliefs and assumptions we created may not apply in today's world. We are no longer children looking at life through children's eyes. We can no longer afford the discrepancies between those long-ago views and the realities of adulthood today.

Became Willing

Step 8 states we "Made a list of all persons we had harmed, and became willing to make amends to them all." It is helpful to remember that working the Steps is a process. We don't have to be completely willing right now. We are **becoming** willing.

This is the only time in any of the 12 Steps that the word "willing" is mentioned, and yet the concept of willingness can first be found in Step 3. We made a decision to turn our will and our lives over to the care of our Higher Power, only through our willingness to do so. That's all it took, the willingness to decide. Our willingness is the critical connection to our Higher Power and the path of true surrender.

> **Dru reflects:**
>
> *The power of willingness made it possible for me to write down the names of people I had harmed. My will was powered by my desire to be the kind of person who could own his part in the relationship. I was willing to accept the truth and be honest. I prayed for willingness to come forth, and it did.*

Willingness is a conscious choice. It creates an inner environment for an opening to appear that was not available to us **before** we became willing. The impact of willingness could show up as trust, faith, confidence, ideas, intuition, peace, or solutions. There are no requirements or limits to willingness. It's available to everyone, always. What aides our will is surrender. Surrender is letting go of our way, of our version of how things should be. We learn how to be our best selves by first being willing to **be with how things and people are** – and create newly out of that.

We may not like or be compatible with the character traits of others. Our healing includes tolerance and understanding as we let go of needing them to be what we think they should be. As we practice this in our lives, we become more peaceful.

Sharon contributes:

I cannot stress enough how important willingness is to me. When I am willing, I don't have to do anything. There is nothing to know, nothing to be good at; there's no skill involved. There is literally nothing to do, but make a choice.

Willingness is always an option for us.

Nancy recounts:

If I am feeling bad and being hard on myself, and don't know what else to do, I become willing to love myself or accept myself, even though I don't think I know how to do that. I find it's not a matter of knowing or being taught. My willingness to love myself leads me to acceptance.

Things take time to grow in accordance with nature's laws. To become willing, sometimes we need to increase our faith, trust, or confidence. Sometimes we just need time. It's a process.

As we become willing, we admit our wrongs and face the amends we must make in Step 9. We become willing with our Higher Power as our partner. It's difficult to take action when we feel small, and the amends feel big. We wouldn't feel up to the task. We need to develop our relationship with our Higher Power as we go along.

> **David states:**
>
> What if I **want** to be willing but can't make myself **be** willing yet? Other than accepting myself where I'm at, all I can think of doing is to remain open to my Higher Power, showing me where my resistance to willingness is. Then I ask my Higher Power to guide my thoughts and actions. I pause and pray to be willing to follow the nudges my Higher Power gives me.

Making amends does not necessarily mean that we apologize. The best amends may be our willingness to change our interactions with a person, an institution, or a group of people. We can and must change **ourselves** in relationship to those we have harmed.

It may be challenging for us to be willing when we justify our resentments because of what was done to us. We can pray to our Higher Power for willingness to move beyond this and come to a place of forgiveness.

As adults abused as children, willingness builds self-respect. We have learned that we cannot change others. We can only **allow** changes in ourselves with the support of our Higher Power. Being willing signifies we are ready to move ahead in our lives without being forced; we are voluntarily participating in them.

Willingness is the ability to accept ourselves and others as they are. As we become more accepting, our lives become more manageable. Our intention of willingness is the foundation of peace. We can begin by having someone else's greater good in mind, other than our own.

Lindsey shares:

When I started to make my amends list, I realized that some amazing changes had already taken place with some significant people in my life. I had become more willing through working Steps 4, 5, 6 and 7 than I was aware of. I had already begun to make amends by treating them with respect and not being as judgmental. One friend started to trust me more when I was less critical of her.

As we become willing to see ourselves authentically, we review our actions and come to a better understanding of how we have harmed ourselves and others. We discover more about our character defects. As we learn more about ourselves, we are able to choose new ways of being and develop new positive feelings about ourselves.

For adults abused as children, willingness is as important as faith. When we feel backed into a corner, overwhelmed with fear or resentment, it is best just to become willing. A state of willingness opens the pathway to inspiration, divine counsel, renewed energy, and guidance. When we are willing, we are naturally open to our Higher Power, and our faith is restored. Our Higher Power gives us what we need to succeed in life. We offer willingness as the fertile ground our success is planted in.

Make Amends

To make amends means to **do something to compensate** for what we did that hurt someone. It may also mean to **shift ways of being** with another or with ourselves. There are no right or wrong ways for us to make amends. **Being sincerely accountable** is the key.

> **Warren realizes:**
>
> When I first began to make my list in Step 8, I was so fearful that I could only think of one way to make amends. I needed to come up with more choices for myself for each of the amends to be relevant. I was so afraid to find things wrong with me, to look at my character defects. Having such low self-esteem, I didn't feel up to the task of looking deeper.
>
> I became willing to think of more choices, by having my Higher Power as my partner, to risk going deeper inside myself. Without my Higher Power, the amends seemed too mountainous when I was feeling really fearful. I had to develop my relationship with my Higher Power anew to be able to make amends.

We may need to apologize and seek forgiveness. We may need to change our behaviors in our relationships with others or with ourselves. We may need to extend compensation for our past wrongs, hurts, or betrayals. There may be times when all of the above is called for.

As adults abused as children, we may think that apologies are the best way to make amends. Sincere apologies might be a crucial step when making amends. However, apologies alone may be insufficient. The most vital part of making any amends is to create a shift in our behavior or attitude. These shifts may even affect our approach to the way we live our lives.

Since we're all human, making amends is a part of life for most people. For us, it is an essential step toward our healing from lives impacted by childhood abuse!

As we begin to look at making amends, it is important to remember that **we** are one of the people we've harmed. For this reason, it is a good idea to put ourselves at the top of our amends lists. Remember, not only have others been affected by the effects of our shortcomings, but we have also.

Stephanie adds:

I want to know other ways of expressing my rage and frustration without hurting anyone. I want to break my old patterns and habits. Otherwise, I'll only have hurtful ways to deal with my anger, and I'll be trapped in them. Making amends to myself involves my learning and practicing empowering and healthy new habits as an adult.

I have begun looking for resources to expand my knowledge of safely dealing with my rage. Then, what I learned from my childhood won't be the only options I'll have available to me.

As we complete Step 8 and Step 9, the results can be profoundly healing for the recipients of our amends. However, even greater benefits come to us by working the Steps and clearing our slates. We may not realize the positive effects on us until after we make our amends. They become evident in our lives over time.

The benefits of making amends are numerous and restorative. Our decision to make amends to them "all" means that we can look forward to no longer having to avoid all those people and situations that have caused us great discomfort. We restore our integrity, self-worth, and overall sense of well-being by making amends. We find we can create lives filled with inner peace and a growing sense of personal freedom.

The willingness to make amends enhances our relationships and helps us regain lost intimacy. Willingness frees us to recover energy that our shame, resentments, and other ill-feelings withheld from us. Most importantly, it gives us an opportunity for true and real closure for the harms we have caused. This is incredibly freeing for everyone involved.

In addition to honoring the other individuals or situations, the willingness to make amends contributes toward our spiritual growth. We continue to turn our will and our lives over to the care of a Higher Power and discover that surrender creates positive changes in our behavior and in our lives. It is accomplished through honest actions that may exist outside of our current comfort zones. We do this from a place of readiness and willingness to be fully accountable.

As a result, our lives are opened to new perspectives and are filled with new possibilities. We reexamine our past actions, or lack of action, and reevaluate what choices we would make today for a better tomorrow.

The process of making amends

1. We look at where we come up short or compromised someone because of our character traits.

2. We see who or what we are judging, diminishing, wanting to control, resenting, or fearing.

3. We become accountable without being self-critical.

4. We admit to ourselves the harm we have done – including self-diminishment – without guilt, shame, or embarrassment.

5. We focus on our willingness, readiness, and the timing of our amends.

6. We let our Higher Power and people we trust support and guide us.

7. We are self-compassionate and self-forgiving when we make amends.

8. We gain clarity about choosing appropriate amends.

9. We add new people or situations to our lists as we discover new harms.

As we look at making appropriate amends, we will need to consider each person, each event, and each harm that was done. No two situations are the same; each is unique to those involved. The willingness to be responsible for our part is the ultimate respect we can offer ourselves and others.

Our amends may not be accepted, welcomed, or wanted. We need to be willing to allow others their rightful responses. When faced with making amends to those not available, we could choose an act of service as our way of apologizing to someone who has passed on. For example, to make amends for wrong deeds to an elder we might volunteer at a senior center if the elder's whereabouts is unknown.

As adults abused as children, we must be totally honest about the extent of our wrongs for us to gain a proper perspective. This is possible if we consider our actions from the others' points of view. Our willingness to share that we didn't have their best interests at heart makes it possible for them to listen without being defensive or accusatory.

Being willing and able to express our remorse or regret can lead to others feeling that we are sincere. We demonstrate that we have owned our past transgressions and that our desires to make amends are genuine.

Steps 8 through 12 are pathways for us to make things right with ourselves, with others, and with our Higher Power. Being willing and accountable are keys to our continued paths of healing. The most effective ways to make amends are to heal ourselves through self-care, self-love, and self-forgiveness. We make conscious choices to deepen our self-respect, self-worth, and self-empowerment. We watch our lives change as we create new possibilities.

Forgiveness

For those of us with child abuse in our pasts, forgiveness does not mean that we excuse, deny, or forget what someone did to us. **Forgiveness is letting go of blaming others or ourselves for how our lives turned out today!**

By now, we have probably experienced many years since our childhood abuse occurred. We have lived in the shadows of our past circumstances long enough and now want to step outside of their constraints. Resentments that we carry from the past prevent us from living fully today.

Our future is not determined by who we've been, what we've done, or what was done to us, but rather what we see possible for ourselves today! That's how new realities and new lives are created. We only have to be **willing** to forgive or be forgiven. Right and wrong are not involved in forgiveness.

One of the gifts of forgiveness is that it allows us to have closure and completion with people and events from our past. We can ask our Higher Power for help when we find ourselves unwilling or unable to forgive others or ourselves.

Forgiveness is not to be forced; it will appear over time. It gives us back our freedom and personal power and is an essential aspect of self-love, self-care, and self-respect. Forgiveness strengthens our internal sense of harmony with the world.

Our ability to forgive does not depend on another's forgiveness of us, even though we may feel it is warranted.

We can find peace within ourselves regardless of how our amends and forgiveness are received. Because we admit our part, we are able to speak our desires to forgive and be forgiven from a place of sincerity, humility, and compassion.

Forgiveness is liberating. It does not change the past. Instead, it gives us a chance for a better future. Forgiveness doesn't condone anything. However, if we hold onto resentments, they have power over us and steal the energy we need to live happier lives. As adults abused as children, forgiveness provides us with the courage to let go of how we thought life should have been and come to accept how it turned out.

Our lists will help guide our prayers, intentions, and affirmations as we move through Step 8. It may be wise to start with someone who we think will be easy to forgive and then venture on to others who may be more challenging. It is important to remember to have compassion for ourselves and others throughout this process.

As we come to ask another's forgiveness, we are asking them to accept our apologies, and let go of any resentments they might hold toward us. It may be difficult for them to do so if we have hurt them repeatedly or have promised to change numerous times in the past but didn't. We may have broken their trust in us. However, these relationships can be rebuilt and mended in time.

Self-forgiveness

Myrna decides:

I need to forgive myself for "taking it" in order to survive when I was little. I can still hear my child's inner voice telling me to do something to stop "it." But by that time, I had learned that any kind of movement or sound would only escalate the violence and torture. So, I did not try to defend myself anymore.

While doing Step 4, I realized that my actual survival as a child was at stake. Wisely, I adapted to the situation by not defending myself. It was safer to accept, rather than to resist. I did not understand any of this when I was little. I just felt bad that I didn't do anything and looked down on myself as a weakling. I remember calling myself "little liver puss." I felt spineless and full of shame for not fighting back.

In Step 8, I was willing to forgive myself for making assumptions when I was a child that were incorrect: I was not weak. I was small. I was a child. And I **was** able to keep myself alive! I was so young; I couldn't possibly have understood what was going on.

I owe myself forgiveness for making erroneous decisions based on my false childlike beliefs about who I thought I was. I've become aware that I've been living them out in *my adult life, too. However, I am no longer willing to live the rest of my life based on these obsolete beliefs.*

I can transform my relationship with myself by seeing and praising my bravery and innate wisdom. I have become grateful for the survival choices I made when I was little.

Anita adds:

I put myself at the top of my amends list. I'm not angry at myself for the adult decisions I made. Yet, I want to straighten out my relationships that were impacted by my mistaken feelings that I was less than I should be. I want to assess what happened to me as a little girl and offer myself an updated view more aligned with reality.

I've worked the previous Steps to get to this point and have not been disappointed in the results. I will ask my Higher Power for help forgiving myself and for misjudging myself when I was little.

As adults abused as children, there were deeds and actions forced upon us. We were powerless to prevent acts that we never would have chosen to take part in, but were forced to do so at the time. We must release our shame, guilt, and blame from our minds and hearts. We can ask for support from our Higher Power to make this possible. As we create self-forgiveness through our thoughtfulness, actions, and changed attitudes, we are on the path to making true and lasting amends in Step 9.

Carol reveals:

I did nothing wrong. I was forced to harm another. Having been injected with drugs by the abusers, I was made to do things that I deeply regret. As a child, I became confused when I thought that I should not have gone along, and blamed myself. Now that I am an adult and have some perspective, I am able to forgive my child-self. I had no choice. They overpowered me.

By being open to forgiving ourselves, we can have true compassion for those toward whom we are willing to make amends. It may be difficult for us to ask for their acceptance of our apologies and ask for their forgiveness. We can be with them, look them sincerely in the eyes, and share that we can appreciate how difficult forgiving us may be for them, as forgiving ourselves might be for us.

All Persons We Harmed

In referring to all persons we had harmed, Step 8 emphasizes the importance of being complete, thorough, and inclusive in our lists. We don't just make amends to the easiest, most accessible ones or to the people we can count on to accept our amends without question.

We are willing to consider our behaviors not only with our close relationships but also, with those who are not close, or those we don't like. As a result, based on our beliefs that we would be happy if only others would change, we became frustrated in our failed attempts to "fix" many of those on our lists. We reacted to them instead of taking action in our own lives.

Naomi contributes:

When I first read the word "all" in Step 8, my perfectionist nature appeared. I thought that meant every living person I'd ever met. I figured I must have harmed them all and had to make amends to everyone I'd ever known. I talked to a trusted confidant who thought I was exaggerating the harms I'd done. We talked for a long time until I had a more realistic view of the actual harms.

Now, when I hear "all," I hear it as a reminder to be thorough, as thorough as I can be. I learned these are not surface amends I'm making. I'm being asked to be searching and fearless again, like in Step 4.

Some questions we can ask ourselves as we complete our amends lists:

- Have we been involved in abusive relationships?

- Have we been discounting expressions of love from others or avoiding intimacy?

- Are we still punishing ourselves for taking responsibility for the abuse itself?

- Who has been impacted by our lack of trust, our perfectionism, or our need to control?

- Who has been affected by our negative attitudes and resulting actions?

- As adults, who did we want to take care of us when we refused to be responsible for ourselves? Were we a burden to them? We list them all.

- Whom have we withdrawn from in our relationships or even written them off completely?

- Where has our hurt and anger spilled over into our dealings with others?

- Whom do we ignore or are irrational around?

- Whom have we neglected?

- Where have we been devious in our past?

- Whom do we have a long feud with refusing to let go of ill-will toward them?

- With whom do we insist on having our own way?
- Whom do we make unreasonable demands of?
- Whose feelings are we unconcerned about, focusing only on ourselves?
- Whom do we pity or feel superior to?
- Did we confuse making mistakes with being human?
- Whom did we assume were bad, unworthy people and showed little respect to? Did we look at ourselves in these same ways and treat ourselves poorly as well?
- How often did we use excuses to keep us from making changes or allowing our Higher Power to help us grow?

Our lists may include ourselves, family members (present and previous), friends, neighbors, creditors, employers and employees, customers, teachers, students, or co-workers. List organizations such as: religious, political, ethnic, gender-specific, economic, or age-related groups. List career or financial biases.

All of these questions, and more, are important to ask ourselves as we complete our amends list. Some names will be obvious to us, others more elusive. But if we are to enjoy the freedom of lives unburdened by the past, we must list who has been harmed by our guilt, shame, erroneous assumptions, or our manipulations. If we continue to hold on to any of these, our healing will be based on shaky foundations.

Healing from child abuse is a process. We can't afford to continue to cling to our unhealthy attitudes and behaviors, or we'll have difficulty realizing the power and strength given to us by our Higher Power. We remember that humility involves accepting ourselves as human beings.

We notice that this Step contains the word "all" twice. Step 8 is not complete until **all** are included in our willingness, even though we may never cross paths with them again.

Step 8 is a **preparation** Step for taking action on each of our amends in Step 9.

We are preparing for the necessary changes in our relationships. As adults, learning to be objective about the events and experiences of our past helps us stop blaming ourselves and others.

Step 8 Summary

At a certain point, many of us suspend trying to figure out our past and why it happened the way it did. Yet some of us know **exactly** why it happened and decided it was because of alcoholism, mental illness, teenage power-testing, misguided parental rights, rage, meanness of spirit, or family and cultural history.

We suspend our rights to assess what happened from our childhood perspective and defer to our adulthood perspective. How would doing that benefit our ultimate intentions of having more satisfying lives today?

When we stay in the present moment as adults, we break the continuity of our mindsets. We stop feeling like victims of our past and fearing our future. Even when we make small changes in the present, our lives are positively impacted in the future as well!

When we try something new, we may begin to trust ourselves. We might gain self-confidence by one small act. When we speak out, we might experience being "able to live through it," even though we were afraid of perishing if we said anything! Clear intentions are helpful in our process of transformation.

Madeleine reminds us:

I see life as a process of forgetting and remembering. I use tools to help me remember when I forget. One tool that I use is gratitude. In doing Step 8, I have used an attitude of gratitude to increase my willingness to accept my part in my relationships. I am grateful that I have the courage to get clear about whom I've hurt and how I can make amends.

When I'm not in touch with my inner resources, especially when I'm feeling hopeless and think I've given up on my Higher Power, I remember the progress I've made and the healthy changes my Higher Power has already helped me make. I become grateful and willing to trust my Higher Power one more time.

It's vital for me to remember that I don't have to know how to change myself. I only have to be willing to work my Steps and have faith that a Power greater than myself knows what I need and meets those needs. I have gained self-awareness from working Steps 4 through 7. They have prepared me for Step 8. I remember that I can change and become willing to treat myself and others with respect.

As adults abused as children who want more satisfying and fulfilling lives, we have discovered that **what we want is possible** when we follow the suggested guidelines in the Steps.

We give ourselves many chances, along with some time to change and to gather courage. Accepting the truth about what has kept us ineffective or off-course is the foundation for making amends to ourselves. We develop self-compassion and the willingness to be honest. We clean our sides of the street and create new lives for ourselves one day at a time in the process.

Without self-forgiveness, how can we make amends to ourselves? Without forgiveness of others, how can we authentically make amends to **them**? We realize that we've wanted fulfilling lives for a long time. Now we are ready to take Step 9 in order to manifest them.

This is our chance to do what is ours to do to promote our healing. We become ready to swallow our pride and make restitution for our mistakes. We no longer wait for others to make the first move toward reconciliation. We release all obstacles to our healing, including self-will and old resentments.

A Higher Power is now in charge of our lives, so anything is possible when we make our lists and ask for help. Willingness will come to yield satisfying and valuable results for us to grow emotionally and spiritually. We choose to work Step 8. It enables us to enjoy new states of freedom and peace from a place of true humility.

> **Morton explains his views:**
>
> For me, willingness to be kind to myself needs to be a conscious choice. Willingness creates an internal environment for me to have access to kindness that I couldn't connect with before I was willing. I didn't do anything different other than decide to be willing to be kind to myself. I haven't found any requirements for becoming willing. I guess it's available to everyone all the time. I simply pray and ask to become willing when I notice that I'm not.

> **Shelly adds:**
>
> Sometimes a willingness to shift my attitude allows new ideas to come to me that my anger had been blocking. I've noticed when I move my attitude from a righteous, hurting place to a compassionate, willing one, a flood of new ideas comes to me. I can't explain how this happens because I don't know. However, I see the results of willingness and goodwill and know that I'm on the right path for my life to be the way I want it to be.

Step 8 Affirmations

1. My Higher Power is helping me.

2. I approve of myself.

3. I gently release my expectations.

4. I am able and willing to courageously look at myself.

5. I orient myself to the present.

6. I choose what's best for me in the long run.

7. I believe in my willingness to forgive.

8. I give myself permission to change.

9. I release the hold the past has had on me.

10. My healing has begun.

11. Prayer restores my connection to my Higher Power.

12. I celebrate myself.

13. Connecting with others is getting easier.

14. I am practicing seeing the "good" in me.

Step 8 Journal Questions

1. What is the spiritual principle beneath admitting a wrong?
2. How has Step 8 restored my integrity and sense of dignity in my relationships?
3. How do I contribute to others?
4. How do I experience compassion for others? For myself?
5. Where have I lacked self-discipline?
6. Where do I feel remorse or regret for how I have acted recently?
7. Am I quick to react with fear, suspicion, or anger? What situations bring these forth?
8. How has trust in a Higher Power given me hope for my future?
9. How has self-centeredness shown up in my life? How has it affected me or others?
10. What progress am I making in one important area of my life?
11. Are there any instances where I justify lying?
12. What negative thoughts about myself need to be released?
13. What are some of my goals and dreams?

Step 8 Prayer

I release all that no longer serves me. My inner life has been filled with thoughts and feelings that are leftover from the past. My heart can feel heavy with obsolete beliefs on which I've based my life.

Help me see where I have clogged my mind with resentments and unforgiveness. I ask for help in being willing to clear away all ill-will that I've caused. I want to be accountable for my part from a place of humility. I seek peace of mind and heart.

I am gentle and compassionate with myself and others. As I prepare to make amends, fill me with knowledge and guidance to be effective and true. I trust healing is possible for me when I take the steps to make it happen.

Thank you, God.

And so it is.

AMEN

Notes

Notes

Step 9

Made direct amends to such people whenever possible, except when to do so would injure them or others.

Step 9

Made direct amends to such people whenever possible, except when to do so would injure them or others.

Table of Contents

Introduction 411

Benefits of Step 9. 414

How to Begin 416

Making Amends 420

Three Kinds of Amends 422

Making Direct Amends to Others 425

Making Indirect Amends to Others 429

Making Amends to Myself 432

Making Living Amends 437

Amends that Could Harm 439

Step 9 Summary 445

Step 9 Affirmations 448

Step 9 Journal Questions 449

Step 9 Prayer 451

Step 9

Made direct amends to such people whenever possible, except when to do so would injure them or others.

Introduction

Step 1 says we admitted; Step 2 states we came to believe. In Step 3 we surrendered; at Step 4 we wrote about who we wound up to be as adults. In Step 5 we shared our inventory. Thankfully, Step 6 has helped us to become ready and Step 7 advised us to ask for help. In Step 8 we made a list. Now in Step 9, we make direct amends to the people on our Step 8 list.

Step 9 is about our willingness to acknowledge and be accountable for the harms we have created in our adult lives and in others' lives. These harms may include what we have said, ways in which we have behaved, and our previous and current attitudes and actions.

As we own the impact of our actions, and choose to come from more empowered states, our self-respect and self-love continue to strengthen us. As a result, our desire to release our past, to identify our character flaws, to make amends, and to forgive become our motivations. Having completed Steps 1 through Step 7, we are recognizing that we have access to our personal power,

Making amends can take many forms. We can meet face-to-face. It may mean that we become willing to be kinder and more considerate or more willing to leave our hearts open to life, others, and most importantly, to ourselves. We may need to make restitution monetarily, by volunteering, or by committing to healthier behavior in the future. Changes of attitude are often appropriate amends we can make. A more detailed discussion of amends follows in this chapter.

As adults abused as children, it is important to remember that completing Step 9 will require us to connect with our Higher Power to ensure that we have the courage to change the things we can and surrender those we cannot. As we become ready to look at our lives and review our actions, we discover more about our character defects and why making amends is core to our personal healing.

Step 9 is the key to creating restitution and restoration in our past and present relationships. Through amends we resolve the harms we have caused. What is **restoration**? Webster defines restoration as, "a bringing back to a former position or condition–reconstruction of the original form." By making restitution we restore our lives. **Restitution** is the act of making amends to those whom we have harmed, including ourselves. It is the actions we take in Step 9.

Making amends is not done once; it is a lifetime commitment. As adults abused as children, we learn to stay watchful of our shortcomings and readily make amends as we recognize where we have caused harm. Restoration, resolution, and restitution are the guideposts of Step 9, helping us make amends and choosing new ways of being and behaving.

Benefits of Step 9

We grow spiritually as we journey through the Steps. Step 9 is the catalyst for our lives to be liberated from regrets, disappointments, and years of pain. As with all the Steps, as time progresses, more and more is revealed. As we dive deeply into Step 9, we discover what's available for us to create peace for ourselves and others.

The willingness to speak and accept the truth helps set us free, and as we do, we restore our integrity, self-worth, and over-all sense of well-being. Taking responsibility helps us create lives of personal freedom. Doors begin to open for us that were not accessible before we made our amends.

Shirley offers:

I grew in awareness as I worked Step 9. I made amends because I finally saw things differently. I saw my part in the hurts I had caused and wanted to admit them so I could feel better and let go of the guilt I was living with.

As we acknowledge our wrong doings, the people we owe amends to may **also** become liberated and feel less harmed. They can release the pain they may have been holding onto.

We help free both of us of any excess baggage. It is a blessing to become free from our past and offer this gift to help free another, as well.

Johnnie reflects:

Step 9 helped me realize that I can handle my life as an adult—a being, fully conscious and aware. Now, I am self-assured enough to say I am sorry and have changed my ways. I am also willing to change my attitudes.

Until I learned how to take care of myself, I would not let my brothers off the hook for not protecting me from the abuse when I was a child. Through working the Steps, I learned I could weather disappointments, stand up for myself, become willing to be fully honest, and forgive my brothers.

Adrienne adds:

As an adult abused as a child, I felt poorly about myself, had low self-esteem, and was quick to judge other people. Working the Steps helped me feel better about myself. Step 9 held me to the highest standards; I was able to tell myself and others the truth. I feel great peace about my past.

How to Begin

As adults abused as children, we are being asked to be honest about the harm we have caused since we were children. We look at how to begin as we consider each person, event, issue, or circumstance involved. These key aspects – person, event, and consideration of the harm done – will help guide us toward the appropriate amends to make.

We see from our Step 8 lists that no two situations are the same; each is unique to the individual and the circumstances related to the harm we have caused. Each is worthy of our time and consideration as we choose the ways to make our amends meaningful and direct when possible, as long as it does not cause further harm.

We may begin our amends by choosing the easiest first. This may help us build courage for the more difficult amends that will be done later. Remember we have developed readiness, willingness, and enough courage through the prior Steps to make amends in our lives now.

We note that the process of making amends is not solely about apologizing. An apology may be needed, but more importantly, we are owning our part, acknowledging where we came up short, and admitting the harm we have done to ourselves and others.

We can pray for courage, humility, and acceptance. We don't want to argue, defend our position, or make other people wrong, even if their responses to our amends are not favorable or accepting of what we share. We may not experience our hoped-for outcomes. We can approach each person in a spirit of humility, offering reconciliation not justification.

We need to be prepared for the possibility that a recipient may decline our invitation to converse with us regarding our making amends. We respect their wishes if they indicate that they would rather not meet to discuss the matter; they may change their minds in the future. We opened the door to be accountable; that is the best we can do for making direct amends at this time.

When the opportunity is available to meet directly, it is good to be brief and specific about the past situation. Details are not necessary.

The purpose is not to explain or describe our side of things. The purpose is to admit where we came up short, the harm we caused, and to commit to something better: better behaviors, better attitudes, better communications, or an apology. We want to make restitution wherever possible.

As adults abused as children, we may be tempted to avoid direct meetings with certain people on our lists. If this is the case, it is a perfect opportunity to go to our Higher Power for help, call a trusted friend, or do nothing in that moment. We are becoming ready and will know when the time is right.

Lastly, as we begin making amends, we will experience times when the person we have harmed is willing to accept our amends and happily does so. This is part of the healing journey. However, there may be times when the person for whom we have caused harm is not yet willing to forgive. Nonetheless, **our** personal healing continues to deepen because we are doing our part by making direct amends.

We remember, as adults abused as children, we may not be comfortable with confrontation. Whether that is confronting situations, feelings, (especially fear and anger), or people, we may find ourselves backing away from them.

To make Step 9 manageable we can focus on one person at a time, one amends at a time. We begin with our Step 8 list that identifies whom we have harmed and review our 4th Step inventory, as well. With these two resources we can develop an action plan for moving forward with Step 9.

After making amends, we may still have a few people we cannot face; this is a very natural response. It does not make us bad, weak, or wrong; we just need more courage, time, or readiness. If we still have anger or fear towards someone, it is often best to postpone contacting them until a later time.

It may be helpful to start with someone who is easy to make amends to. It can give us confidence when we deal with tougher situations along the way. It is also helpful for us to focus on self-love, self-compassion, and self-forgiveness. We can go to our Higher Power and ask for help.

We pray for courage, humility, acceptance, and strength to help us become ready. We can focus on the positive reasons why restitution and reconciliation will help everyone involved. If we do these things and are patient, our Higher Power can give us the ability, willingness, and readiness to reconcile with everyone on our lists.

Making Amends

Willingness to make amends and accountability are keys to our continued paths of healing. As adults abused as children, making amends is a conscious choice we make to deepen our self-respect, self-worth, and self-love. We become responsible for the things we have done. Everyone benefits from forgiveness.

When we consider making amends to others, we may face a lot of fears, false expectations, and outdated beliefs about what may happen. We may be afraid of rejection, retaliation, making financial amends, or hosts of other possible outcomes. The intention of making amends is not meant to hurt anyone, nor to create further harm than that which has already been done. We need to make appropriate choices so that does not occur.

Making amends does not have to be a dreadful or scary experience. We may find that we actually feel relieved about the possibility of healing a relationship, or happily anticipate the relief after making a particularly scary amends. We may even feel unburdened by paying off a past debt. There is great freedom gained by cleaning up our pasts.

As adults abused as children, we may think that an apology is the best way to make amends. A sincere apology may be a crucial aspect of our amends, but an apology alone may not be enough. The most vital aspect of making amends is created by changes in our behavior, in our thinking, and seeking new approaches for living our lives. As we explore how to make amends through reparation, or compensation for past loss, damage, or injury, we are creating greater peace of mind and unburdening our heavy hearts.

When we make amends, we make changes toward others as we **allow** changes in ourselves. We demonstrate that we have evolved beyond whom we used to be. Through Step 9 we are growing more self-aware, choosing our actions more wisely, and exhibiting new positive traits affecting our relationships.

Three Kinds of Amends

1. **Direct Amends:** *We go directly* to the person, group, or organization and address the harm that we have caused. It involves taking personal responsibility by communicating openly and honestly, being willingly to explore how to make reparation.

   It takes a lot of courage to do this. If possible, it is done in the presence of the other person to whom we owe the amends. We may begin with a heartfelt apology and ask for forgiveness. We may share how the wrongs we did have impacted them.

   For example:
   If we stole money or damaged property:
   - We can work to repay the debt, or repair, or replace the item.

   For example:
   If we tarnished someone's reputation by lies or gossip:
   - We can communicate with those whom we gossiped about or lied to, own our part, apologize, and commit to ending our behavior in the future.

2. **Indirect Amends:** *We are unable to communicate directly* due to death, an inability to locate the individual, or the potential for further harm. We can share the amends we desire to make with someone else, such as a counselor or a trusted friend.

   Through selfless acts we can do sincere service indirectly helping someone like them instead and make reparation in symbolic ways.

   For example:
   If we took our pain and anger out on strangers:
   - We can enroll in an anger management class.
   - We can do random acts of kindness.
   - We can volunteer at a hospital and help lessen someone else's pain.

   For example:
   If we were prejudiced toward a group of people:
   - We can volunteer to work in a community kitchen for people in need.
   - We can donate money to a religious group of whom we were intolerant.

3. **Living Amends:** *We make genuine life changes* by making amends through changed behaviors, attitudes, and beliefs. We choose and commit to living differently. These shifts reveal our changes to others and have a positive and direct impact on everyone, including ourselves. Through living amends our actions reflect new ways of being.

We show others and ourselves that we have become adults who want to expand and improve how we handle our lives. As adults affected by childhood abuse, we have grown beyond whom we used to be. Our behaviors and attitudes reveal our changes as we commit to our healing. As a direct result of the Steps, we grow more self-aware and able to make the necessary shifts we desire.

Making Direct Amends to Others

When we make direct amends to the people on our Step 8 lists, we also decide how to carry out those amends. We listed whom we harmed, the harms done, and our choices for making amends. One way to begin to make direct amends is to start with the safest people and make small, personal changes as we try out new behaviors.

Deciding how to make amends for the harms we created is especially important. To know that we have choices helps us balance our black and white thinking about perfection or failure. We might think there is one right way to make amends. Remembering we have choices helps us acknowledge that there is more than one way to right our wrongs. In addition, there may be times when we will have no idea how to make amends. It is helpful to talk to support people or pray about it and ask our Higher Power for guidance and clarity.

When we make amends, some of those on our lists may minimize the events or deny the need for our apologies or restitution. They may not have the tools to deal with their own feelings or choose not to. They may not even remember the events we're addressing. It is important that we stay in integrity with ourselves and do the best we can to make the amends in ways we feel are necessary and respectful for all concerned.

Angel courageously admits:

When I started Step 8, I went to the person I owed financial amends to and spoke directly to him. "I was working for you three years ago and stole $800 from you. Although I cannot pay you back all at one time, I would like to start paying you $50 a month for the next 16 months. I am terribly sorry. I want you to know that this will help me forgive myself and make amends to you all at the same time. I also want you to know that I am not stealing anymore and I commit to never doing it again."

That is how I was able to make my amends. The outcome was satisfying for both of us; I was able to forgive myself and make restitution. My previous employer chose to forgive me and was grateful that I was willing to expose my wrongdoing and come forth with honesty and integrity. He accepted my amends.

Norton explains:

In working Step 8, knowing what to say to make amends did not come easily for me. I prayed for guidance to be clear. In time, I discovered my guidance through a feeling in my gut. It also appeared as fleeting thoughts. With the help of my Higher Power, my heart knew how to express my amends. On my own, I had no idea where to begin.

One of the ways we may have done harm to others was to expect them to fulfill that which we did not receive in our childhoods. Though it was not their responsibility to provide that for us, we sought their affection, attention, praise, consolation, encouragement, and acceptance.

As adults abused as children, some of us have been, or still are, needy for love, starving for attention, and wanting to feel that we matter. We may expect our spouses, siblings, friends, or even our children to provide what our parents, caregivers, and previous significant others did not.

There are other ways that we may have caused harm, which may be easy to overlook or discount as insignificant. We may have been totally impatient with people for reasons that have nothing to do with them! We may have to make amends if we betrayed a confidence. Even if we told someone who promised to keep the secret private, we were still betraying a confidence.

Some people may need to make amends for stealing things at work. One way of making direct amends to our employer is to stop taking things or replace the items we have stolen. We could also tell our employer what we have done. Stealing from our places of employment is not uncommon; it is worthy of making amends.

As adults abused as children, we may have created a dynamic of separation from others. To include people whom we once excluded is another way of making direct amends.

The pattern of creating separation alienates us from others. We do not want to feel separate from others. That can promote fear, anxiety, loneliness, and isolation.

It is good to get clear about whom we avoid, whom we feel uncomfortable around, or whom we exclude from our lives. We may find the need to exclude certain people for our own healing or personal safety. Some others may choose to exclude us from their lives. We respect the choices of all.

> **Nancy adds:**
>
> *Another way I made direct amends was to start paying attention to people I used to ignore. I finally gave them a little extra time and attention. I acknowledged their style of dress or admired the flattering color of their shirt.*

It is important to focus on being willing to amend our ways and choose to include those whom we have avoided in the past, even as we take the time to discover why we've done so.

One of the goals of our 12 Step journeys is to see how we humans are more alike than we are different. In time, we can become comfortable with our differences. To openly choose to be inclusive and break the pattern of separation between us require us to behave in new ways. It takes courage, willingness, and practice to overcome our habits, patterns, and beliefs that cause separation.

Making Indirect Amends to Others

We may have lost contact with a person whom we harmed. We may not know how to contact them or they may have died. We consider if direct amends would cause further harm to us or to them. The last part of Step 9 says "except when to do so would injure them or others."

An example of indirect amends might be if we had an affair with someone and they have not told their partner. We do not go to the partner and confess the affair. We might share our admission of wrong to a trusted confidant to make amends for our actions and we end the affair.

If we gossiped about a person whom we no longer have contact with or has died, we stop gossiping. There are many ways to make amends indirectly. Some of us may choose to write a letter and then burn it, bury it, flush it, or throw it away. We can say in the letter everything we would have said to the person had he or she been available.

Sherri shares:

I know a woman who stole a ring from an elderly person. The elder died and the woman was not able to give the ring back directly. As a result, the woman had the ring appraised and donated that amount of money to a senior organization. The important thing to me was the motive in her heart. She willingly took responsibility and was able to make amends indirectly.

Bernard reflects:

I was only twenty-one when my father suddenly died. When I was older, it was important to me to make amends to him by asking a man I knew to sit in a chair opposite me as I told him everything that I would have said to my father had he still been alive. I asked this gentleman to be a substitute, a proxy for my father. I really got into it.

As an adult, I wanted to tell my father how I felt about him. I wanted to thank him for what he **did** do for me, instead of only focusing on what he had neglected to do. I blamed him for being an abandoning father, for not protecting me when my mother molested and physically abused me. Since he didn't protect me, I resented him. That became the central dynamic of our relationship. When I got the opportunity to make amends in Step 9, I told this man sitting opposite me what helpful things my father had taught me, what positive things I remembered about him, and how much I really loved my dad.

I chose to make these amends and experienced satisfaction by making sincere amends to my father in my heart.

Making Amends to Myself

The key to making amends to ourselves is our willingness to change our perspective **about** ourselves. This can be a new and challenging endeavor. We may have thought we were inferior to others. Thus, we could not afford to let them see our authentic selves. We felt rejection was too high a price to pay for revealing who we really were. We may have believed we were unlovable, or true happiness was only for others. It can feel risky when we finally reveal who we know ourselves to be.

As we awaken and become better informed about the nature of our self-harm, more is revealed about our inner beliefs. This deepens our paths of self-forgiveness. One of the best ways to make amends is to choose self-love, self-care, self-acceptance, and true self-forgiveness for the harm we have caused others and ourselves.

Elyse adds:

I started loving myself. I started trusting that some people could handle who I really was. I wanted to be around those people. I realized that I could distance myself from others who wanted me to continue to act out my old behaviors that were no longer appropriate. They treated me as if they knew what was best for me and that I didn't.

When I finally spoke up, some friends didn't want to be in a relationship with me anymore. It was challenging, but I was proud I chose to live an honorable life.

Marion reflects:

I had to encourage myself to let who I was on the inside, out into the world. I was terrified. I have memories of things going terribly wrong in my childhood when I tried to survive my household violence by revealing what was going on inside of me to my abusive father.

As an adult, I have had to encourage myself to express myself more often with safe people in safe situations, risking being seen for whom I really was.

By making amends to ourselves, by releasing self-harming patterns, and by treating ourselves as the precious beings we truly are, we claim the wonderful and meaningful lives we so deserve.

Monica shares:

In the abusive home I grew up in, I wasn't given a doll or even a stuffed animal. So, when I was little, I named my pillow "Clarabelle." She became my best friend and ally. She was my symbol of someone who loved and cared about me.

One day, by mistake, I told my mentally ill and abusive mother about Clarabelle and how special she was to me. My mother immediately stormed up the stairs to my bedroom, grabbed Clarabelle, and threw her out, never to be seen again! The grief I felt was unbearable because I knew my mother wanted me to suffer.

Thirty years after that event I bought myself my first doll...a Raggedy Ann.

We may want to consider some helpful practices as we make amends to ourselves. Practices are the activities of repeated focus and attention. Choosing a practice is usually motivated by an intention, a goal, a desired outcome, or a way of being.

Some choices for making amends to ourselves.

We may start by focusing on one or two from this list.

- We treat ourselves as if we count and take good care of ourselves. We demonstrate through self-love that giving to ourselves assures that we give to others from over-flowing and abundant states of love.
- We accept our humanity.
- We forgive ourselves for our past mistakes and for judging others as being wrong.
- We get clarity about what's important to us. We take action in those directions.
- We align our lives with our values. This is where our healing lies.
- We ask for help for support and guidance.
- We become aware and accountable for our character traits and shortcomings with self-compassion.
- We consciously look for blessings and are grateful for them.
- We're good for our word.
- We notice what puts a smile on our face, what lights us up, what we're interested in. We take action in those directions.
- We're honest with ourselves.

- We update our beliefs and replace obsolete ones with current, appropriate beliefs.
- We are generous and kind to ourselves.
- We trust in our Higher Power.
- We claim our good.
- We experience ourselves as being enough.
- We pray.
- We aim to act from our personal best as it fluctuates each day.
- We make decisions for our highest good.
- We are humble and willing.
- We expand our possible choices to include new ways of being.
- We set limits for ourselves and healthy boundaries for others.
- We listen to our self-talk about waiting to go for what we want. We may hear our thoughts, such as: I'm waiting until I deserve it. I'm waiting until I have time. I'm waiting until I feel more confident and less afraid. I'm waiting until I can do it my way...and so on. It may help to make a list of everything we're waiting for that comes to mind.
- We give ourselves permission to be all that we can be.

Making Living Amends

Living amends literally means amending the way we live. Instead of repeating old behaviors and making apologies for them, we commit to living our best possible lives. We stay conscious of old patterns and choose new ways of being that are best for all involved. We might stop reminding others of past hurts.

We can fulfill a promise we made to help someone but did not keep it. It could have been as simple as cooking a meal when they really needed to know that we cared, but we didn't show up or follow through. Instead, we made excuses explaining why we didn't keep our word. Living amends means delivering a meal or showing up in the future when we say we will.

We actively work on improving relationships in our lives. We include others we may have excluded. We connect with relatives more often. We can mentor young people or volunteer to teach people skills that we have mastered.

Living amends means to offer the best of our true selves. As appropriate, for many of us we centered on ourselves and our past needs as we were developing. Now, as adults, we can include others in our focus as well. We can volunteer our time to help with a charity or a worthy cause.

We learn we make an impact on others and that we have the personal power and ability to affect our relationships. We are accountable for the consequences of our actions and are able to investigate new choices. We find ourselves having access to greater wisdom and becoming ready to make our amends.

Alice recounts:

When I make amends, I am doing it for my healing, as well as for the other person. I want to clean up my side of the street. They may not feel that I have done anything wrong or remember the incident. However, I want to release guilt and feel a sense of resolve. When I make amends, whether they accept my amends, understand what I am doing, give me a warm reception, or forgive me, I know I am healing and forgiving myself by making amends.

Amends that Could Harm

How can we injure someone when we're seeking to be accountable for our part? Knowing if making amends would injure someone is tricky. Our trusted confidants can help us in confusing situations. Together, we look at our motives in making amends.

We learn to be aware of the effects of our honesty. Are we looking for a way out of undesirable consequences for ourselves? Are we using this process as a way to meet our own needs at the expense of others' well-being? Are we merely trying to unload some guilt? We need to be clear about our motives with humility, awareness, and honesty.

Charlene offers:

How do I know what really doesn't need to be said when I make my amends? For me, it's a sense, a feeling in my gut, or a fleeting thought. Most of all, my heart knows. I've learned that I need to allow myself some errors in judgment of what I need to say.

Making direct amends may involve harm to others. At their expense, we cannot be selfish and unburden ourselves for our own peace of mind. In other instances, omitting words that could create harm is an act of caring. We can simply change our past behavior in the present. This may be the kindest way of making amends in delicate situations.

For those of us who are parents who neglected or abused our children, as they mature into adults, we may have become overprotective and over-responsible to make up for our past harms to them. Making amends to our children may focus on encouraging their independence, self-esteem, and self-reliance.

Some of us may have confronted our abusers. We may have been told by them to apologize for making up false accusations and creating upset in our families! To make amends would be to compromise ourselves and act like we're still victims. This would be an injury to ourselves! However, as a way of making amends, we may choose to focus on improving our relationships with the abusers instead. At some point, we may even find that we are able to forgive them. It is most important that we are in harmony with **our** values and feel that we are in good standing with ourselves.

Some of us find making amends to our Higher Power is in order. We may have failed to love, be appreciative, or let go of resentments. As we become open to other people, we heal the separateness we have created. Anything that comes between us and other people cuts us off from connection with our Higher Power. Through prayer, we make amends by asking for help from that Power and shifting the ways in which we choose to live our lives.

There are times when our anger was valid, when raising our voices may have been needed and appropriate, and when our frustrations were justified. There are circumstances when such behaviors and responses do not require us to make amends. We still need to take personal inventory to discover if we need to make amends for our actions, but there is no absolute rule. We may have thought of ourselves before another or hurt their feelings. Each situation is unique. Talking with a trusted confidant can help us gain clarity about whether amends are appropriate or not.

We are learning the importance of evaluating the impact of our choices and actions. We are no longer denying our feelings. Instead, we are learning to experience them and recognize and honor our needs. We are learning what actions are healthy and justified and which create harm and injury to others or to ourselves.

Lois's heartfelt remembrance:

I knew my needs had to come before my son's. I had promised to take him to his best friend's house while he was on winter break. However, when the day came, I needed to see my dentist and could not do both. I went to the dentist on the promised day. Yes, my son was upset, but I did not injure him, as I am reminded in Step 9.

This time, I knew my needs had to come before his. I could appreciate why he was upset while still taking care of myself. I communicated this to him. Just because he had hurt feelings didn't mean that I was wrong or that I had any amends to make to him.

When we choose to take better care of ourselves, other people may not support that. We need to allow them to have their feelings about us. We now have the courage to stand up for ourselves, though others we care about may be uncomfortable with our choices. When we come from a place of self-love and self-respect, we do not need to make amends just because our choices caused someone else discomfort.

It may be an old habit for us to please others and put our care, needs, and feelings after theirs. Many of us learned to be people-pleasers to ensure security, to feel like we had value, and to experience connection in our lives. Relationships built on these old habits are unhealthy for all involved. As we begin to consider our own well-being, we learn it is each person's responsibility, including ours, to take care of ourselves.

What if making amends could bring harm to us? What if we stole money or other valuables from a bank, a store, or a person, and our need to be accountable puts us at risk for going to jail or other punitive actions?

Facing this question and concern is why it is important that we have good support systems. An insightful confidant with more objectivity may see options that we do not see. We need to pray about our choices of amends and ask our Higher Power for guidance.

Brian offers:

I have a friend who was willing to go to jail because he wanted to clear his conscience and clean up his past misdeeds and start over. He told me that he was moved by his Higher Power to confess. Knowing the possible risks involved, it took a lot of courage and support for him to choose to do what he felt was right for him.

Rita reflects:

I have appreciated the objectivity and guidance of my support system. After discussing my errors, I have new insights and even changed my mind about some actual harms I thought I had done and the amends I thought I needed to make.

As adults abused as children, assuming we are not harmed or injured by looking at our pasts and owning the things we have done wrong, we may feel tremendously sad, disappointed, self-loathing, or guilty. However, those feelings do not injure us. They can demonstrate our inner strength and integrity by speaking our truth to those whom we harmed. As we admit our part, we don't condemn ourselves as bad people. In fact, we remember we are on paths of healing from the effects of childhood abuse and want our lives to improve.

Step 9 Summary

The word **amend** means change. When we make amends to someone, we change ourselves in relation **to** that person, group, or institution. Step 9, as with all the Steps, is not something we do just once in our lives. This is a new way of living for us, as we will continue to make mistakes, harm others, and make errors in judgment. The need to make amends will be ongoing. Step 9 is a process, not an event.

Step 9 guides us toward the creation of resolutions for our past wrongs. We made a lot of mistakes with good intentions. We also made mistakes from places of inexperience, immaturity, ignorance, lack of role models, or misguided beliefs. Making amends is part of our recovery from lives impacted by childhood abuse. It is vital for our healing to own our past misdeeds and admit our wrong doings.

Claudia makes amends in this way:

I use the process of "let go, let God" that I practiced in Step 7. I am willing to be accountable when I face my resistance or get upset about something. Often, I want to blame outer circumstances or past circumstances for my reactions. But usually, I find my character traits responsible for my part. I learned to ask for help in Step 7, but I need to keep asking for clarity in Step 9 to know what proper action to take.

As I admit my harms, I feel a freedom for new ideas to surface and new attitudes to be born. I am free to create new beliefs. Through this cleansing, I can develop a new way of life for myself.

Step 9 takes time, effort, and intention. It also takes willingness. If we intuit that it's not the right time to make amends, we can wait for our Higher Power's timing. We may still be attached to things working out the way we want. We don't know how long completing our amends might take. What is important is that we are willing - whenever possible.

Stephanie has learned:

*Often, I don't know **what** I did wrong, only that I feel that I have done **something** wrong. That's when I go to my Higher Power for clarity and guidance about making amends. I pray and ask for help so I can better assess what my part was. I don't know when my answers will come. I also pray for patience. I want the uncomfortable feelings to go away and learn to be brave in the face of discomfort. I trust my Higher Power will show me what I need to know.*

As we clean up our pasts, we have new possibilities for handling difficult situations constructively. Our relationships are being restored to sanity by working Step 9. We remember that there are profound benefits to owning the consequences of our past behavior. Even if we do not get caught, it does not mean that there are no consequences. We cannot fool ourselves. When we pray for help and are open to accept our Higher Power's guidance, it is then that we are ready to humbly take action in making amends.

As adults, we are now responsible for our own lives. We want to heal from the abuses of our pasts and move on to live the kinds of lives we desire. We remember that the purpose of the 12 Steps is to uncover and discover who we really are and to make healthy decisions out of those new discoveries. We want to realize what our Higher Power's will is for us and to live it out with joy!

Step 9 Affirmations

1. I am willing to live in present time.
2. It is my job to love myself.
3. I forgive.
4. I value and honor myself.
5. Peace begins with me.
6. Life is a gift.
7. My Higher Power wants to help me and keep my faith strong.
8. A peaceful day is possible for me.
9. I deserve to feel good.
10. I know the difference between blame and accountability.
11. My highest good is always seeking expression.
12. I am feeling more gratitude every day.
13. Sharing with others is getting easier.
14. I accept "what is so" in life.

Step 9 Journal Questions

1. What actions contribute to my sense of peace?

2. How does sharing give me breathing room to acknowledge with another what I might dismiss privately?

3. Only when I have an honest heart is good-will possible. Why is that?

4. How would I describe my life through eyes of gratitude?

5. What do negative thoughts make me feel like? How do they impact my actions?

6. What is the trend of my thoughts today?

7. Before I can forgive, I need to accept. Who or what would benefit from my practicing acceptance?

8. What aspects of mine are challenging for me to accept? What is standing in my way?

9. In which areas of my life have I grown beyond my expectations? What supported my growth?

10. What new action could I take that would contribute to someone else or myself?

11. Where can I reduce my demands on others when they are not meeting my needs?

12. If I have a tendency to lie or exaggerate, how do I rationalize this to myself? How does it relate to any fears I may have?

13. What is my understanding of a Higher Power today?

14. Describe areas in my life where self-will is dominant. What relief would I expect to experience when I become ready to let go?

15. Can I increase compassion for the people who are challenging for me? Can I increase compassion for myself? What stands in my way?

Step 9 Prayer

May I continue to practice forgiveness as it is one of the most powerful actions I can take. Though it doesn't change the past, by using forgiveness to shift the present moment, it gives me a chance for a different future.

As I make amends, I ask for help in discovering my courage to let go of the way the past should have been. I seek compassion for myself and other people. As I connect with them, I experience the awareness that I am not alone.

Help me to admit what attitudes still linger from my childhood abuse and impact my adult life in ways that create unmanageability.

May I practice affirmations which are statements of truth to support what I want to be present in my life today. May they keep me focused on my Higher Power and offer me renewed hope.

Thank you, God.

And so it is.

AMEN.

Notes

Notes

Step 10

Continued to take personal inventory and when we were wrong and when we made progress, promptly admitted it.

Step 10

Continued to take personal inventory and when we were wrong and when we made progress, promptly admitted it.

Table of Contents

Introduction 459

Continuing the Inventory 461

Personal Inventory 465

Step 10 Daily Guide 468

When to Do an Inventory 473

Promptly Admitting When We Were Wrong and When We Made Progress 477

Benefits of Step 10 481

Step 10 Summary 483

Step 10 Affirmations 485

Step 10 Journal Questions 486

Step 10 Prayer 488

Step 10

Continued to take personal inventory and when we were wrong and when we made progress, promptly admitted it.

Introduction

Step 10 asks us to continue to take personal inventory so we can stay current in our journeys of healing through daily self-check-ins. The purpose of Step 10 is to help us keep our spiritual houses clean and our personal affairs in order.

As humans, we are bound to make mistakes and have errors in judgment. With the help of Step 10, we continue to discover and address our short-comings and our progress. We are reminded that we can resolve any of our wrongs and do so promptly.

As adults abused as children, we have admitted and chronicled our abuse, our abusers, and our feelings of being wronged by them. Through the Steps, we have also gained courage and willingness to look at ourselves in our current lives.

Admitting when we erred today is necessary to maintain and create better lives for ourselves and to make continued spiritual progress.

The gift of Step 10 is to help us become increasingly aware of how we show up in our relationships. As we journey through the Steps, we are gaining new perspectives, new attitudes, and new understandings about others. We are learning and applying basic spiritual principles to our lives.

There can be an impact of our childhood abuse on our families and friends. Those who live with us may or may not know about or believe our past. But they **are** affected by it. One day at a time, we are claiming, owning, and releasing the negative effects. We understand and appreciate this can be challenging for our loved ones.

We may temporarily become moody, quiet, or impatient with others. Our perspectives can become temporarily jaded. When appropriate, it helps everyone involved to have conversations about this and ideally have a plan when needed.

Continuing the Inventory

In Step 10, we continue to take personal inventory and promptly admit our shortcomings, as well as our progress. The word continued reminds us that our healing is a process and not an event. It implies movement and reminds us to move forward with hope. We remember that we will not always be who we appear to be today. We will change.

We will not always have to make the same amends tomorrow because we have been willing to make them today. By continuing to do our personal inventory, we stay connected to our path of healing, personal growth, and our Higher Power.

Henry looks at it this way:

Step 10 reminds me that the Steps are not something that I do once in my life and never again. There is no way of being that I am expected to attain forever. I continue to move along my path maturing and growing.

Repetition is an aspect of perseverance. It is an essential part of our continued development, learning, and maturing. We need repetition. All of nature demonstrates this through the repetition of the seasons. As adults abused as children, we **develop** familiarity and ease of doing things in new ways through repetition. We become authentic through continued practice of living out our values one day at a time.

Perseverance is vital at this point since our personal progress depends on it. These new habits and patterns of living are the foundations for our improved lives. We have learned to retain these new ways, being accountable on an ongoing basis is necessary.

Useful qualities that can contribute to perseverance may appear as stamina, stick-to-it-ive-ness, commitment, tenacity, or endurance. Any of these supports daily maintenance for our growth.

Shirley contributes:

Even if I don't feel up to a task in a particular Step, seeing the word continued in Step 10 keeps me going. I like knowing there is no graduation, just a keep on, keeping on.

Perseverance is possible through self-discipline, inner strength, self-love, dedication, faith, and willingness. Those focuses build our self-confidence and self-respect. Looking at ourselves on a regular basis requires a new level of self-awareness and self-love. Step 10 requires a great deal of humility as we create new lives for ourselves. We are rewarded as we realize our intentions of healing the effects of our childhood abuse.

We no longer solely rely upon hindsight to see if we have created harm. Now we are blessed with the ability to call upon self-honesty in each moment! We can acknowledge uncomfortable feelings when we have misspoken or acted inappropriately, if not immediately, soon after. We promptly choose the opportunities to make it right.

We have newfound attitudes toward integrity and hope. We hope that we will not always be confused or feel negative about ourselves. We hope that we will overcome our shortcomings. Hope can bring opportunities for making peace with our past that we thought were impossible. Deepening our connection with our Higher Power brings us back to hope. Just when we might think or feel that all hope is lost, the Steps reconnect us to self-acceptance and self-forgiveness.

Step 10 gives us permission to take time to practice taking our inventory as we continue to make progress. We have ample opportunities to develop healthy rituals and ways of thinking and being that guide us to better lives.

Mark reveals:

Time has helped me discover who I am and who I was truly meant to be. As I am able to be authentic and accountable, my relationship with my Higher Power deepens. I begin to understand what is mine to do. I am experiencing personal, mental, emotional, and spiritual growth.

It is suggested that we take a daily inventory, as one day is a workable amount of time to check in with ourselves while the events and attitudes of the day are still fresh in our minds and hearts.

Personal Inventory

There is no right or wrong way to take a personal inventory. As adults abused as children, doing our inventory keeps us focused on ourselves. It reminds us to be aware of how we are expressing ourselves and discovering what gives us the results we desire in our lives.

As we listen to our thoughts, acknowledge our feelings, beliefs, and self-talk, we are in personal contact with ourselves. We witness that we are not avoiding, denying, or minimizing our actions. We are neither grandiose nor arrogant. We are living with honesty and humility.

The 12 Steps are designed to foster humility. Humility comes most easily when we refrain from self-judgment and self-criticism. It helps us stay aware and be honest in present time. It is our responsibility to keep monitoring our actions, thoughts, and emotions. We do this because we want our lives to function better than they have been up until now.

Shelley reflects:

My actions are easy for me to watch because they are a part of real life. It is a more subtle process to take personal inventory of my feelings or attitudes. Looking at my belief systems or thoughts takes inner resources that I had to develop.

In the beginning, I had no idea how to figure out what I was feeling. Step 10 reminds me that as I continue to take inventory, I can pray for a better understanding of my thoughts and feelings.

When we are looking at our part in our daily lives, we continue to seek improved relationships with our families and friends. It could be that we long for a stronger connection to our Higher Power. Our motivation stems from our desires for inner peace, increased sense of self-fulfillment, or pure joy. Working the 12 Steps guides and helps us succeed in our intentions.

Shirley adds:

*As an adult who was abused as a child, I was taught that everything was my fault and my responsibility. Today, I need to remember to be aware of and own my part, but **only** my part, not another's. Sometimes I get confused and need to find out what my part is, so I ask my Higher Power for clarity. There are still areas in my life where I'm not clear where my life ends and someone else's begins.*

We remember this is a personal inventory only of ourselves. We don't spend time taking other peoples' inventories as it doesn't support our healing from our childhood abuse. Taking personal inventory regularly allows us to focus on a small number of things in a 24-hour period.

Step 10 helps us move our awareness into our **present** lives, as we did with the past in Step 4. We acknowledge what aspects of ourselves need refining and which ones are working well in our and others' behalf.

Step 10 Daily Guide

We take time each day to contemplate these questions as we take an inventory of our day.

When we are complete, we give it all to our Higher Power. As we promptly admit, we tell our Higher Power we are ready to have our unhelpful traits removed and acknowledge our paths of progress.

For an upsetting situation:

We pray for ourselves and the other people, if they were involved. If needed, we ask for guidance as we explore where we need to look within and be accountable.

1. What was the incident that upset me?

2. What about it upset me?

3. What happened (recall details)? Who was involved? What was said?

4. Where and when did it happen? What significance did I give it?

5. What were my reactions? Why did I react? How did my reactions impact me or others?

6. Was my pride hurt in any way?

7. Do I have any amends to make?

8. What could I have said or done differently for a better outcome?

9. What are the character traits I want to release?

10. What shortcomings have appeared?

11. Am I willing to "Let Go and Let God"?

Comments:

_____
_____
_____
_____
_____
_____
_____
_____
_____
_____
_____
_____
_____
_____

For our daily progress:

We are grateful for each small step forward.

1. In what area of my life that's important to me have I been slowly and steadily improving?

2. What inner quality is becoming easier to manifest?

3. In what situations am I more open-minded than I used to be?

4. For whom did I experience compassion today?

5. Did my faith help stabilize my reactions in challenging circumstances?

6. Did I maintain my integrity when faced with a difficult choice?

7. Did I take a risk today that would have been unheard of not too long ago?

8. Did I treat someone with respect whom I don't care for?

9. Where do I notice my spiritual practices positively affecting my actions? My attitudes?

10. Was I able to hear another's views without judgment or righteousness?

11. Did I help someone today out of the goodness of my heart?

12. Where was I able to be brave, even though I was afraid?

13. Did I exhibit self-kindness or self-generosity today?

Comments:

When to Do an Inventory

Taking a personal inventory can be done at any time. It can be done as an evening reflection or in the morning when we're setting our intentions for the day. We can do it when it comes to our awareness in any moment. We are learning that we can do a personal inventory even in the midst of difficult times as we are becoming able to self-reflect with honesty.

As adults abused as children, we are using what we have learned in the previous Steps and applying it to our daily lives. Our inventory is about taking personal responsibility for ourselves and our actions.

We remember that there is no one way or right way to do a self-check. We need only to be honest about how we're showing up in our lives. We build our adult lives on the truths we are willing to own, including how far we've come.

1. ***We can take a personal inventory at the end of each day.***

    It is helpful to look back and notice how we acted, how we felt, and what we might have handled differently. We ask ourselves if there is anything for which we need to make amends.

    We take a look at our motives. Are we proud of the way we took care of some situation or could we have chosen a more effective way to express ourselves? In looking back, we might create possibilities that will be more readily available to us in the future.

By reviewing our day and taking a personal inventory, we have distance from those previous moments and are more able to be objective.

Marla creates her nightly inventory this way:

Before I go to sleep, I review my day in three ways. I find three things I could have done better, three things I made progress in, and three things I handled well.

Yvonne practices:

I chose to focus on patience today. At the end of the day, I was able to look back and was happy to notice how much more patient I was with my co-worker. By choosing to focus on patience, I became more patient. I prayed for my Higher Power to bring me moments that would help me practice being more patient. I succeeded today.

2. **We can take our inventory in any moment.**

Looking back, we can see where we have grown or where we might still need further growth. We are more self-accepting and self-aware. We practice self-reflection without being critical, judgmental, or arrogant.

When we consciously check in with ourselves in the moment, we might be able to shift gears to a more effective or productive outcome right then! We notice our willingness to positively affect the situation for the benefit of all concerned. We take appropriate action in that direction.

3. *We can do an inventory when starting something new.*

   The journey through the 12 Steps is not just about attending to our past. The Steps guide our lives in the present. Being able to apply the Steps is liberating. It can be helpful to take a personal inventory when we begin a new activity so we anticipate not only how we might show up based on our pasts, but also our new intentions and growth in the present. We want to know what we can realistically count on within ourselves.

   > **Belinda explores it this way:**
   >
   > *While working on Step 10, I realized that I was wanting a new love relationship. In the past, jealousy had been my response to my fear of being abandoned. I badgered my ex-boyfriend to find out every place he went, what he was doing, and who he was with. It was a disastrous experience for both of us.*
   >
   > *I decided to check in with myself now to see how I was doing in my tendency toward jealousy before I considered a new relationship. Was it still showing*

> up in other areas of my life? I was willing to look at what attitudes and beliefs about abandonment I still held that could influence present-day relationships. I did not want to repeat the past. I looked at how far I'd come in my healing from childhood abuse and began feeling more confident in pursuing an intimate relationship at this time. I'm glad I decided to use Step 10 as a reality check.

Promptly admitting our wrongs and progress is not a one-time thing. We are being guided to make self-examination a habit, a way of living conscious lives. This can assure us that we will continue to grow, maintain our integrity, and heal.

Promptly Admitting When We Were Wrong and When We Made Progress

In Step 10, we are asked to promptly admit. To whom do we admit our wrongs or our progress? As in Step 5, we admit to ourselves, to God, and to another human being. Step 9 reminds us to make direct amends to people we harmed and admit our errors to them. We may be at the point in our healing when admitting to ourselves and our Higher Power is enough. We will know.

Why would it be beneficial to admit promptly and not wait a while? Acknowledging and handling our errors right away leaves less room for exaggeration, minimization, avoidance, gossip, drama, or even denial. The less time we take postponing our accountability, the less time in which our mistakes can create harm. We clean up our sides of the street as soon as appropriate.

What about admitting our progress promptly? Why would that be beneficial? Being aware that we choose healthy actions or attitudes shows us we are able to carry out our intentions to heal. Each small success becomes part of the new foundations we are building for our lives. It is vital for us to see that one day at a time, we are shifting into being the kinds of people we want to be.

Irene shares:

By promptly facing my mistakes and taking responsibility, it prevents situations from festering into resentments and anger that can become real problems for me. I don't have to hold on to guilt, shame, embarrassment, or all the negative feelings I have about myself. My Step 10 work releases the feelings I have about making an error.

Inga reveals:

I can't always admit that I am wrong in the moment, or even the same day, but I can still be prompt. I can choose to wait awhile, another day or a week and allow for the continued examination of myself. I choose not to procrastinate too long, though.

As we continue to take inventory of our shortcomings in Step 10, it benefits us to promptly move on to self-forgiveness and forgiveness of others. There is no limit to the number of times we need to extend forgiveness and that we need to be forgiven. As adults abused as children, we can no longer afford to feel like victims any longer. Forgiveness can eliminate that feeling.

As a foundation for our healing, we need to admit when we are handling our lives well or taking right actions. This builds our self-confidence. We acknowledge the impact of what is working on our behalf and what is preventing it. The 12 Steps focus on progress, not perfection. Every bit of our progress deserves to be celebrated.

When we are right on target with our thinking, attitudes, and actions, we admit it. As adults abused as children, it may be challenging to admit when we have done something appropriate or well. We may have a tendency to minimize ourselves, so admitting our progress is a much-needed, self-loving practice. It is a discipline that gives our healing process a firm foundation.

Jason sees it this way:

Admitting what I have done right is as important to me as admitting what I've done wrong. Why wouldn't I admit what I'd done right? I'm not coming from a place of arrogance or ego. I just want to admit all of what I see about me.

When we were children, our successes, talents, or positive traits may not have been noticed or rarely mentioned. Many of us did not realize that there was much good about us. We may have been living out those same skewed views in our adult lives. Through Step 10 we can undo that conditioning and let go of those erroneous, deep-seated beliefs. We note our gradual tendencies toward mature, healthy decisions and the actions that follow them.

Charles says:

I wasn't born a mistake. I make mistakes.

Admitting progress is the foundation upon which to admit our wrongs. We may have been overzealous in admitting our mistakes as well as minimizing our progress. An unbalanced assessment of ourselves is not useful for our healing. Every day we are becoming more aware of our blossoming into the kinds of people we aspire to be. With humility we admit and own all that we are.

We may ask ourselves some simple questions to assess our progress:

- Do we appreciate the people and situations that inspire our growth?
- Have we been facing difficult circumstances with faith and confidence?
- Are we exhibiting wisdom based on our past experiences?
- Is our spiritual strength increasing?
- Do we have courage to try new endeavors?
- Are we remaining open to our Higher Power's guidance one day at a time?

Benefits of Step 10

As adult abused as children, we may overlook the benefits of regular inner reflection. Our Step 10 journey continues to support new healthy and helpful ways of thinking, doing, and being. We have grown to be insightful, courageous, compassionate, humble, honest, forgiving, and more loving individuals. **We have a path worthy of following.**

Promptly admitting our short-comings is a shortcut for our healing. Step 10 has restored our hope as we see something better for ourselves has already started happening.

> **Neil comments:**
>
> *I choose not to establish blame; I just want to know my part.*

We self-correct and self-acknowledge every time we do a 10th Step inventory. It helps us find easier ways through life without letting the past deeds accumulate for a long time before we deal with them. Cleaning our slate leaves room for new ideas, new growth, and new seeds that are germinating and waiting to blossom.

Self-observation is another aspect of being self-aware, self-reflective, and introspective. It gives us hope and the knowledge that we are making progress. We are continuing to realize the impact we have on others. We become accountable for our mistakes and move beyond justification, explanation, and defensiveness.

In addition, we are able to see how others impact us without shaming, blaming, or making them wrong. We experience the benefits of choosing healthier ways of communicating, responding rather than reacting, and creating healthier attitudes.

Our willingness to be observant leads us back to focusing on ourselves. This is the practice that will enable our healing from childhood abuse. It is very powerful.

Step 10 Summary

The main intention of Step 10 is to look at our part in our present lives. We consider our actions, reactions, attitudes, words, and emotions. We look at where we omitted showing up when it was ours to do so. The things we could have said but didn't, the things we could have done, or done better, but didn't.

Step 10 is where we integrate and practice Steps 1-9 in quick succession. With practice, Step 10 becomes simpler and easier. Done regularly, it offers us the opportunity to acknowledge how far we've come since beginning our path through the Steps. Its benefits are easily recognized in our everyday lives.

We ask our Higher Power to help us become more aware when our minds tend to cloud our thinking, limit our choices, and hinder our growth. We ask it to help us with our admitting, our amends, and our letting go. We continue to ask our Higher Power to help us make healthier choices.

The prior Steps have led us to experience how instrumental our Higher Power has been in moving us forward on our healing journey. Our Higher Power has helped us be more honest, deepening our self-trust, and guiding our transformation to the people we had hoped to be.

As adults abused as children, most of us have had critical, judgmental inner voices waiting to find fault in our every choice and our every word. Those voices, left over from our past, tend to put too much blame and responsibility on us, leaving us confused, disappointed, and ashamed. These voices are our inner critics. They are not true.

These critical voices soften as we welcome support from our Higher Power. We are learning that we deserve and need a connection with a Power greater than ourselves. With that connection, we can reshape our thoughts and beliefs.

Emil contributes:

I learned that life is not a black-and-white picture but grey, especially when I think about responsibility, about my job, and about my relationship with myself and others. When I get confused, I ask my Higher Power for guidance to let me know when I am taking myself off the hook too soon or when I am accepting the wrongs of another. I have a voice in my head that tends to hold myself far too accountable for everyone's mistakes. I need to learn what is my part and what belongs to another. This is how I'm using Step 10...to figure that out.

We can't create our new lives until we release the personal traits standing in our way. Each day our responses bring different aspects of us forward. It helps us be aware of how we are expressing ourselves today so we can praise ourselves or self-correct as appropriate.

Step 10 Affirmations

1. One day can change my whole life. A new 24-hour day can begin right now.

2. I do not let the past define who I am today.

3. Shifting my awareness to my progress brings the good **already** existing in my life into focus.

4. I make a difference in the world just as I am.

5. My words are kind and bring peace to my life and to the lives of others.

6. I am learning to reveal the best of who I am.

7. I celebrate myself and hold thoughts that nourish and support me.

8. I am responsible for my satisfaction in life.

9. Self-change can only be realized in the present.

10. I make choices coming from my gifts rather than my wounds.

11. I trust that my highest good is unfolding.

12. This is my life. I am in it. It is not fixed.

13. I stay true to myself and real with others.

Step 10 Journal Questions

1. How do I feel about myself right now?

2. What do I have to be grateful for today?
   How has this day blessed my life?

3. Am I worrying about yesterday or tomorrow?

4. Am I treating myself with respect?
   Am I treating others with respect?

5. Is this a good time to increase my level of self-care?

6. For what do I acknowledge myself today?

7. Did I say or do anything today that would warrant an apology?

8. Have I allowed myself to become too hungry, angry, lonely, or tired?

9. What better choices could I have made to improve on today?

10. What is my Higher Power inviting me to choose today?

11. Where am I being inauthentic?
    Who am I pretending to be or how am I covering up who I am?

12. As I get to know myself better, what if I discover I'm someone I don't want to be?

13. What or who contributed to my view of myself?

14. Do I have the feeling that if you REALLY knew me, you wouldn't like me? Why?

15. Am I creating my life by design or by default?

16. What progress have I noticed as I release unhealthy behaviors?

17. Where am I still blaming outside circumstances for the conditions in my life?

18. In what areas of my life have others noted that my progress has already begun?

19. What actions or attitudes could I adopt to create ease?

Step 10 Prayer

One day at a time, I reach for the spiritual goals I've set for myself. Little by little, I create new habits as I let go of old ones that no longer serve me.

Let me remember that I'm only one decision away from an entirely new life. Help me to have increased faith and courage as I try out new ways of being. Guide me to see both helpful and unhelpful aspects of myself that have been hidden until now.

Thank you for my inner resources that support me in taking chances today that I would not have ventured to consider in the past. I invest in my unborn tomorrows by living authentically in the present. Help me to choose my personal best each day.

Thank you, God.

And so it is.

AMEN

Notes

Step 11

Sought through prayer and meditation to improve our conscious contact with God, *as we understood Him*, praying only for knowledge of His will for us and the power to carry that out.

Step 11

Sought through prayer and meditation to improve our conscious contact with God, *as we understood Him,* **praying only for knowledge of His will for us and the power to carry that out.**

Table of Contents

Introduction 495

God, *As We Understood Him* 498

Seeking 501

Improving Our Conscious Contact 503

Making Contact Through Prayer 508

Making Contact Through Meditation 521

Benefits of Prayer and Meditation. 524

Praying for Knowledge of God's Will 529

Praying for Power 532

Step 11 Summary. 536

Step 11 Affirmations 539

Step 11 Journal Questions 541

Step 11 Prayer 543

Step 11

Sought through prayer and meditation to improve our conscious contact with God, *as we understood Him,* **praying only for knowledge of His will for us and the power to carry that out.**

Introduction

For adults abused as children, the foundation of Step 11 is built upon reliance on a Power greater than ourselves. We continue our journey through the 12 Steps because we desire better lives for ourselves. Step 11 answers the question of how to deepen our relationship with our Higher Power as we admit the need to connect. This Step requires a tremendous act of humility. It affords us the opportunity to look more deeply into who we have become, which assists us in our connection with Spirit.

Judd explores:

I prayed for awareness of my distorted thinking, which led to actions that were revealed in Step 10. Now I'm practicing shifting my consciousness to a Power greater than I am before I take action.

Step 11 reminds us we need to maintain the new way of life we've been working toward. It can be seen as practicing Steps 2 and 3 on a daily basis. Step 11 can be our guide for our spiritual growth for the rest of our lives. We can recharge our spiritual batteries by getting in touch with the Source of our strength and find direction one day at a time. We are open to whatever insights come our way as we see we are given exactly what we need for us to heal.

Roland remembers:

When I was a boy, my home life was a nightmare. Trying to act normal was a willful act of survival. My problem was I didn't know what normal was. That's what I needed to learn. Through the 12 Steps, my Higher Power has been teaching me what that could look like for me. Step 11 is crucial for my continued sanity. **My needs become my Higher Power's opportunity to help me.**

The unmanageability recognized in Step 1 is the result of our reliance upon ourselves. Step 11 helps to reaffirm we do not rely solely on ourselves, and we are not alone. Step 11 is very specific. It tells us how to rely upon our Higher Power by praying only for knowledge of His will for us **and** the power to carry that out.

A basic principle of the Steps is to become reliant on our Higher Power. We were not thinking about reliance when we started our journey through the Steps. The previous Steps were the preparation and path of readiness enabling us to rely on this Power. This is the core theme of Step 11. Working Steps 1-10 has created the ability for us to have come this far. We have worked diligently toward the lives we have longed for. Before this, we might have thought it was impossible to achieve this.

We have arrived at Step 11 and this is something to celebrate. As adults abused as children, we have made great progress. We are not the same people who began Step 1.

God, As We Understood Him

The reference to a Power greater than ourselves may not be comfortable for some of us. When the word God is used, we may feel mixed emotions or remember unpleasant experiences from our past. Some of us, however, may have developed a fulfilling relationship with God, as **we** understood it.

The references to a Higher Power, Source, or Spirit, are intended to be neutral terms that allow each of us to decide whom or what we focus on as we seek connection. As we find or discover a personal source of guidance and power, it may not matter to us what its name is. We can name it anything we choose. Some of us create in our minds exactly what we want our Higher Power to be: our best friend, a parent, the wind, universal intelligence, an enlightened being. In addition, we are not told what to believe about our Higher Power's nature, only that it is a loving Power that has our best interests in mind. As we accept protection and care from it, our lives are enriched beyond belief.

> **Charlotte reflects:**
>
> *As a child, my whole existence was dedicated to taking care of others. Even after I matured, I realized I didn't know how to change this behavior. The way of life I knew didn't feel worth living; I was not yet a resource for myself. I knew I was powerless.*

Once I admitted I was powerless to change myself or my history of childhood abuse, I learned there is a Power greater than me. That Power was my resource for the transformation I needed that I couldn't create by myself. Eventually, I had experiences of a Power far greater than the limits of my human realm.

The issue of trust appears again for many of us. We are gradually learning to trust ourselves and have begun to selectively trust others. Step 11 asks us to extend trust even further and believe there is good within us and around us, if only we dare to seek it. We can look back and notice how our lives have developed so differently from the ways they would have had **we** been in charge. Now, as adults, we know we were truly not alone. We are relying on our Higher Power and are not disappointed. Ever.

Alexis reveals her confusion:

When it came to my emotions, I relied on my personality traits to be my Higher Power and be in charge. Then I saw where I was allowing my immaturity to run the show. I also watched myself consider others to be my Higher

Power when I wanted their love or approval. Sometimes, I still try and control things to be the way I think they should be, taking the reins and insisting I know best.

As a child, I had no idea of any Higher Power, let alone one that cared about me. It's been challenging to allow my old patterns to be restored by my current working version of a Higher Power. However, now I'm releasing them slowly, one pattern at a time.

Seeking

Step 11 is an invitation that guides our seeking. It is worded in such a way to put us in a state of being where we can be available for our Higher Power to reach us through prayer and meditation. We are guided to be open to our Higher Power's influence to know what help is available to us in the present.

Step 11 is an action step. It is we who are doing the seeking through connection to a greater Power. There is an implied openness and willingness to live more satisfying lives through seeking and staying in contact with that Power. We may have become passive when earlier attempts to deal with our childhood abuse on our own failed to bring us peace. Step 11 offers new possibilities for success as we recommit to our healing by shifting our attitudes and our actions guided by our Higher Power.

God always chooses the best methods for meeting our needs when we leave the decision up to it. We have often been surprised by unexpected improvements in our lives when we do. We may only be able to see a part of the big picture. Some things, seemingly attractive and reasonable at present, may not be for our highest good. That will be made clear to us in time.

Seeking can initiate the beginning of change as the quality of our lives improves. Trying on new ways of being can help us overcome our fears and resistance to change. We are blessed with the gift of free will and use it to access options we may not have seen before.

Raoul discovers:

The more I am aware of my own human nature through connection to God, the more aware I am of my inner divinity. I find I am more able to live from the consciousness of not being better than or less than others—but part of the whole of humanity.

Improving Our Conscious Contact

The wording of Step 11 tells us directly that prayer and meditation will improve our conscious contact with God, **as we understand Him.** It is telling us that, through **conscious** contact, we continue to grow into the kinds of people we want to be, have the kinds of attributes we desire, and find greater ease and peace in our lives.

We are reminded not to sit back and wait for our lives to improve on their own. Seeking ensures our participation in our healing. It is made possible with the guidance and support from our Higher Power.

> *Gloria offers:*
>
> *I like a very simplified version of key messages that I can follow, so I have propped up a 3x5 card on my table where I sit and have my morning coffee. The card says: "seek contact."*

Conscious contact is always with a Higher Power of our understanding. We began to develop this relationship in Step 2. However, it may or may not be the same version of a Higher Power that we chose in an earlier Step. The word "conscious" reminds us that we are asked to be present and make a decision, just as we were asked to do in Step 3. We are making conscious decisions to seek, to be aware, to make contact, to pray, and to meditate.

Danielle contributes:

I am grateful for the previous 10 Steps. I have formed new ideas that allow for a loving, caring Higher Power to be a part of my life. I have grown to believe in and am consciously aware of this Power.

In Step 3, I learned to trust my Higher Power's guidance. When I sat down to work on Step 4, I was filled with a quiet certainty that I could trust the process, because I felt and knew the presence of a Higher Power would be with me moving forward. Today, I welcome conscious contact and a better understanding of God's will and desires for me. I am deepening my surrender one day at a time.

The task of Step 11 is to find ways to improve conscious contact and connection with God. Our consciousness is like a stream, constantly changing and flowing. Our spirituality and powers of understanding are developing and shifting as well.

A lot happens during our times of prayer and meditation that we may not be aware of. These times are beyond our will, our control, and our knowing. Our unconscious minds exist below the level of conscious awareness and are not readily available to the conscious mind without altering or raising our states of awareness. God can be known in these higher states.

We awaken our unconscious minds through prayer and meditation. They are the activities on the path to open what is not actively known to us. In addition, they help us know our Higher Power's will for us. Seeking to make contact creates the door for new possibilities to emerge.

Our lives are improved on our spiritual paths by our connection to a Higher Power that is always there for us. We are reminded that making contact any time we need or want to is a conscious choice. Earlier in the Steps, we have seen evidence of our improvement. This strengthens our beliefs that better lives are in store for us.

Improve

To improve implies that we have already begun the journey. It reminds us this is a practice, a path, a way that has taken time and will continue to require our attention. Improvements will happen without the expectation of perfection.

As we worked through the earlier Steps, we witnessed our progress and maturity. Over time, our awareness has deepened with ease and clarity. We are awakening to our true essence, accepting who we have been, who we are, and who we desire to become as we expand.

The desire to improve allows for consideration of our humanness. It challenges our black and white thinking, that we're either right or wrong, a success or a failure, good or bad. Improvement takes time. We allow for openness, flexibility, ease, and acceptance. We notice we are making progress and trust it will continue. Our compassion for ourselves increases.

Improving reminds us there is no special place to get to. If we are always seeking to improve, as we arrive at one goal, we can then set the next one. Our connecting will improve naturally as it gets deeper, stronger, and easier.

Mary admits:

I have come to understand when I am unwilling to let go of the desire for perfection, I do not want things to improve. I think most often I am afraid of failing. I used to believe the only way to be happy and feel fulfilled was through perfection. But perfection never came.

My perfectionist nature limits my access to improvement and achievement. I learned perfection is unattainable! Why would I strive for something I cannot achieve? Maybe I do not feel deserving? Instead of trying to figure it out, through Step 11, I am choosing to surrender my will to my Higher Power with the desire for conscious contact.

As we improve our relationship with a Higher Power, it deepens our relationships with others and with ourselves. Because we are more conscious and aware, we feel safer to be open to share ourselves authentically.

April adds:

Step 11 has helped me approach Source willingly, openly, and consciously. The level of trust I have attained is huge for me. So much of my life has improved, and I believe it will continue.

Making Contact Through Prayer

Some of us may believe we do not know how to pray. We may think we don't know the language of prayer. We might we believe we are not religious enough, or we may have simply never prayed before. Talking to our Higher Power can be just as easy as talking to our best friend. We feel heard, understood, and cared for.

Letting go and letting God does not mean we will not be involved in the evolution of our lives. Rather, it means we are open to **divine** ideas beyond our current human perspectives. We realize there is an entire ocean of possibility beyond the small coves we can see through our minds' windows.

Prayer changes our perceptions of life and opens us to these new possibilities. Prayer uses our thoughts and our wills to connect our inner and outer worlds. Under its influence, we are grounded and intentional. Our Higher Power changes hearts, heals wounds, and grants wisdom. As we pray, we release the power of God's blessings on our lives and circumstances. We ask our Higher Power to take care of things.

Prayer is a tool for communication. Whether it be with our Higher Selves, our Higher Power, or with others, when we consciously seek union through prayer, we commune with Source. That which we were otherwise unconscious of becomes available to us. What is important is our desires, intentions, and willingness to be present and open. There are no right or wrong words to use; there are no right or wrong ways to pray.

Natalie contributes:

I communicate with a Greater Power. I talk to it, think about it, and sometimes I write about it. In prayer, I can ask for help and express thanks.

As I progress in my healing through the 12 Steps, I learned there is no special way to pray or form of prayer. There are no good or bad prayers. Flowery language is no better than simple, everyday words. While praying, what is important is my intention to connect and be present. Throughout my work with Step 11, **prayer has proven superior to my willpower.** As prayer renews my mind, it has become a practical skill for everyday life.

Steve reflects:

My prayer work makes contact and says, "Hello, here I am. I want to talk to you; I need help." Or "This is what is happening; I just wanted you to know." Prayer opens the way for me to extend gratitude, ask a question, have a conversation, and so much more.

Are there things we should not pray for? We can pray for anything that does not cause ourselves or another harm. We can pray for our enemies or for people who have died. We can pray for our Higher Power to help others and never know the outcomes. Prayer is a desire of our hearts and spirits, a sacred privilege given to any one of us who chooses to use it.

Prayers Can Change

The forms of our prayers may change. The types of prayers we need today may not be the same as tomorrow. We go to our Higher Power with our willingness to listen, to be heard, to be guided, to be helped. We not only ask for help but also have a willingness to receive it. We remember we are deserving and worthy to receive the guidance our Higher Power desires for us. As *we* are changed, our worlds change with us.

> **Prayer is like this for Ben:**
>
> *I admit my powerlessness and surrender when I pray. My admission of humility is my intention. That is the state of mind I go to as I pray.*

The following are some examples of experiencing prayer. We are always free to create our own paths to connect.

Ways to Pray

- Commune with nature/garden
- Create art
- Dance
- Exercise
- Listen to music or play an instrument
- Memorize and repeat meaningful passages of others
- Read spiritual literature
- Sing/chant/hum
- Visualize desired circumstances
- Write/Journal

How to Pray

- Be alone/be with others
- Be silent/pray aloud
- Bow head
- Close or open eyes
- Kneel
- Light a candle
- Sit, lie down, stand, walk, run, sway, rock, skip
- Use finger/hand/posture positions
- Use prayer beads

What to Pray For

- Abundance/prosperity
- Comfort/encouragement/support
- Courage
- Forgiveness
- Gratitude/blessings
- Grief/sorrow/loss
- Guidance/clarity
- Health/healing
- Help/inner and outer resources
- Inner strength
- Patience/tolerance
- Peace for self, others, the world
- Power
- Relationships
- Releasing the past
- Self-love
- Transformation
- Wisdom/insight

Other Kinds of Prayers

- **One-word prayers** (for a specific need or for a day): Amen, Help, Lead, Now, Thanks, Yes.
- **Memorize an affirmation** and have it ready in our minds when needed.
- **Breath prayer:** count our blessings in a single breath.

When to Pray

Prayer can be done at special times, on certain days, spontaneously, or with no thought of time at all. We tailor the time to our individual schedules. We might find ourselves praying when we're stressed, at a crossroads, or needing inspiration. We might be unsure of our next actions, needing answers, or inner strength. We pray when we need help of any kind.

We also pray when we give thanks. Many of us say prayers of gratitude before we eat a meal, when we tuck our children in at night, when we pet our furry family members. Prayers of thanksgiving keep us focused on our blessings.

When we pray for others, we remember that their Higher Power knows their needs and what is in their best interest. Praying for others frees us from worry as we envision the best possible outcomes unfolding in their lives. We bless them with our words, thoughts, and loving care. We feel fulfilled as we release them to the care of their Higher Power. We remember they are not alone with whatever they are facing.

As we pray for them, we are blessed as well. The sincerity of our prayers raises our spirits. We experience renewed hope and faith that our prayers are making a difference in the lives of the ones we are praying for.

Christie prays for others this way:

I get so invested in thinking I know what's best for others. I have to put my Higher Power between me and who I'm praying for.

We pray for those we care about and those we do not. We pray for people we've never met, for people we disagree with, for anyone in need. Some of us like to pray with others. We can pray over the phone, create prayer partners, or attend a silent retreat for prayer. The right time to pray exists in every moment.

We may find first thing in the morning is a good time to pray to set the tone for the day before it has begun. Some of us find praying before we go to bed helpful. If we choose, we can combine prayer, meditation, and reviewing our day with the 10th Step each night.

As adults abused as children, when we are afraid, in terror, rage, or anger, we might take five minutes to become aware of our feelings through prayer instead of being overwhelmed by them.

Prayer can be a daily practice. It can be done throughout the day at different times or at the same time each day. It can be done whenever we want or feel the need. We remember it is a practice. We seek connection to live better lives.

Cheryl admits:

Sometimes, I just don't feel connected to my Higher Power. My willingness to be honest about how I feel, when I do not have the enthusiasm or desire to pray, is enough. Prayer does not require me to be in a perfect space or have a certain mindset. It simply asks for my willingness and intention. I have to keep letting go of expecting my prayer time to look and feel a certain way.

Answered Prayer

We may sometimes feel our prayers have not been answered. We hear about answered prayer, but what do we do when we think that ours have not been answered? How do we decide what prayers are answered or unanswered? These are all good questions. We can pray to be able to discern the signals of answered prayers. Our peace of mind might be one way to tell. In addition, we can pray for "knowledge of His will for us and the power to carry that out."

Our Higher Power may answer in ways that are quite different from what we expected. We may assume our prayers were not answered when the results did not resemble our wishes. It may be we did not recognize or understand the unfolding yet. It is like asking for a red apple and getting a green one instead. That is not an unanswered prayer; it is simply different from what we thought the answer would be.

Don looks at prayer this way:

It is best for me to pray and let it go. I have learned to trust that whatever is meant to happen, will. I follow the promptings of my Higher Power in my mind and heart and take whatever actions I am guided to take.

Affirmative Prayer

Affirmative prayer is not about asking our Higher Power for something. It is about connecting with our Higher Power, asserting a positive belief about what we want. Our thoughts have energy that attracts other energy of the same frequency. When we remain focused on our intentions, we can draw those things into our lives. This is one way to manifest what we need or want.

Step 2 reminds us to believe, one day at a time, that our Higher Power is guiding and restoring us. As we put power (good use of our self-will) and faith into our thoughts, new possibilities come to mind. We come to believe our needs are being met. We practice this spiritual tool for our sure and steady progress on our paths of healing.

Examples of Affirmative Prayer

- **Prayers for self:** I am blessed with health, happiness, and love. I have all the strength, wisdom, and imagination I need for the tasks at hand. I feel the divine presence within me, guiding me to right action. I am peaceful.

- **Prayers for healing:** I am whole and complete. I am sustained by the love of God. I am awake to God's healing presence. I am freed from all concerns. I am blessed by God's harmonizing power expressed in me. I am guided to the perfect resources for complete healing.

- **Prayers for love and comfort:** The love of my Higher Power flows through me, comforts me, and assures me I am not alone. Source is nearer than my breath. The presence of peace has no bounds and fills my heart and mind.

- **Prayers for prosperity:** I am thankful for abundant supply. My life is enriched by God. My highest and best is manifesting now. Mighty currents of God's power are prospering me. I flow along with my good.

- **Prayers for protection:** The presence of my Higher Power is greater than my fears. God is in charge of today. I am safe, secure, and at peace. I trust in God's guiding presence.

With faith in these truths, our potential is beyond anything we can imagine.

Making Contact Through Meditation

Meditation is focusing on a thought, idea, or even silence. As with prayer, there is no right way to meditate. The intention of Step 11 is to use meditation and prayer to consciously seek contact with God, **as we understand Him.** Meditation is a spiritual practice that opens communication with our Higher Power. Many of us find regular meditation with others an effective way to keep our practice consistent.

We can meditate on a single question until an answer comes. We can meditate to clear our minds and accept whatever comes forward. While meditating, we can sit, stand, lie down, walk, have our eyes open or closed. We can focus on the flame of a candle or a word. We can focus on a spot between our eyebrows, our third eye. We can meditate on a spiritual passage, a sacred object, on love, or on peace. Many of us focus on our breath. We simply relax and follow our breath as we inhale and exhale.

The ways of meditating are only limited by our lack of imagination or education. There are many resources available for us to learn from: books, retreats, classes, videos, groups, audio recordings, and teachers.

As adults abused as children, we meditate for answers, guidance, stillness of mind, or clarity. Our reasons vary. If we go into meditation to get something out of it, we are working in opposition to it. Meditation is the spiritual practice of surrendering our thoughts and minds. Through surrender, we seek and receive knowledge of the will of our Higher Power.

Meditation stills the chattering of our conscious minds. It puts us into contact with the divine so we can have a deeper relationship with our Higher Power. There are many popular types of meditation practices. Some of us practice loving-kindness, mindfulness, conscious breathing, yoga, repetition of a mantra, transcendental meditation, or movement. Concentration is focusing on one thing. Meditation is focusing on God.

Bridgette adds:

I am not as angry as I once was. I have more patience and am more peaceful. Struggles in my life are less painful or shorter-lived. Sometimes I go through the process of working the Steps deeper than before. I receive answers in my meditations.

Thinking vs. Meditation

The difference between thinking and meditating is important. Thinking about a problem is not meditating on it. Meditating involves our whole being, including our bodies, hearts, spirits, minds, sensations, feelings, and thoughts. When we are meditating, we are conscious, open, and receptive. It expands our consciousness and heightens our awareness.

Thinking occurs in our minds. When we are thinking, we are musing about our own thoughts. In meditation, we are seeking what our Higher Power wants us to know or do. In meditation, we seek, not think. In the beginning, some of us may have had to exercise faith and trust that meditation will work for us. It may take time to experience the benefits, but with consistent practice, most of us see the positive impact on our lives.

We are not chasing our thoughts with our minds. We are learning to still the mind and be open to receiving our Higher Power's guidance, insights, and desires for us.

> **Mabel surrenders in this way:**
>
> *I am committed and willing to pray and meditate. I am more peaceful when I am not working to come up with answers on my own. I have great help. I am connected to the best Source of all. I will receive what I need, and the answers will come from my Higher Power.*

Benefits of Prayer and Meditation

The key that unlocks the treasures of Step 11 is regular practice. **We** decide when we will be available to our Higher Power. We follow whatever individual plan we have for prayer and meditation, whether we feel like it or not. If we want the peace of mind and serenity that comes from this conscious contact, we have to be willing to cultivate that relationship.

> **Scott shares:**
>
> *When I withdraw myself from my outside world in meditation, it is easier for me to see my true nature. With childhood abuse in my past, this is helpful for me, as I hid who I really was, even from myself, for so long. When I can view my true nature without judgment, I can understand why I did certain things in my past. My self-compassion increases as a result.*

As we quiet our minds and focus our energies inward, we find out who we are beyond our thinking minds. We have access to the presence of the divine **within** us. We discover states of just "being," states of aliveness and peace. When we stay in the present moment in meditation, we experience doorways to integrate our bodies, minds, and spirits. These states allow us to transform the obstacles on our paths to opportunities to return to wholeness, or who we really are. Step 11 can be our guide for the rest of our lives.

Results of Prayer and Meditation

Step 11 includes a plan for adults abused as children to enter the realm of Spirit. The search takes place within us. The purpose of prayer and meditation is to improve our conscious contact with God.

The more we practice nourishing, conscious, and loving thoughts, the greater the positive effects they create in our world. There will be signs along the way revealing we're on the right path.

This list of well-documented benefits is lengthy and worthwhile to note. Many of us experience these results of prayer and meditation:

- A deep sense of gratitude
- A feeling of belonging
- A feeling of worthiness
- A sense of being guided
- A sense of nurturance
- A sense of peace
- A sense of serenity
- Enhanced sense of inner knowing
- Improved learning and memory
- Increased ability to focus
- Increased access to creativity

- Increased courage
- Increased effectiveness
- Increased emotional stability
- Increased energy
- Increased inner strength
- Increased mental clarity and decreased confusion
- Increased present moment awareness
- Increased self-esteem and enhanced confidence
- Increased sense of being loved
- Increased sense of connection
- Increased wisdom beyond our normal capacity
- Lessened anxiety and depression
- Lessening of irrational fears
- New options and possibilities
- Physical improvements: lowered blood pressure, sounder sleep, ease of digestion, easier to control pain
- Reduced stress
- Renewed hope
- Sharpened discernment

Marian shares:

When I pray, I receive comfort and peace. I feel loved and taken care of. This brings me back to Step 3, which says that my Higher Power will take care of things. Receiving guidance and clarity is how my Higher Power takes care of me.

Yolanda adds:

I notice changes since I have begun meditating. Unanticipated benefits continue to occur when I follow the Steps; spiritual principles and universal laws become clear. I experience synchronicities when I seek to know the truth from my Higher Power through prayer and meditation.

Meditation and prayer can help us release and let go. For some of us, having experienced the powerlessness of childhood abuse, letting go may be challenging. Our lives continue to change for the better. We become happier and more peaceful people. We realize who we are at the core of our beings. We are able to overcome our obstacles to peace, happiness, and vibrant aliveness.

We are not avoiding or denying our feelings. Rather, we have found ways to be with our feelings, breaking the isolation they can create. We experience not being alone.

As adults abused as children, we have found a safe refuge to commune with our Higher Power; that is the best benefit of all.

Praying for Knowledge of God's Will

The recommendation to pray for the knowledge of God's will is a direct route to our serenity. If we could have created sane lives for ourselves, we would have. If, by our sole efforts, we could have manifested what we believed possible, we would have, but we did not have the ability to manipulate others and situations to our liking. Oftentimes, we didn't even know what the best outcome for all concerned was. At a certain point, we admitted we needed something greater than ourselves to experience our lives to the fullest.

We realize we are not in control. We do not have all the answers. It is ours to seek and accept what comes. As we come to know God's will, we are learning to accept life as it is—and as it isn't. With the assistance of knowledge of God's will, we are able to co-create the lives we desire for ourselves.

To some of us, guidance is defined as knowledge of our Higher Power's will for us. We follow, rather than lead. We leave matters to our Higher Power, which only has our best interests at heart. It is our personal source of guidance. We may have a sense of being sustained, and we may be surprised by unexpected improvements in our lives.

Shannon learns:

After working Steps 4-7, I saw how my self-will had impacted my life. It became evident to me how **I had relied on my character defects, instead of relying on my Higher Power.** *No wonder my life wasn't working the way I wanted it to. Now, I fully believe my Higher Power's will for me is to know I have the ability to face life with dignity and peace when I follow the guidance I receive.*

How do we know God's will for our lives? If we are unsure, the support of other people can be an important part of Step 11. We do not have to make major decisions by ourselves. We involve others whom we trust, believing a Higher Power works through other people too.

Often, time will tell us whether we're headed in the direction our Higher Power wants for us. Since we work the Steps one day at a time, we do the best we can to discern the guidance we receive today. We pray our thoughts and actions will be on target in the present, letting go and letting God work out the future. We may assume we each have a part to play in life; we have things only each of us can do. If **we** don't do it, it might never be done.

We need not second guess what God intends for us. It is not our responsibility to figure out God by trying to know its mind or will. In addition, we cannot assume we know what God wants for us. We are asked to pray and meditate, being patient for an answer. It is in our best interest to pray and let go of the outcome we think should occur. We simply seek to merge our wills with our Higher Power's will.

Praying for Power

We may have a glimmer of what our Higher Power's will for us might include. The crunch comes when we think about actually carrying out some of these possibilities. It may not be enough for us to know what's good for us; we need to do the footwork to bring about the results we desire. Often, the courage to take a first step on a course of action will generate the power to take another step. Growth is possible when we are willing to move ahead. We may not know what the outcome will be, but with faith, we will be guided and given the power and inner strength to continue. We act on the insights we receive. Power to do God's will is available to us.

The power is found within our ability to trust, have faith and hope, and be willing to be honest. We ask for power and use it. We have the power to make amends, to admit our errors, to feel compassion, gratitude, and humility. These are just a few of the powers we have been skillfully developing through the 12 Steps. We may have failures and successes. We may hurt and be afraid, but our emotions will not destroy us. We will be grounded in a Source of power beyond ourselves. We will be given the means to carry out our Higher Power's will for us.

To consciously invoke the presence of God raises our consciousness to connect with and be receptive to our Higher Power. We may become vessels through which this presence expresses itself. It allows us to experience life from a higher perspective while positively influencing our thoughts, words, choices, and actions. The power of Source provides whatever is needed. It's a reminder we always have access to the realm of the Divine.

Lois shares:

Through regular prayer and meditation, I experience clarity and calmness in the middle of frantic situations. I simply remember that my Higher Power is present, and its power is moving through me with ease. Often, it works like clockwork.

Bryan looks at it this way:

I feel like my destiny, my future, depends on surrendering to a Greater Power. **I think my motives to change for good are the outworking of this Power's will for my life.** *Otherwise, I hold onto the past or old beliefs and stay stuck.*

We have access to inner powers to carry out God's will. Some of them appear as imagination, faith, wisdom, strength, will, enthusiasm, release, love, and understanding. We see the potential of these powers to help us lead richly blessed lives. They are helpful spiritual tools, providing support for our growth. We can link ourselves to our Higher Power through these powers. We exercise the power of resilience through practicing this connection.

David explains:

I use the power of will to attune my mind with God's consciousness. Clearing my negative thinking is my first step. I breathe deeply for a while to allow a strong, healthy thought to be present. Often what comes to mind is: "I am enough." I have witnessed my actions following that thought; what I affirmed became real. The source of this power is God.

Step 11 Summary

As adults abused as children, the time we spend getting in touch with our Higher Power will multiply our effectiveness in everything we do. When we are in contact with God, we find we can live many moments according to inner direction beyond our egos. We encounter a slow growing sense of assurance and a feeling of being guided.

> **Kim experiences assurance in this way:**
>
> *When my thoughts are muddled, I go within and seek divine presence for spiritual vision. When my mind and heart are centered on my Higher Power, outer matters don't distract me as much.*
>
> *I need to spend time each day in prayer and meditation, pausing to refocus my mind. I know that I am always divinely guided. From this consciousness, I think, act, and speak with clarity. I am guided by Spirit within.*

We may need to let go of the need to control our Higher Power. Up until now, we may have continued to pray for what **we** thought should be happening, i.e., our wills. We believed we knew what was best for us and others. In retrospect, we find we are still lonely, often feeling helpless and re-victimized. When we rely on a Power greater than ourselves, we experience life as thriving adults, not as victims. We have learned to trust this Greater Power.

As adults abused as children, the Steps have helped to reveal our human limitations, the roadblocks to our healing. Hope arises as we learn what to do with these obstacles. We are being motivated to seek consciously, to create better lives, to know we are truly not alone, and have a Source to turn to when we need it. We are deepening our surrender to this Power's influence. The 12 Steps are uniquely effective as guides for our spiritual growth.

It may help to have a regular place and time to pray and meditate, as it may breed familiarity and comfort. We may have a specific room, or a chair, blanket, or pillow to sit on. There are traditional ideas, but it is for us to find the ways with which we are most comfortable. **The more we practice loving thoughts, deeds, and actions, the greater effect we can have on the world around us.** Many of us simply start following our breaths. We may inhale to a count of four and exhale to a count of four. We relax into breathing. There is nothing else to do.

We have experienced surrender; we have become ready. We asked for help. We have looked within and became honest—while deepening our trust in our Higher Power.

Steps 10, 11, and 12 teach us how to maintain the manageability of our lives, our sanity, our versions of self-satisfaction and self-fulfillment. We enjoy peace of mind. These are some of our motives in seeking to heal through conscious contact and connection with our Higher Power, praying only for knowledge of His will for us and the power to carry that out. We are learning to follow our true natures and reap the rewards.

Marni reflects:

My Higher Power is the Source. I am a piece of the Source and strive to connect with this Greater Source. My Higher Power is the best resource for me to have the kind of life I want.

Chandra affirms:

My small acts of kindness become my living prayers.

Step 11 Affirmations

1. I weave joy into my daily activities.
2. My love is expressed by giving and receiving.
3. I choose nourishing and supportive thoughts.
4. I am at peace with life.
5. Prayer changes things.
6. I cannot touch truth and come away unchanged.
7. Through prayer and meditation, I keep resiliency alive.
8. I focus my attention on the present moment.
9. I move toward the light instead of fighting darkness.
10. I trust in the power of Source.
11. I am bigger than my circumstances.
12. Hope radiates from my heart.
13. Centered in the awareness of my Higher Power, my thoughts turn to compassion.
14. I have spiritual solutions to deal with physical plane problems.

15. Starting now, I truly feel alive, awake, and enthusiastic.

16. My prayers are manifesting.

17. I have been given the power to do Source's will.

Notes

Step 11 Journal Questions

1. What is my prayer for myself today?
2. What actions help me feel connected to my Higher Power?
3. What steps could I take that speak of my desire for inner peace?
4. What problems did I encounter this week and how did I resolve them through prayer?
5. What can I do to feel more fulfilled in my life?
6. What are some of my outdated beliefs?
7. What new perspectives could I create that would benefit me or another?
8. What traits could I develop that would empower me to keep the will of my Higher Power?
9. What's the value of my being centered?
10. What am I here to contribute?
11. What is it like to live inside of me today?
12. How have patience and understanding affected my ability to further my healing?

13. Step 11 has a spiritual foundation. What does this mean to me?

14. What forms of power do I imagine are within me? What actions could I take to practice using them?

15. Do I express the desires of my heart?

16. How do my beliefs about my Higher Power affect my life?

17. Why do I pray and meditate?

18. In my prayers each day, I ask what is mine to do today. What have been some of my answers?

Notes

Step 11 Prayer

I let go and let the awareness of my Higher Power pour into me. I allow Spirit to flow unimpeded when I practice gratitude and faith. It is then I experience divine order in my life.

The love of God restores me. The power of God heals me. The grace of God is always present. The peace of God comforts me. These blessings no longer feel elusive, as I have discovered them within. I relax and center my thoughts on being a conduit of these gifts.

I commit myself to see the blessings from God that enrich my life today. I am grateful to Spirit for providing for me in both seen and unseen ways. I continue to do my part with prayerful consciousness, listening and following the promptings from Source within. I gratefully accept the gift of grace.

Thank you, Spirit.

And so it is.

AMEN.

Notes

Notes

Step 12

Having had a spiritual awakening as the result of these Steps, we carried this message to others and practiced these principles in all our affairs.

Step 12

Having had a spiritual awakening as the result of these Steps, we carried this message to others and practiced these principles in all our affairs.

Table of Contents

Introduction	551
A Spiritual Awakening as a Result of These Steps	554
Step 12 Is Written in the Past Tense	563
Spiritual Practice	565
Asleep and Awake	568
Carrying the Message	571
The Spiritual Principles of The 12 Steps	578
Practicing the Principles	579
In All Our Affairs	582
Service	584
Step 12 Summary	588
Step 12 Affirmations	595
Step 12 Journal Questions	597
Step 12 Prayer	599

Step 12

Having had a spiritual awakening as a result of these Steps, we carried this message to others and practiced these principles in all our affairs.

Introduction

As adults abused as children, we have journeyed through the prior Steps and arrived at Step 12. Whether we are aware of it or not, we can be assured that a spiritual awakening has already happened. We are being asked to acknowledge this awakening, as we practice the principles and carry the message of the Steps to other adults abused as children.

The dictionary defines the spirit as a vital principle or animating force within us. The definition of spiritual is something of the **spirit's** nature, distinguished from that which is tangible and related to physical nature or matter. Spiritual can be a quality, trait, idea, understanding, or tendency of humans in life.

The 12 Steps are a set of spiritual principles, a way of life governed by universal laws that apply to every living being. They are a guide or action plan that, when followed, awakens us spiritually, connects us to our Higher Power, and helps us contribute to others.

Our spiritual awakening does not occur just once. It is ongoing, never-ending, and meant to inspire us throughout our lives as we continue to practice the spiritual principles of each Step.

Step 12 carries us beyond ourselves to the world around us. Before this, we have been primarily concerned with ourselves. Now we begin to reach out to others and talk to them from our hearts, being our true selves. Being true encompasses aspects of ourselves unaffected by circumstances or events. We remain stable, no matter what is going on around us.

As we take Step 12, we simply share our stories, past experiences, spiritual growth, and healing. We find our own healing and personal insights expand as well. The gift we bring to other adults abused as children is the gift of ourselves. We have something of value to share. We can take satisfaction from the fact that someone else may find the help they need when we reach out to them.

Step 12 includes three distinct themes. The first speaks of a spiritual awakening, the second encourages us to carry the message of hope and healing to others, the third invites us to practice the principles learned in these Steps in all aspects of our lives. We wake up physically, emotionally, and spiritually. We are grateful we are able to re-awaken our spirits and find peace of mind.

A Spiritual Awakening as a Result of These Steps

We realize we are connected to a new source of strength, a Power greater than ourselves. As we live from a spiritual perspective, we may encounter new challenges. We find our guidance and answers in the spiritual principles imbedded in these Steps. We are able to lay old fears and anger to rest. We witness inner transformation which propels us into new states of consciousness and new experiences.

For some of us, this happened quickly, but for most of us it's been a gradual process. It cannot be forced or hurried. It happens naturally as we work the Steps. Waking up to who we really are and becoming aware of our relationship with a Higher Power are the foundations for our transformation. This is the basis of our spiritual awakening.

Claudia explains:

Spiritual awareness requires that I see with new eyes. When I observe challenges or even obstacles, I need to look beyond them to see new possibilities. I connect with my Higher Power, which increases my faith and inner strength. I see things I never saw before and feel a sense of power within me. I know living my life based on spiritual ideas changes my life.

We may think our spiritual awakening will be similar to someone else's. We may believe we are not yet deserving. The truth is, through the Steps we have had many spiritual awakenings. Step 12 helps us become more aware that it is **not only possible,** but has already happened.

We may be unable to acknowledge, or hesitant to accept, that we have had a spiritual awakening. We may have believed it had not been grand, extraordinary, or supernatural enough. We may deny ourselves because it seemed too easy. As we read further through Step 12, the spiritual awakenings for each Step are highlighted.

Owen affirms:

I do not think it is necessary for me to intellectually know what the words "spiritual awakening" mean. It feels more important to sense and be aware of the experience of awakening.

Who decides if we have had a spiritual awakening? We do! Looking closely, we see we have already had a spiritual awakening as a result of these Steps. We understand why Step 12 is written in the past tense. Each of the Steps is meant to expand our spiritual growth and understanding beyond the physical realm.

- **Step 1's awakening** is created as we admit our lives have become unmanageable and as we became willing to accept that we are powerless. We may not have been able to admit how unmanageable our lives had become before this. We are spiritually seeking and wanting something better for ourselves.

- **Step 2's awakening** offers us the discovery that we aren't responsible for own restoration; we have a Power greater than ourselves to help us. We discover we are not alone in improving our lives. Many of us are relieved to learn this.

- **Step 3's awakening** occurs once we make the decision to turn our will and our lives over to the care of our Higher Power. Many of us have not had a spiritual relationship with a Source greater than ourselves. We did not have a spiritual frame of reference, nor did we realize we have a Higher Power that cares about us. This woke us up to a new comforting realization.

- **Step 4's awakening** is affirmed as we made the decision to do a searching and fearless moral inventory while calling upon the strength of our Higher Power's help to do so. As an adult abused as a child, it is a miracle we can now alter the focus from our abuse, our abuser(s), as well as those who did not protect us - and bring it back to ourselves. We have begun to awaken to who we were as children and discover who we are **as adults.** We have become aware, awake, and willing to look at the less desirable aspects of ourselves as adults and to note those aspects working well for us. We have entered a spiritual realm that asks us to reveal ourselves authentically.

- **Step 5's awakening** is born of our admitting to God, to ourselves, and to another the exact nature of our wrongs **as adults.** This is the first time we have actively included another person in our Steps. It involves trusting someone who accepts us and cares about us exactly as we are. This can truly be a revelation for us.

- **Step 6's awakening** creates space for a deeper spiritual dimension. We discover we do not have to fix ourselves; it is not our job. Our Higher Power is doing the clearing for us and removing what prevents us from releasing the limiting effects of our childhood abuse. All we need to do is admit, do some soul searching, deepen our commitment to self-honesty, and know we do not have to clean up our acts. We are not responsible for improving or changing ourselves. We let ourselves become more alive to who we really are.

- **Step 7's awakening** is our willingness and readiness to ask for help. Our asking is an admission of powerlessness and reveals our true humanity. It may be an eye-opener to realize we are not in control of ourselves. We are admitting we are not the Creator. When we admit what is true, we experience spurts of growth, feel more alive, and open the doors to possibilities for continued change and healing.

- **Steps 8 and 9's awakenings** are born of the admission to ourselves, to our Higher Power, and to another that we can change. Admitting and making amends is what changing is all about. Our willingness to change is met with forgiveness for ourselves, others, and the world. This is a profound awakening as we step from the past into the present. We are rewarded with easy access to new clarity and self-responsibility.

- **Step 10's awakening** is realized through our continued willingness to do a regular self-check. We explore who we have become, the decisions we made, the beliefs we chose, and the actions we took. We become self-observant, deepen our self-awareness, and remember to stay focused on ourselves with compassion. Our shortcomings are the blessings that move us closer to our Higher Power. Our progress continues to demonstrate our healing. As we admit our shortcomings and progress, we have awakened our inner humility and connected with ourselves through self-acceptance.

- **Step 11's awakening** is gained through prayer and meditation as we improve our conscious contact with our Higher Power. These practices help reinforce our awareness of our Higher Power's presence in our lives. We connect and listen for guidance to align our lives with the divine plan. As we awaken, we discover we **do** have the ability to do God's will. The relationship with our Higher Power creates direct access to our spirit!

- **Step 12's awakening** is experienced as we share our spiritual growth and healing with others. As we live these principles, we realize we are valuable human beings and have much to contribute to our world. We see we do make a difference by being who we truly are.

Penny shares:

I feel the words "spiritual awakening" in my gut, in my core. It feels like a seed was planted and it is growing. One day, the seed wakes up and out comes a flower. The seed and the flower are waking me up, growing, blossoming, and becoming my true self.

Spiritual awakenings are not limited to these 12 Steps. However, our healing through **this proven model** is focused on the spiritual awakenings as a result of the 12 Steps of **ADULTS ABUSED AS CHILDREN ANONYMOUS.** Reading a book, taking a class, seeing a movie are other avenues of awakenings. In this guide, however, we follow the Steps and reap the benefits.

Our Individual Spiritual Awakening

Many of us may not have known we had a spirit to awaken. We share common, yet unique, awakenings through each Step. As our own personal spirits awaken, we enjoy increased understanding of our spiritual natures and have access to being more authentic. We recognize the benefits our new lives can offer us.

Our individual and personal spiritual awakening can happen over time in subtle and gradual ways. This awakening is often realized in moments of clarity, when we can say ahhh...now I understand. As we journey through the Steps, we experience miraculous changes in our lives and in our personal transformation, as well. These occurrences are possible because we have awakened to another way of being as we follow this spiritual path. We found ourselves inviting Spirit to express itself in us and in our lives.

> **Joni tells us:**
>
> I had an awakening to who I was in relation to the Creator in a way that completely altered my self-perception and how I navigate my life each day. I found out the difference between my role as a human being and that of my Higher Power. Now I understand what true humility is.

Being an adult abused as a child, a lot was expected of me from my perpetrators that was inappropriate and not mine to do. Some wanted me to fulfill roles for them that were not my responsibility – parent, caretaker, lover, confidant, or the one to serve them. I became very confused about where I fitted into my own world and other peoples' worlds too. Through the 12 Steps I'm seeing what it is to be truly human. It's a far cry from what I thought it was! I desperately need the structure of the Steps to risk revealing my humanness, especially to myself. One day at a time, I do this as a spiritual practice. I count on my Higher Power's care to be there with me. My job is to love myself no matter what!

Our personal awakening may have begun when we became willing to believe in a spiritual presence greater than our human selves. **We are the benefactors of our Higher Power's desires for our lives.** It may be a huge awakening to discover that there is a Source greater than ourselves that is here to guide and help, because that Source cares about us. This may be the first awakening for many of us.

Some of us were not aware that there is a Higher Power we can rely on to guide us on our life's journeys. The spiritual awakening described in Step 2 says, "Came to believe that a Power greater than ourselves could restore us to sanity." Step 2 initiates our personal spiritual awakening. It addresses the true nature of being human. We are spiritual beings learning about Spirit, having a spirit, and being human. We are human beings learning and deepening our trust in a Higher Power. Some of us want to integrate our human aspects with our spiritual ones in our everyday lives. The 12 Steps can help us learn how to do that and be one with ourselves.

> **George reveals:**
>
> *Living a spiritual life, after having had a spiritual awakening, has become as significant as breathing. I discovered that my spirituality is as essential to my everyday life and well-being, as eating and sleeping.*

As **we** expand, we become part of a much larger awakening in our world. We do not have to have it figured out or analyzed in advance. Our individual awakenings do not have to be clear to us. We only need to continue to practice the spiritual principles and accept that we have awakened.

Step 12 Is Written in the Past Tense

Step 12 states, "Having had a spiritual awakening as a result of these Steps...," not only as a result of counseling, attending a house of worship, or reading spiritual or religious writings. It simply says if we work these Steps, we are going to have a spiritual awakening. This Step is written in the past tense implying we may have been asleep and now we are waking up.

When we become spiritually awake, we decide to allow our lives to be governed by spiritual laws or principles. Every being on the planet is subject to spiritual principles. We are encouraged to live our lives according to these laws.

We reap the benefits each time we do. We have a chance to wake up to reality, to what is really going on, and to who we really are. We discover our work is to become the people we had hoped to be.

Iris acknowledges:

Most of my life, I walked around with rose-colored glasses on. I did not know I could afford to take them off. I feared I couldn't handle life as it appeared to me without them. The glasses jaded my views of life.

Through working the Steps, I discovered how skewed my vision was. I had only allowed myself to see what I thought I could handle. The life I envisioned behind those rose-colored glasses was not real. I made it up. I was not accepting life as it was, and I realized that I wasn't living my life according to universal and spiritual principles. I was living in fantasies, avoiding reality. I imagined life on my terms, thinking it was the only life I could successfully live in. Working the Steps woke me up to my previously limited choices. Now, I have new possibilities and am able to live by universal truths that have been there all along.

Spiritual Practice

The 12 Steps are a spiritual practice. We are winding down the 12 Steps and continuing with them at the same time. Those of us who choose to live these Steps as a structure for our lives understand the possibilities of healing from the effects of childhood abuse are **unending** on this path.

We may have personal spiritual practices we include as we work the 12 Steps. We remember we can create what works for us and do it our own way. The journey through the Steps is personal and unique to each of us.

We are promised a spiritual awakening; our spirits have awakened. Life does not ask us to be well-educated, have a good job or relationship, or have the right amount of money to have an awakening. Step 12 simply states, "Having had a spiritual awakening **as a result of these Steps...**"

Unless we, as individuals, have other spiritual paths that have guidelines we choose to follow, there are no set rules, structure, or focus for our spiritual awakening. The 12 Steps allow for individual paths of spirituality and spiritual practice. The 12 Steps for adults abused as children do not say this is the only or best way for spiritual advancement. We do not exclude any other paths for healing or spiritual practices. However, it does say we will have a spiritual awakening as a result of working **these** 12 Steps!

Carli offers:

I really like the fact that the Steps do not say this is the only way for me to heal. They say it is a **proven** way. I discovered these 12 Steps for adults abused as children spoke to me.

I found a way for myself, and I like that. I had never had a path for living before I started working the Steps. They enhanced other areas of my spiritual life and helped me seek more spiritual insights too.

Asleep and Awake

Our actions have shifted to those activities which propel us in the directions we wish to pursue. We can lay old fears and resentments to rest as we discover new options for ourselves. Because we are linked to a new source of strength, our relationships can offer us opportunities to experience connection, contribution, and personal healing. Waking up is an internal shift of consciousness and our awakenings may have shown us that spirituality makes a positive difference in our daily lives.

> **Linda remembers:**
>
> *I couldn't see the truth because I had protected myself by living in a fantasy world. I closed my mind and heart, unwilling to see, hear, or accept. I protected myself and stayed asleep inside my cocoon, insulated from the real world.*

> **Ray shares:**
>
> *Since the first thing Step 12 says is, "Having had a spiritual awakening..." I assume at some point in my life, I was asleep and now, to some degree, I am awake.*

Miriam discovers:

I had a spiritual awakening with the 12 Steps. I discovered I had been asleep until Step 1 helped me realize what I was powerless over. I had a true spiritual awakening since I had no idea it was okay to be powerless in my life.

Before I started working the 12 Steps, I tried so hard not to be powerless over anything! When I accepted that I was powerless over things I had no control over, my life changed. I had misinterpreted what powerlessness was and wrongly thought I didn't have what it took to live my life well. During my working Step 1, I gained the spiritual understanding that it was not my job to control others, my life, or the world.

As we progress through the previous Steps, they are the help and preparation for our spiritual awakening from a deep slumber. We are not slow; we are becoming ready for a series of awakenings. We are waking up to who we really are. For most of us, it appears to be gradual, not an event. An event might be called a spiritual experience, with a beginning and an end. Spiritual experiences can be a sign we're making progress in our spiritual awakening. These experiences can be common, everyday happenings with a spiritual element to them. Watching a sunset or seeing a baby's smile can be a spiritual experience. Having moments of insight or seeing something clearly that had been hidden up until now are spiritual experiences. Consciously or not, we had an awareness of our Higher Power's presence within us. Our spiritual awakening is continuing as we make progress.

Dave reflects:

When I think about having a different kind of life from this moment forward, that really wakes me up! It offers me hope, and hope speaks to my spirit and awakens me. I feel a quickening of my spirit and feel more alive.

Sonya shares:

I awakened to the realization it was normal that I still had so many unexplored and undeveloped aspects of myself. I had previously determined them as "bad." I saw how I had incorrectly assumed I had to hurry up and change those unwanted, undesirable aspects in order to be loved, valued, and wanted. My belief that I needed to be a different kind of person to be of value ran deep.

Talk about an awakening! My whole adult life has been focused on trying to be who I thought I should be, without considering who I already was. It took courage and a lot of prayers to admit who I was and to consider that I might be lovable and valuable as I am.

Carrying the Message

The first word of each of the 12 Steps is an implied "We." We are human beings having had a spiritual awakening as a result of our working these 12 Steps. This is the message we carry in Step 12.

As adults abused as children, we are embodied spiritual beings awakening to the spiritual laws that govern our lives in our human bodies.

We have chosen to heal our childhood abuse through the 12 Steps. Our lives have been transformed through them. We want to share what we've learned (carry the message) and contribute to other adults abused as children. We want them to have access to and experience more satisfying and joyful lives as we do!

In all Step 12 work we share ourselves. Often, we tell our childhood abuse stories and healing from them so that other individuals can identify with us, experience a sense of hope, and accept the current adult realities we all face. It's a way of saying it's okay to be the way we were and the way we are now. We let them know they are not alone. We also share how our spiritual awakenings took place and the difference they make in our healing today.

Claudia remembers:

When I talk to another adult abused as a child who doesn't know about the 12 Steps, I talk about my own healing. I tell them I finally had to admit I was powerless over my past abuse when I kept choosing partners who were self-absorbed and not really interested in me. I realized I was repeating my childhood family relationships in which I was not considered valuable or important. As a child, it seemed to me, I was an afterthought.

As we share with others, we are contributing to our own healing. There is value in giving of ourselves. We can see how much we've grown since Step 1. This reinforces our commitment to continued personal transformation.

Andy shares his thoughts:

*When I was growing up, I thought I was all alone with the sexual abuse from my brother. Through working the 12 Steps, I awoke to the understanding through all the abuse, that I was not alone. To my knowledge, in physical reality, I **was alone**. But I was very little, and the abuse happened a lot.*

Now I'm an adult. I have not abused my children; I broke the family chain. I may never know how my Higher Power helped me survive my childhood sexual abuse. But I do know that I would never be as emotionally healthy as I am today without its help. I was too little to know how to get through the abuse by myself. I am eternally grateful I was helped by my Higher Power. I call my Higher Power the help that was unseen and unknown to me as a child.

We are carrying a message of universal truth, transformation, hope, trust, and honesty. We are living proof that the 12 Steps for adults abused as children create valuable and welcomed changes in our lives. We are modeling our spiritual awakening for others. When we are working the Steps in our daily lives, we are walking examples of healing in action.

We carry the message by sharing our stories. We lend a compassionate ear, offer support without judgment, and keep an open door to any who seek healing. We share how we were able to change our lives for the better because of the 12 Steps.

We carry the message, **not the person** who is troubled by the abuses of their past. The message we carry lives in our hearts. Our message is one of lives free of victimhood and inspired by personal freedom. We have done our part whether or not others accept our message. We may have planted a seed; it is not ours to know. We do not know their journey; we are not their Higher Power. When we do Step 12 activities, we turn the results over to our Higher Power. It is the joy and gratitude we feel for having a path of healing that we want others to see and want for themselves. We pray they find a healing path as we did.

> **Maria reflects:**
>
> *I found out who I am is ok; I am lovable just as I am. My spiritual awakening does not mean I am perfect, all better, or forever healed. I am who I am today with whatever stuff remains I may not like. I am living my life guided by the spiritual principles found in the Steps. I did not know that I could be so human and messed up and still have a spiritual life available to me. I know I had spiritual awakenings such as this as I went through the 12 Steps. This is the passionate message I wish to share with others.*

Our messages are unique and yet similar. We are adults who experienced childhood abuse. We each carry a beneficial message based on our willingness to live our awakening, do our Step work, embrace our shortcomings with honesty, trust in a Higher Power, and live a surrendered and humble life. This way of living and being is enough to carry the message.

Words are only one way to carry the message. Showing up authentically in our lives is an effective and powerful way, as well.

We are guided to continue to use the 12 Steps. We've gained courage, strength, faith, and hope. Sharing the message is to be done carefully and with consideration. Some helpul thoughts:

- **Talk to people when they are ready.**
  We draw people in by our own example. We can pray to share the right words, at the right time, with the willingness and compassion to do so.

- **Keep it simple.**
  Share our story as simply as we can. Be mindful not to overwhelm the other person. There is always time to share more. Pray and ask what is appropriate to be shared in this moment.

- **Tell them what difference the 12 Steps have made** in our lives and tell them they have access to it as well. Share how life has taken on new meaning as a result.

- **Offer insight, support, and understanding**, but not advice.

- **Have no expectations.** We plant seeds of hope and thought. We show we care and respect them without judgment.

Bella says:

When I share my message, my story, I get excited. I feel hopeful. I hear what I am sharing with someone else and often, they are the exact words I need to hear. I found I have the ability to alter my future and the future of others.

Some of us may find ourselves reluctant to talk about our childhood abuse. We pray to be guided for the highest good of all, including ourselves. Sharing our pasts with others is a personal decision. It may depend on how centered and safe we feel in the moment, how inspired we are by our Higher Power, or the level of interest by the other person. Each of us has a unique story to tell. It is up to us if and when we tell it.

Our Higher Power can let us know what, if anything, is appropriate to be shared at this time.

The Spiritual Principles of The 12 Steps

Step 1	Powerlessness
Step 2	Faith
Step 3	Surrender
Step 4	Self-Honesty
Step 5	Trust
Step 6	Readiness
Step 7	Humility
Step 8	Willingness
Step 9	Restitution
Step 10	Accountability
Step 11	Spirituality
Step 12	Service

Practicing the Principles

In Step 12, we are asked to practice these spiritual principles in all our affairs. We may not express ourselves effectively in the beginning, nor is perfection the desired outcome. All we are asked to do is practice to bring about our learning. We do this through repetition. Sometimes it takes a lot of repetition for us to grow our understanding and appreciation of the benefits of practicing these principles.

J.J. looks at it this way:

The principles for me are statements of truth on which I base my beliefs and actions. When I live my life in line with my values, things go well for me. When I don't, I get upset and things fall apart. I feel stressed and dissatisfied.

Here are some ideas for practicing spiritual principles. There are many others. We are encouraged to create more for ourselves.

- Continuing to hold ourselves accountable for the lives we want

- Keeping a self-inventory journal and checking our emotional state throughout the day, noticing any triggers

- Maintaining self-awareness of the impact we have on those around us
- When appropriate, promptly admitting any wrong-doings and forgiving ourselves
- Praising ourselves for our progress
- Modeling the spiritual principles of forgiveness, empathy, and surrender in all our relationships
- Making daily healthy decisions that benefit our lives
- Giving selflessly and asking nothing in return
- Accepting life on life's terms
- Transforming our character defects into assets and strengths
- Making our spiritual growth our highest priority
- Sharing our healing with another adult who was abused as a child
- Doing our personal best and trusting the outcomes to a Higher Power
- Asking for help when we need it
- Focusing on our blessings with gratitude
- Willing to let go of our resentments
- Adjusting our attitudes when appropriate

- Seeking and maintaining close contact with a Higher Power
- Listening without judgment
- Offering compassion to others
- Being fully known and understood by someone
- Letting go of circumstances beyond our control and turning them over to a Power greater than ourselves
- Sinking deeply into the present moment responding from a place of maturity

In All Our Affairs

In all our affairs simply means we practice the spiritual principles of the Steps in every aspect of our lives, not only in relation to our childhood abuse. They become a way of life for many of us. We use them in our relationships, at home, in our jobs. They offer us the joy and self-fulfillment we had not yet discovered on our own.

We look at how our behavior has changed since we began waking up. There are some signs that tell us we're making spiritual progress. Are we more open and honest about our shortcomings? Do we contribute to others whom we don't particularly care for? Do we refrain from gossiping or walk away from people who engage in it? Do we complain about the state of affairs in the world or take some positive actions to move things in a healthier direction? Do we procrastinate less? Are we eager for the day ahead of us?

Our affairs don't have to be big ones. Flossing our teeth can be an act of self-care. We are responsible for the health of our bodies. We make hundreds of small decisions all day long. As we create new, positive, beneficial habits, the practice of following spiritual principles gains momentum and takes on a life of its own.

We are aware of some Power operating in our lives as our healing and spiritual growth increases. We learn how to apply the principles in everyday situations and our lives get easier to handle.

George expresses it this way:

Now I know what it's like to be a human being with a spirit. As I have awakened, the Steps taught me what the true nature of my spirit really is. I have found myself a changed person as I go through the day focused on practicing the principles to the best of my ability.

I feel like I have more spirit toward life. Others have noticed my new serenity and the shift in my behavior toward them. They see me as more giving of myself and more understanding of them. I am grateful every day for my Higher Power in my healing from the effects of my childhood abuse.

Service

The type of service we are talking about here includes anything that benefits or enhances someone or something other than ourselves.

As adults abused as children, we carry the message to others who are like us, share similar backgrounds, and have common needs. As we carry the message, we receive as much as we give. We "serve" as we carry the message.

Being of service to others and asking or expecting nothing in return is essential to Step 12. We are not responsible for others, but instead, care enough about them to share how the 12 Steps have made a difference in our lives.

Ingrid remembers:

Doing service in Step 12 reminds me I'm not alone. I'm not alone in having been abused. I'm not alone in working the 12 Steps or in my feelings toward the effects of the abuse.

I know I'm not alone in my desire for healing. This gives me comfort and hope. However, it saddens me that so many other people have had similar childhood experiences as I had. This guides me to include others in my progress by doing service.

Equally important, being of service strengthens our personal healing. It reinforces our learning, keeping us focused on our path. It helps open doors for others to heal as well. We may need to put aside our personal life challenges in the moment, if appropriate, and simply share our story, offering support without judgment to any who seek healing from their childhood abuse.

Without even seeking it, we may find a shift in our consciousness away from lack and toward fullness. Letting others know we care about their welfare expands the hearts of all of us. Service strengthens our connection with our Higher Power. We recognize our efforts toward others are outer expressions of our Higher Power's caring within us.

Roger affirms:

If escaping the bondage of my past was my last act on earth, it would be worth it to me. I do this by being of service to others who have childhood abuse in their pasts. I listen to them without interrupting and let them know I'm available if they'd like to learn more about the 12 Steps.

Being of service is not the same thing as helping. It is not helpful to do for another what they need to do for themselves. **We** help through service by carrying the message, practicing the principles, being present, and continuing to work the Steps.

Service can be done through volunteering or other physical acts. It can be done by listening to someone through a lens of compassion, holding a door for someone, or delivering an anonymous bouquet of flowers. Anything we do to contribute to someone else is service. **Service is a spiritual practice.**

All Step 12 work is service. **Any act of kindness is service.** It's an acknowledgment that we're part of a larger community and have something valuable to share.

Step 12 asks us to carry the message to other adults abused as children who are still struggling. Service is a healthy way of using what we've learned from our childhoods for the good of ourselves and someone else. This benefits all of us. Being of service to others can:

1. Prevent us from becoming complacent in our lives

2. Give us a sense of purpose and continue to build our self-esteem and self-confidence

3. Enhance our fellowship with others, which can balance our sense of isolation

4. Offer us an opportunity to encourage, support, and understand others

5. Inspire us to stay present in our lives

6. Make a difference in someone else's life

7. Contribute to the community from a place of hope and healing

8. Remind us we're not alone

9. Remind us how we found a path to live with our pasts unchanged. Accept the past as it was, and as it wasn't

10. Help us remember our spirit while integrating it into our human selves

Step 12 Summary

One of the beauties of human life is that we are able to live and impact not only our own lives, but also those we care about. We contribute to others on a regular basis, as we are called to do so.

We are committed to a Source-centered consciousness which fosters our ability to share our authentic selves in the world. We have experienced building our lives on spiritual ideas.

This gradual shift has empowered us to allow the changes we have been wanting since we began to work the 12 Steps. We keep ourselves available to others and model the healing possibilities for all of us.

We made the decision to trust a Higher Power and deepen our spiritual commitment to journey through the 12 Steps as adults abused as children. Our lives took on new meaning.

We became willing to identify our fears, confront hidden aspects of ourselves, and deepen our commitment to wanting a better life for ourselves.

We have openly admitted our progress and faults to another and discovered we are not alone in having shortcomings and goals.

We have created the possibility of living in the real world, not in our fantasies or worlds of denial. We live with honesty, courage, and trust as our guides instead of the lies we believed to survive.

We are living in ways we had long hoped for and have taken responsibility for how we conduct ourselves. True healing has become a reality and the burdens of our pasts have begun to be lifted.

Ferdinand offers:

I have the sense of Source's presence in my awareness as I go about my day. This connection has been available to me since I began focusing on the here and now. What was once unmanageable, I can handle one day at a time now.

I am learning to cope with good feelings and upsetting feelings, keeping anxiety at a minimum. When I stay in the present and focus on what is happening right now, I respond appropriately and worry less about the future.

Through the Steps, we have awakened to realize there is more freedom for our spirit to become what it truly is and for us to discover how magnificent we are as humans. We share this knowledge with others and our Higher Power. We observe ourselves, release as necessary, and connect with our Higher Power with humility, grace, and self-acceptance. We are blossoming and becoming our authentic selves. There is an expansive aspect to our lives as we live our spiritual awakening and demonstrate it daily.

The 12 Steps for adults abused as children are a blessing. We will continue to grow to know ourselves and recognize our true selves. As adults, we are meant to simply trust we are enough, as we are. Our Higher Power is our partner in our lives and on our paths of healing. Step 12 is our way of saying thank you to our Higher Power.

Instead of wishing we could change the past, we can choose our relationship to it and create new possibilities in the present. We have inner and outer resources as adults that were not available to us as children. With the help of our Higher Power, we have journeyed and grown through the support and guidance of the 12 Steps.

We have access to awareness, which is a state of mind that can bring us to freedom from the hold the past may have on us. As we identify our thoughts and innermost feelings, we see they are the sources of creating our current reality, our views of the world.

We open our minds and consider points of view beyond our current vistas. We experience the power within to do what is ours to do. We consciously structure our lives by praying and taking guided action steps. We learn how to shift our perspective from the past and experience life differently today by working the 12 Steps.

Claudia says:

As I let go of past hurts, I am committed to allowing inner changes to surface, making space for new ways of thinking and being. It's taken a while for the new to manifest, even though I've been dedicated to my healing for a few years. It seems my job is to trust, be patient, and be self-compassionate.

I had no idea how powerless I was to become the person I thought I should be. Only in partnership with my Higher Power am I in touch with the power I do have as a human being exactly as I am.

In working Step 12, I ask to be used in healthy ways for the benefit of my fellows. I pray to say what is mine to say and hear what I need to hear. This prayer is all I need to share a message of healing from the effects of my severe childhood abuse. I seem to be given the words others need to hear when I remember to relax and speak my truth.

The more I admit my powerlessness, the more expansive I become in my consciousness. This is an expression of an awakened spirit in me. I experience the integration in myself as a human being and a spiritual being.

A Quick Review

Step 1: We admitted we were powerless over our childhood abuse and the unmanageability of our lives today.

Step 2 : We came to believe in a Power greater than ourselves.

> The 12 Steps for adults abused as children are based on the belief in a Higher Power. For some of us, this Higher Power may be God. For others, it may be a belief in a Universal Source, a Greater Good, or a Higher Self. Our healing begins as we seek the guidance and connection of this Power.

Step 3: We began to learn about the necessity and healing power of surrender.

> God can be known in many forms and can be referred to by many names. We decided to surrender to this Power. The purpose of this Step is to further acknowledge we are not meant to do this healing journey by ourselves.

Step 4: We wrote our fearless and moral inventory.

> We do not inventory what we did or did not do as children as a moral issue of right and wrong. We looked at the facts of the abuse, how we appeared to ourselves as children, and how the childhood abuse still impacts us today as we explore our adult selves. We included our assets and our liabilities.

Step 5: We shared what was in our inventory with another person and our Higher Power. We revealed the nature of our erroneous thinking, beliefs, and actions as adults.

Step 6: We became ready to have God remove all the adult character traits that diminish us.

Step 7: We asked for help from our Higher Power to remove those adult traits where we came up short and to increase the ones which enhanced or expanded us.

Step 8: We made a list of all persons we had harmed as adults and became ready to make amends and be accountable.

Step 9: We made amends to the people on our Step 8 list, as long as the amends did not cause anyone harm.

Step 10: We continued to take moral inventory and promptly admitted when we were off the mark as adults and when we were progressing.

Step 11: We learned to seek conscious contact with our Higher Power through prayer and meditation. We prayed for knowledge of God's will for us and the inner power to carry out God's will.

Step 12: We shared our stories of childhood abuse and healing through the 12 Steps. We lived our spiritual principles in our everyday lives.

Healing is a journey, yet accessible and possible for each of us. We are not the same people as we were when we began the 12 Steps. We look at where we are now and notice the great difference.

Our journeys are unique, yet similar. Though our specific needs for healing may vary, the outcomes are consistent. We are empowered to release shame, build resilience, break cycles of abuse, heal relationships, and create safety for ourselves in our environment. These are some of the impacts of learning new skills and developing new resources.

Not only do we explore how our childhood abuse has impacted us negatively as adults, we also acknowledge our strengths, assets, and actions of healthy self-esteem.

By unlocking the power within us, we discover we have everything we need to create lives of joy, have peace of mind, and contribute to others in our communities. Our attitudes of appreciation of who we truly are, support our shifts toward greater self-love and self-acceptance. We begin to appreciate our humanity and our inspiring qualities already apparent to us. This is what makes all the difference toward our success in healing.

Step 12 Affirmations

1. I am committed to allowing changes in my life.

2. I welcome my Higher Power's presence.

3. I summon courage to manage any denial that may arise.

4. I am human. That is enough.

5. I am worthy of being loved.

6. I am willing to transcend and release old patterns of perception and beliefs that keep me hooked into the past.

7. I expect my prayers to be effective because I can contact my Higher Power.

8. I am becoming more authentic every day.

9. I pray to be the kind of person I would want for a friend.

10. As a result of these 12 Steps, I am accepting life on life's terms one day at a time.

11. I believe in a benevolent universe.

12. I practice spiritual principles in all my affairs today.

13. I am creating new possibilities with the help of my Higher Power as I stay in present time.

14. I am aware the behavior of others has little to do with me.

15. I am discovering how to better care for myself.

16. I radiate peace in the midst of conflict.

17. Awareness is the fertile ground for change.

18. I am grateful for my health.

19. My Higher Power approves of me.

Step 12 Journal Questions

1. What prayers have been answered for me?
2. How do I act when I feel empowered?
3. What actions can I take to free myself from blame and bitterness?
4. What paths am I following that answer the call of my heart?
5. How am I expressing my true self today?
6. What might I set aside, so I may "travel lighter" in life?
7. When I forgive, I do not excuse or forget what I or someone else did. What is one thing I could do to demonstrate that forgiveness has occurred?
8. In what areas of my life do I deceive myself and look to the outside world as the source of my discomfort or upset?
9. What activates or triggers my behavior that prevents me from functioning in a healthy manner in my adult world?
10. List specific situations that demonstrate my humility.
11. What childhood or adult experiences inspire me to contribute to the quality of other people's lives?
12. Where is my personal growth enhanced by my willingness to surrender to my Higher Power?

13. Where have I held back sharing my past for fear of another's judgment?

14. What characteristics have I discovered within me that empower me to reveal myself to other adults abused as children?

Step 12 Prayer

Upon awakening, I face each day with infinite possibilities. My world feels new and full of promise. I ask my Higher Power to guide me so I may know what is mine to do today. I am given everything I need to carry out the will of my Higher Power. My divine birthright offers me freedom from obsolete notions and opens new doors through which I am able to contribute fresh ideas unencumbered by the past.

As I awaken on my spiritual journey, I embark anew on my path with a more open mind and heart, seeking a stronger connection with my Higher Power. I feel the oneness with this Power as I go within; it is always available to me.

May I respond with humility and begin this very moment to express myself from new perspectives that will benefit myself and others. I feel my Higher Power's care flowing through my life like a river which never runs dry.

Thank you, God, for awakening me to a new potential and extraordinary insights to be used for the good of all. I can see clearly now; I am awake.

And so it is.

AMEN.

Notes

Notes

Notes

Notes

About the Author

El (Ellin) Chess has been called a miracle, and rightfully so. Her story includes triumph over adversity. Her first 20 years were dominated by torture, extreme child abuse, and trauma. This was followed by 20 years of discovering what is really going on in the world and who she really is. During her mid-life, she began her journey of actualizing who she wound up to be, and for the last 15 years has been in the act of successfully creating the life she always hoped was possible for her.

El has multiple facets that show up in her life. From those dramatic beginnings, she has become a wise woman, truth sayer, storyteller, warrior, world bridger, re-writer of history, an empath, a sensitive healer, mother, grandmother, wife, sister, friend, world lover.

In the world, she has played many parts. They include: personal life coach for 40 years, seminar leader, keynote speaker at conventions, teacher, self-love educator, Executive Director of The Attitudinal Healing Center of Sonoma County, 10 day wilderness quester, business administrator, and business owner.

Today she is enjoying recovery, having joined her first 12 Step program 40 years ago. It was at that time that she started on her spiritual path of self-love as a way to self-realization. Through the years, she has given seminars, workshops, and private consultations on this self-love path. She is a gifted teacher who inspires and empowers others to learn how to live happy, healthy, and satisfying lives.

El is the founder of a new 12 Step Program called **ADULTS ABUSED AS CHILDREN ANONYMOUS.**

Her enthusiasm for life springs from her obvious deep caring and commitment to offering hope to others who have had a difficult childhood. She demonstrates that healing from childhood abuse is certainly possible for them.

El credits her living a fulfilled life today to: developing courage, wanting to be happy, deep inquiry inside herself, and especially grace.

Contact El
Ellin (El) Chess
708 Gravenstein Highway North #424
Sebastopol, CA 95472
707.861.0144
admin@adultsabusedas children.com

Appendix

Websites

adultsabusedaschildren.com

Visit this website to learn more about the fellowship of ADULTS ABUSED AS CHILDREN ANONYMOUS

Follow Us on Social Media

facebook.com/adultsabusedaschildrenanonymous/

facebook.com/EllinChess

Stay in Touch

Sign up to get a free copy of the Program Newcomer Packet in exchange for your e-mail. We promise never to share your information. We will keep you informed about the fellowship and when new materials are available.

Give Us Your Honest Feedback

Please leave your honest feedback/thoughts as a customer review of this book at your favorite online retailer.

You can also post a book review on Goodreads, Facebook, and Twitter. Thank you.

The 12 Steps of Alcoholics Anonymous®

1. We admitted we were powerless over alcohol — that our lives had become unmanageable.

2. Came to believe that a Power greater than ourselves could restore us to sanity.

3. Made a decision to turn our will and our lives over to the care of God *as we understood Him.*

4. Made a searching and fearless moral inventory of ourselves.

5. Admitted to God, to ourselves, and to another human being the exact nature of our wrongs.

6. Were entirely ready to have God remove all these defects of character.

7. Humbly asked Him to remove our shortcomings.

8. Made a list of all persons we had harmed, and became willing to make amends to them all.

9. Made direct amends to such people wherever possible, except when to do so would injure them or others.

10. Continued to take personal inventory and when we were wrong promptly admitted it.

11. Sought through prayer and meditation to improve our conscious contact with God, *as we understood Him,* praying only for knowledge of His will for us and the power to carry that out.

12. Having had a spiritual awakening as the result of these Steps, we tried to carry this message to alcoholics, and to practice these principles in all our affairs.

The Twelve Steps of Alcoholics Anonymous have been reprinted and adapted with the permission of Alcoholics Anonymous World Services, Inc. (AAWS). Permission to reprint and adapt the Twelve Steps does not mean that Alcoholics Anonymous is affiliated with this program. A.A. is a program of recovery from alcoholism only. Use of A.A.'s Steps or an adapted version in connection with programs and activities which are patterned after A.A., but which address other problems, or use in any other non-A.A. context, does not imply otherwise.

We honor our agreement with A. A.
to reprint their 12 Steps as we adapt them for
ADULTS ABUSED AS CHILDREN ANONYMOUS.

The 12 Traditions of Alcoholics Anonymous®

1. Our common welfare should come first; personal recovery depends upon A.A. unity.

2. For our group purpose there is but one ultimate authority — a loving God as He may express Himself in our group conscience. Our leaders are but trusted servants; they do not govern.

3. The only requirement for A.A. membership is a desire to stop drinking.

4. Each group should be autonomous except in matters affecting other groups or A.A. as a whole.

5. Each group has but one primary purpose — to carry its message to the alcoholic who still suffers.

6. An A.A. group ought never endorse, finance, or lend the A.A. name to any related facility or outside enterprise, lest problems of money, property and prestige divert us from our primary purpose.

7. Every A.A. group ought to be fully self-supporting, declining outside contributions.

8. Alcoholics Anonymous should remain forever nonprofessional, but our service centers may employ special workers.

9. A.A., as such, ought never be organized; but we may create service boards or committees directly responsible to those they serve.

10. Alcoholics Anonymous has no opinion on outside issues; hence the A.A. name ought never be drawn into public controversy.

11. Our public relations policy is based on attraction rather than promotion; we need always maintain personal anonymity at the level of press, radio, and films.

12. Anonymity is the spiritual foundation of all our Traditions, ever reminding us to place principles before personalities.

The Twelve Traditions of Alcoholics Anonymous have been reprinted and adapted with the permission of Alcoholics Anonymous World Services, Inc. (AAWS). Permission to reprint and adapt the Twelve Traditions does not mean that Alcoholics Anonymous is affiliated with this program. A.A. is a program of recovery from alcoholism only — use of A.A.'s Traditions or an adapted version in connection with programs and activities which are patterned after A.A., but which address other problems, or use in any other non-A.A. context, does not imply otherwise.

> We honor our agreement with A. A.
> to reprint their 12 Traditions as we adapt them for
> **ADULTS ABUSED AS CHILDREN ANONYMOUS.**

Notes

Notes

Notes

Notes

Notes

Notes

Permissions

Each quote was given anonymously to
ADULTS ABUSED AS CHILDREN ANONYMOUS
to use in this publication.

Step 1 Affirmations

1. I am learning to trust others.//
2. I admit with honesty what really happened.
3. I love myself as I am.
4. I am learning to appreciate my body as it is.
5. I am powerless over the past abuse.
6. I am courageous.
7. I am no longer silent.
8. I have what it takes to handle life today.
9. I am able to change.
10. I am not alone.
11. I am no longer a victim.
12. I am lovable.
13. I live in the present.

Step 2 Affirmations

1. I am restorable.
2. I give faith a chance.
3. My Higher Power has no limits.
4. My thoughts create my world.
5. I have what it takes to handle my life.
6. I am enough as I am.
7. I look for new possibilities in my life.
8. I leave abusive situations with ease.
9. I treat myself as if I count.
10. I protect myself from abusive people.
11. I am no longer a victim.
12. I let nature takes its course.
13. Restoration is a process.

Step 3 Affirmations

1. I am never alone.

2. I am patient with myself.

3. I believe I can be restored by surrendering.

4. I believe that my Higher Power cares about me.

5. I decide to align my will with the will of a Power greater than me.

6. I turn my life over to a Higher Power one day at a time.

7. I release my grip on problems.

8. I let go of control.

9. My Higher Power inspires me.

10. I discover I have many choices.

11. I let go and let a Higher Power lead me.

12. I love myself no matter what.

13. I step out in faith.

Step 4 Affirmations

1. By releasing the past, I am creating space for new possibilities today.
2. I find peace of mind as my life becomes more manageable.
3. I choose to trust the process of doing my inventory.
4. I align my mind, attitude, and actions with the truth of my being.
5. I am healing through the 12 Steps.
6. I have ample opportunity for enjoyment today.
7. I have what it takes to handle real life.
8. My Higher Power cares about me.
9. With courage, fearlessness is made real with my Higher Power.
10. Self-love creates a life that is worth living.
11. Being authentic feels good.
12. I am coming out of hiding and revealing who I am.
13. Just for today, I accept what is and what is not.
14. I am enough.

Step 5 Affirmations

1. I accept my own worthiness.
2. Gratitude helps me accept.
3. I live as if I have value.
4. I honor myself.
5. There's nothing wrong with me.
6. I live as if my body matters.
7. Insecurity is a feeling. I let it pass through me.
8. I accept my past one day at a time.
9. I love myself no matter what.
10. I honor my courage as an adult.

Step 6 Affirmations

1. I give myself time to mature.

2. Difficulty is not a sign of failure.

3. I release fear and choose faith.

4. I openly welcome something better that what I have now.

5. I let nature take its course.

6. I shift my beliefs to a more positive point of view.

7. As I release, my inner light reveals what once appeared in the shadows.

8. My ability to make wise choices increases.

9. I am filled with the expectation of good.

10. I offer compassion to myself as I am healing.

11. I am a healthy, whole, and productive person.

12. I am grateful for the Higher Power of my understanding

13. It's becoming easier to express my true nature.

Step 7 Affirmations

1. I trust my Higher Power and allow changes in me.//
2. I have courage.
3. My life is unfolding in wondrous ways.
4. All my needs are met.
5. I want to be all I can be.
6. I am healing.
7. Peace fills my heart and mind.
8. I release that which no longer serves me.
9. Listening connects me to this present moment.
10. I am loved as I am.
11. I make life-affirming choices.
12. I have compassion for myself.
13. Wholeness is my true nature.
14. I am worthy of releasing my family's perceptions of me.
15. I release my demands of the outer world.

Step 8 Affirmations

1. My Higher Power is helping me.

2. I approve of myself.

3. I gently release my expectations.

4. I am able and willing to courageously look at myself.

5. I orient myself to the present.

6. I choose what's best for me in the long run.

7. I believe in my willingness to forgive.

8. I give myself permission to change.

9. I release the hold the past has had on me.

10. My healing has begun.

11. Prayer restores my connection to my Higher Power.

12. I celebrate myself.

13. Connecting with others is getting easier.

14. I am practicing seeing the "good" in me.

Step 9 Affirmations

1. I am willing to live in present time.
2. It is my job to love myself.
3. I forgive.
4. I value and honor myself.
5. Peace begins with me.
6. Life is a gift.
7. My Higher Power wants to help me and keep my faith strong.
8. A peaceful day is possible for me.
9. I deserve to feel good.
10. I know the difference between blame and accountability.
11. My highest good is always seeking expression.
12. I am feeling more gratitude every day.
13. Sharing with others is getting easier.
14. I accept "what is so" in life.

Step 10 Affirmations

1. One day can change my whole life. A new 24-hour day can begin right now.

2. I do not let the past define who I am today.

3. Shifting my awareness to my progress brings the good **already** existing in my life into focus.

4. I make a difference in the world just as I am.

5. My words are kind and bring peace to my life and to the lives of others.

6. I am learning to reveal the best of who I am.

7. I celebrate myself and hold thoughts that nourish and support me.

8. I am responsible for my satisfaction in life.

9. Self-change can only be realized in the present.

10. I make choices coming from my gifts rather than my wounds.

11. I trust that my highest good is unfolding.

12. This is my life. I am in it. It is not fixed.

13. I stay true to myself and real with others.

Step 11 Affirmations

1. I weave joy into my daily activities.
2. My love is expressed by giving and receiving.
3. I choose nourishing and supportive thoughts.
4. I am at peace with life.
5. Prayer changes things.
6. I cannot touch truth and come away unchanged.
7. Through prayer and meditation, I keep resiliency alive.
8. I focus my attention on the present moment.
9. I move toward the light instead of fighting darkness.
10. I trust in the power of Source.
11. I am bigger than my circumstances.
12. Hope radiates from my heart.
13. Centered in the awareness of my Higher Power, my thoughts turn to compassion.
14. I have spiritual solutions to deal with physical plane problems.

15. Starting now, I truly feel alive, awake, and enthusiastic.

16. My prayers are manifesting.

17. I have been given the power to do Source's will.

Step 12 Affirmations

1. I am committed to allowing changes in my life.

2. I welcome my Higher Power's presence.

3. I summon courage to manage any denial that may arise.

4. I am human. That is enough.

5. I am worthy of being loved.

6. I am willing to transcend and release old patterns of perception and beliefs that keep me hooked into the past.

7. I expect my prayers to be effective because I can contact my Higher Power.

8. I am becoming more authentic every day.

9. I pray to be the kind of person I would want for a friend.

10. As a result of these 12 Steps, I am accepting life on life's terms one day at a time.

11. I believe in a benevolent universe.

12. I practice spiritual principles in all my affairs today.

13. I am creating new possibilities with the help of my Higher Power as I stay in present time.

14. I am aware the behavior of others has little to do with me.

15. I am discovering how to better care for myself.

16. I radiate peace in the midst of conflict.

17. Awareness is the fertile ground for change.

18. I am grateful for my health.

19. My Higher Power approves of me.

Step 1 Journal Questions

1. Notice where the past is still showing up in the present. Pick at least one thing that is happening in my life that isn't the way I want it to be. What action could I take that would help me change this area to be the way I would like it to be?

2. What secret is the hardest to admit? Why?

3. What progress am I experiencing as a result of shedding some light on an aspect of myself or my past that had been previously hidden or unclear?

4. Where am I no longer experiencing life as a victim today?

5. What am I doing today to try to get others to love me?

6. How am I creating safety for myself in my relationships? What healthy boundaries am I setting?

7. Which self-care strategy would be helpful today?

Step 2 Journal Questions

1. Who or what do I think a Higher Power is?
   Who or what am I afraid it is?

2. Who or what would I like a Higher Power to be and why?

3. Do I believe my thoughts and feelings create my reality?
   Do I notice a dominant theme in my thinking?
   Is it helpful?

4. What do I believe I deserve?

5. What would I be like if I were restored?

6. What progress have I already made in being restored?

7. How do self-care and self-love help me to be renewed and allow my very nature to be transformed?

8. What would a sane life look like?

9. How are my needs being met by a Power greater than I am?

Step 3 Journal Questions

1. What are three of my most important values? Am I living them out in my life?

2. What does the right use of my will mean?

3. What preconceptions of a Higher Power have I relinquished?

4. When did I change my opinion or my mind about something? What did I learn from this?

5. In which area(s) of my life is my willpower in charge? Am I successful in getting what I want?

6. Where have I found it easier to decide to surrender, even if I didn't know what to do next?

7. What beliefs left over from childhood are standing in my way of being happy? Which ones would I consider changing?

8. What am I attached to that is keeping me from attaining my spiritual goals?

9. What pain am I afraid of facing and avoid it by using my self-will?

10. What measuring sticks do I use to make my decisions – integrity, respect, love, or fear and resentment? Am I satisfied with the results?

11. What do I fear by letting go?

Step 4 Journal Questions

1. How is my distorted thinking still affecting my life?

2. Am I aware that avoiding pain makes my life unmanageable? When is this most evident?

3. What strengths do I see in myself that were revealed in my inventory?

4. In what areas of my life do I demonstrate balance?

5. Who is part of my support system?
   How do I express my trust in them?

6. List some ways I have asserted myself recently.

7. How do I still treat myself as if I don't count?
   How does it feel when I do this?
   How does it feel when I treat myself as if I matter?

8. Do I notice areas of excess in my life?
   What are they?
   Have I considered surrendering them to a Higher Power?

9. Where have I taken responsibility for things that were not my fault?

10. What was it like for me the last time I said "No" and meant it?

11. Where do unrealistic expectations of me still trigger my need to be perfect?

12. Do I ask for what I need? Is it becoming easier?

13. List some "mistakes" I have made recently. What positive changes did I make as a result?

Step 5 Journal Questions

1. Where have I put my life on hold waiting for something to change on its own?
2. Do I still think I am what I do and how well I do it?
3. What decisions do I make when I lose faith in my goodness?
4. What decisions do I make using my free will poorly?
5. What false ideas have I believed that I need to relinquish?
6. In my practice of self-awareness where is my self-talk still harmful?
7. Where am I letting circumstances direct my life instead of taking right action from the cues within me?
8. Do I get upset when someone else is upset with me? Who does or doesn't this happen with?
9. Where and when do I treat myself as if I don't count? Where do I see progress?
10. Where do I see myself as not enough?
11. Where do I think I have the right to make decisions for others because I know better?
12. How have I used Step 5 as a path to personal freedom?
13. What obstacles do I need to overcome to achieve peace of mind?

14. Where do I give unwarranted power to my fears and anxieties?

15. What decisions did I make as a child that are no longer appropriate or necessary as an adult?

16. Where do I try to play the Higher Power to get some control over something or someone?

17. In which areas of my life do I come from a victim mentality? What part of my nature is being revealed?

18. What do I want to create or work toward in my life?

19. When did I have the courage to say something difficult lately?

Step 6 Journal Questions

1. Which of my traits do I find challenging to let God remove?
2. Who would I be and what would I look like after God removes my defects?
3. Which traits diminish who I am or limit me in some way?
4. What traits expand or enhance who I am naturally?
5. In what areas of my life am I still living from my fears or anger?
6. What do I want to create in my life?
7. What decisions did I make as a child about who I should be that are no longer appropriate?
8. What do I want to shift now that has stopped me before?
9. What would I find inside myself if I slowed down?
10. What am I committed to?
11. What could I do that would be an expression of my commitment?
12. What help do I need today?
13. Where in my life am I aligned with my Higher Power? Where am I not?
14. Where have I fallen short in thought, word, or action?

15. What past behaviors, thoughts, or feelings make me feel guilty or ashamed?

16. What effect has insecurity or low self-esteem had on my life?

Step 7 Journal Questions

1. Where in my life do I still try to get control over something I can't?

2. What qualities do I have that contribute to my success in an important area of my life?

3. Where do I assign unwarranted power to my fears?

4. When I get upset what could I do that would help me?

5. What possibilities do I see for myself today that I hadn't seen before?

6. Where do I experience a lack of compassion for myself?

7. What is the nature of my Higher Power?

8. Is my life going in the direction I want it to go? If not, why not?

9. Am I quick to be angry?

10. If I tend to fabricate the truth, how do I rationalize it to myself? Does it relate to any fears I may have?

11. What is it like to live inside of me these days?

Step 8 Journal Questions

1. What is the spiritual principle beneath admitting a wrong?
2. How has Step 8 restored my integrity and sense of dignity in my relationships?
3. How do I contribute to others?
4. How do I experience compassion for others? For myself?
5. Where have I lacked self-discipline?
6. Where do I feel remorse or regret for how I have acted recently?
7. Am I quick to react with fear, suspicion, or anger? What situations bring these forth?
8. How has trust in a Higher Power given me hope for my future?
9. How has self-centeredness shown up in my life? How has it affected me or others?
10. What progress am I making in one important area of my life?
11. Are there any instances where I justify lying?
12. What negative thoughts about myself need to be released?
13. What are some of my goals and dreams?

Step 9 Journal Questions

1. What actions contribute to my sense of peace?

2. How does sharing give me breathing room to acknowledge with another what I might dismiss privately?

3. Only when I have an honest heart is good-will possible. Why is that?

4. How would I describe my life through eyes of gratitude?

5. What do negative thoughts make me feel like? How do they impact my actions?

6. What is the trend of my thoughts today?

7. Before I can forgive, I need to accept. Who or what would benefit from my practicing acceptance?

8. What aspects of mine are challenging for me to accept? What is standing in my way?

9. In which areas of my life have I grown beyond my expectations? What supported my growth?

10. What new action could I take that would contribute to someone else or myself?

11. Where can I reduce my demands on others when they are not meeting my needs?

12. If I have a tendency to lie or exaggerate, how do I rationalize this to myself? How does it relate to any fears I may have?

13. What is my understanding of a Higher Power today?

14. Describe areas in my life where self-will is dominant. What relief would I expect to experience when I become ready to let go?

15. Can I increase compassion for the people who are challenging for me? Can I increase compassion for myself? What stands in my way?

Step 10 Journal Questions

1. How do I feel about myself right now?

2. What do I have to be grateful for today?
   How has this day blessed my life?

3. Am I worrying about yesterday or tomorrow?

4. Am I treating myself with respect?
   Am I treating others with respect?

5. Is this a good time to increase my level of self-care?

6. For what do I acknowledge myself today?

7. Did I say or do anything today that would warrant an apology?

8. Have I allowed myself to become too hungry, angry, lonely, or tired?

9. What better choices could I have made to improve on today?

10. What is my Higher Power inviting me to choose today?

11. Where am I being inauthentic?
    Who am I pretending to be or how am I covering up who I am?

12. As I get to know myself better, what if I discover I'm someone I don't want to be?

13. What or who contributed to my view of myself?

14. Do I have the feeling that if you REALLY knew me, you wouldn't like me? Why?

15. Am I creating my life by design or by default?

16. What progress have I noticed as I release unhealthy behaviors?

17. Where am I still blaming outside circumstances for the conditions in my life?

18. In what areas of my life have others noted that my progress has already begun?

19. What actions or attitudes could I adopt to create ease?

Step 11 Journal Questions

1. What is my prayer for myself today?

2. What actions help me feel connected to my Higher Power?

3. What steps could I take that speak of my desire for inner peace?

4. What problems did I encounter this week and how did I resolve them through prayer?

5. What can I do to feel more fulfilled in my life?

6. What are some of my outdated beliefs?

7. What new perspectives could I create that would benefit me or another?

8. What traits could I develop that would empower me to keep the will of my Higher Power?

9. What's the value of my being centered?

10. What am I here to contribute?

11. What is it like to live inside of me today?

12. How have patience and understanding affected my ability to further my healing?

13. Step 11 has a spiritual foundation. What does this mean to me?

14. What forms of power do I imagine are within me? What actions could I take to practice using them?

15. Do I express the desires of my heart?

16. How do my beliefs about my Higher Power affect my life?

17. Why do I pray and meditate?

18. In my prayers each day, I ask what is mine to do today. What have been some of my answers?

Step 12 Journal Questions

1. What prayers have been answered for me?
2. How do I act when I feel empowered?
3. What actions can I take to free myself from blame and bitterness?
4. What paths am I following that answer the call of my heart?
5. How am I expressing my true self today?
6. What might I set aside, so I may "travel lighter" in life?
7. When I forgive, I do not excuse or forget what I or someone else did. What is one thing I could do to demonstrate that forgiveness has occurred?
8. In what areas of my life do I deceive myself and look to the outside world as the source of my discomfort or upset?
9. What activates or triggers my behavior that prevents me from functioning in a healthy manner in my adult world?
10. List specific situations that demonstrate my humility.
11. What childhood or adult experiences inspire me to contribute to the quality of other people's lives?
12. Where is my personal growth enhanced by my willingness to surrender to my Higher Power?

13. Where have I held back sharing my past for fear of another's judgment?

14. What characteristics have I discovered within me that empower me to reveal myself to other adults abused as children?

Step 1 Prayer

Dear Spirit,

You know how hard it's been for us living with the abuse that happened in our childhoods. We'll be going along just fine in our current lives and BAM some event occurs and the effects of the abuse are right inside or right in front of us in the present! We can become triggered and often surprised by the impact the past abuse has on us after so long a time.

Not only were we powerless in all ways while the abuse was happening, but even today, as adults, we're powerless over it coming up again! Our adult lives definitely can become unmanageable.

Pausing and assessing ourselves and the situation can help us get back into the present moment. We become curious about what we reacted to. We discern what we need to do to take care of ourselves.

We need a Power greater than we are, especially when our lives become unmanageable. Thank you, Higher Power, for being there for us.

And so it is.

Amen.

Step 2 Prayer

Higher Power,

We trust that you have a plan for each of us to discover and follow. When we are confused or lose our way, we trust you are there to guide us toward what is best for us and what we need to know. We have only to bring our attention to our minds or hearts to consciously connect with you.

In the quiet we are given direction, new ideas, inner strength, or the courage to move forward. All our needs are met. You are our hope for a fulfilled future. We are learning to trust your help, though sometimes we allow change very slowly.

Please be patient with us; we are doing our best. Our challenges seem very large to us. We become overwhelmed or despondent sometimes. We need you to be able to create new ways of handling life for us.

We know we are not alone. Please show us the way...Thank you.

And so it is.

Amen.

Step 3 Prayer

Higher Power,

We know that your will is being made known to each one of us. We make ourselves receptive to your power by surrendering our will to you. We allow your power to flow though us, to manifest what is for our highest good. We know with you we can accomplish our greatest desires.

Our thoughts and actions can develop a new force of their own by aligning our will with yours. We are guided by your wisdom for right action in our best behalf. Free will is a gift from you, our Higher Power. A violation of the purpose of will brings harm to ourselves and others.

As we are guided by wisdom, we find fulfillment and happiness. We make up our minds to receive that which we need to evolve and grow. Help us to be active in our efforts to be authentic. We must never give up, our well-being depends on it. Thank you for caring for us.

And so it is.

Amen.

Step 4 Prayer

As an adult abused as a child, I realize how important it is to discover the part I play in my own life. I seek to know and understand why I react to certain people and circumstances in the unhealthy ways I do. I ask for help to uncover what is triggering me. I want to learn what is it about me that gets upset or scared.

As I find out these answers and more, I remember to turn them over to my Higher Power and ask for guidance and clarity. I pray that I'll have the inner strength to direct my will to follow these promptings.

I am grateful for whatever courage I can muster. I trust that I do have what it takes to create a new life for myself with my Higher Power's help. I begin with self-honesty. That is enough for today.

Thank you, God.

And so it is.

AMEN

Step 5 Prayer

As I discover where I've erred in my thinking or my actions, I simply acknowledge it. I am willing to be responsible for where I was off base and the impact that has had on my life. I pray to treat myself as if I matter, especially when I make mistakes or make errors in judgment. I am no longer afraid to reveal to another what it's like to be an adult abused as a child.

I have faith in the power of healing through these 12 Steps. I intend to reap the benefits as I work them. I am grateful to my Higher Power for the help I receive with every effort I make. I direct my attention to my Higher Power's care of me and release any anxiety that may appear and watch it dissipate. I remain calm and trusting as I reflect and share.

Since I do this journey with my Higher Power, I enjoy a sense of peace. I share myself from a place of nonjudgment. I am learning to accept myself and love myself as I am today. I experience a sense of well-being, for which I am grateful.

Thank you, God.

And so it is.

AMEN

Step 6 Prayer

I offer to my Higher Power what I have learned about myself by working these Steps. I come from a place of humility and self-love. I am patient with myself as I grow. I practice willingness to be transformed by keeping myself available to God; I remain open and vulnerable as a human being.

My imperfections are not an indication of anything wrong with me. They are merely manifestations of my humanity showing up as traits or characteristics. I remember that I have an eternal connection to Source – my Creator. I turn to that Source for guidance, trusting what I receive.

When I stop thinking about my problems and focus my attention inward, I move beyond my thoughts to a place of stillness. In quiet communion with my Higher Power, I am able and ready to receive the guidance I am seeking one day at a time.

Thank you, God.

And so it is.

AMEN

Step 7 Prayer

Each time I ask for help from my Higher Power, I am placing my trust in it. By choosing to take this Step, I am open to receive. I go directly to the source of help.

I know answers and guidance are available to me; my healing path is being made clear. I confidently allow new ideas to be expressed by me as they assist in planning my new future.

I step out in faith as I anchor these opportunities with action. The place to begin is always with my Higher Power as I move in the direction of the guidance I receive. My concerns fall away, and I am peaceful.

Thank you, God.

And so it is.

AMEN

Step 8 Prayer

I release all that no longer serves me. My inner life has been filled with thoughts and feelings that are leftover from the past. My heart can feel heavy with obsolete beliefs on which I've based my life.

Help me see where I have clogged my mind with resentments and unforgiveness. I ask for help in being willing to clear away all ill-will that I've caused. I want to be accountable for my part from a place of humility. I seek peace of mind and heart.

I am gentle and compassionate with myself and others. As I prepare to make amends, fill me with knowledge and guidance to be effective and true. I trust healing is possible for me when I take the steps to make it happen.

Thank you, God.

And so it is.

AMEN

Step 9 Prayer

May I continue to practice forgiveness as it is one of the most powerful actions I can take. Though it doesn't change the past, by using forgiveness to shift the present moment, it gives me a chance for a different future.

As I make amends, I ask for help in discovering my courage to let go of the way the past should have been. I seek compassion for myself and other people. As I connect with them, I experience the awareness that I am not alone.

Help me to admit what attitudes still linger from my childhood abuse and impact my adult life in ways that create unmanageability.

May I practice affirmations which are statements of truth to support what I want to be present in my life today. May they keep me focused on my Higher Power and offer me renewed hope.

Thank you, God.

And so it is.

AMEN.

Step 10 Prayer

One day at a time, I reach for the spiritual goals I've set for myself. Little by little, I create new habits as I let go of old ones that no longer serve me.

Let me remember that I'm only one decision away from an entirely new life. Help me to have increased faith and courage as I try out new ways of being. Guide me to see both helpful and unhelpful aspects of myself that have been hidden until now.

Thank you for my inner resources that support me in taking chances today that I would not have ventured to consider in the past. I invest in my unborn tomorrows by living authentically in the present. Help me to choose my personal best each day.

Thank you, God.

And so it is.

AMEN

Step 11 Prayer

I let go and let the awareness of my Higher Power pour into me. I allow Spirit to flow unimpeded when I practice gratitude and faith. It is then I experience divine order in my life.

The love of God restores me. The power of God heals me. The grace of God is always present. The peace of God comforts me. These blessings no longer feel elusive, as I have discovered them within. I relax and center my thoughts on being a conduit of these gifts.

I commit myself to see the blessings from God that enrich my life today. I am grateful to Spirit for providing for me in both seen and unseen ways. I continue to do my part with prayerful consciousness, listening and following the promptings from Source within. I gratefully accept the gift of grace.

Thank you, Spirit.

And so it is.

AMEN.

Step 12 Prayer

Upon awakening, I face each day with infinite possibilities. My world feels new and full of promise. I ask my Higher Power to guide me so I may know what is mine to do today. I am given everything I need to carry out the will of my Higher Power. My divine birthright offers me freedom from obsolete notions and opens new doors through which I am able to contribute fresh ideas unencumbered by the past.

As I awaken on my spiritual journey, I embark anew on my path with a more open mind and heart, seeking a stronger connection with my Higher Power. I feel the oneness with this Power as I go within; it is always available to me.

May I respond with humility and begin this very moment to express myself from new perspectives that will benefit myself and others. I feel my Higher Power's care flowing through my life like a river which never runs dry.

Thank you, God, for awakening me to a new potential and extraordinary insights to be used for the good of all. I can see clearly now; I am awake.

And so it is.

AMEN.

How to Get Involved and Start Your Own Meeting

Want to start a group in your area?
See pages 45 – 61.

Get more information at:
adultsabusedaschildren.com

Help spread the word about the fellowship
by following us on Facebook and sharing this information
with people you care about.

facebook.com/adultsabusedaschildrenanonymous/

Index

A

abandonment, 363

abuse,
    child, types of, 13, 76
    effects of child, 15, 75, 82-84
    others' versions, 77
    what is it, 12

acceptance, 127, 190, 327, 377, 529

accountability, x, 380, 386

act as if (see also *fake it*) 34, 104

action, right, 32, 153

addictions, 16

admit, 73, 79, 226, 238-239, 241, 245, 247, 249-251, 477-480

adult abusive patterns, 369

adult perspective, 74

adult power, 537

ADULTS ABUSED AS CHILDREN ANONYMOUS, 3-8, 47-48, 51-52, 54-56, 66-67, 144-145 advice, 50, 552

affirmations, 28-30, 89, 118, 151, 214, 260, 301-303, 339, 401, 448, 485, 539-540, 595-596, 621-634

Alcoholics Anonymous
    12 Steps, 608-609
    12 Traditions, 610-611

alignment, 129-133

alignment, with values, 435, 440

all our affairs, 582-583

alone, 537, 571

amend, 445

amends
    choices, 380-383
    direct, 417-419, 422, 425-428
    indirect, 423, 429-430
    living, 424, 437-438
    process of, 384, 411-413
    purpose, 417
    that could harm, 439-444
    to all, 382-383
    to others, 385
    to self, 382, 432-436

anger, 441

anonymity, i 4

anonymous, 4

apology, 381, 416

ask for help, 323-325

asleep and awake, 568-570

assessment scale, 176

assets (character), 336

authentic, 134

avoid (feelings), 80

awakening, see *spiritual*

B

be specific, 38-39

becoming, 375

beliefs, 100-103, 189, 233, 242

boundaries, 365-366

C

came to believe, 105-106

carry the message, 571-576

change, 336, 421, 445

character
   assets list, 296-297
   defects, 271-273, 278, 282-286
   defects list, 294-295
   defects remove, 288-289, 291-293
   traits, self-diminishing, 209-210, 274
   traits, self-enhancing, 207-209

child abuse-types, 13, 76

child selves, 369, 392

choices, 116-117, 146-149, 354-358, 435

clearing up the past, 103

communicate, 331

compassion, 88

confidentiality, 50

confusion, 319, 323

connection, 109, 463, 483-484

conscious choices, 420-421

conscious contact, 501, 503-507
    through prayer, 508-509, 521-522, 524-528, 501

consciousness, 34

continued, see *inventory*, 461

control, 85, 102

courage, 229, 314, 416-419

created life, vii, 28, 38, 84-86, 117, 139-140, 145, 280, 298, 388

critical inner voice, 175

D

daily practice, 461-464

danger, 439-441

decision, 128, 132, 146

defect of character, see *character defects*

denial, 196-198, 231-232, 375-378

desire to heal, 110

divinity, 502

E

effects of child abuse, 15, 18, 84

ego, 315

encouragement, 279

entirely, 275

exact (nature), 235-236

F

faith, 116-117

fake it/pretend as if, 34, 104

fearless, 175, 186-188, 193

feelings (emotions), 202-204, 478

fellowship, 60-61

focus, 39, 40, 332

forgiveness, 249, 351, 359, 388-389
    of self, 390-392, 399-400, 478

freedom, 315, 388, 414-415, 420, 573-574

G

God (see *Higher Power*), 65-67, 105-106, 107-109, 144-145, 498-500

God's will, 129, 529-531

gratitude (thankfulness), 590

group, 46

growth, 537

guidance, 529

guide (daily), 468-471 (see *inventory*)

guilt, 234

H

happiness, 139

harm, 349, 360-366
    self, 362-366
    to others, 371-374, 393-396, 427-428

healing, 381-383, 399, 412, 418, 438, 463, 573

hiding, 83, 194-195

Higher Power, 65-66, 100
    See *God*, 105-106, 107-109, 144-145, 497

honesty, 100, 217, 227-228, 249

hope, 100, 116, 463, 481-482

humanness, 33, 39

humiliation, 318

humility, 248, 316-319, 465, 560

I

improve, 496, 505-507

insanity, 112-114

inventory, 162-164, 165-166
    moral, 174
    personal, 465-467
    ways of writing, 177-179, 459-467
    when to do an inventory, 473-476

J

journaling, 90, 119, 152, 215-216, 261-262, 304-305, 340, 402, 449-450, 486-487, 541-542, 597-598, 635-653

judgment, 171, 175

K

knowledge, of God's will, 529-531

L

let go let God, (see also *surrender*), 279-281, 285-286, 288-290, 445-447

lists, 350, 370
   amends, 352-359
   character assets, 296
   character defects, 294

love, 82, 84

M

maturity, 417

meditation, 503, 521-528
   benefits of, 524-528

meeting format, 47-61

meetings, 47-48
   agreements, 50
   closing, 60-61
   format, 57-58
   guidelines, 49
   sharing, 58
   service positions, 59

memories, 24

message, 571

minimization, 15, 196

mission statement, 5

mistakes, 380-381, 445, 460

motives, 32, 212, 439, 473

my part, 484

N

nature (of wrongs), 230-232, 233

near death experience, v

non-judgment, 171, 175, 370

O

options, 33

others affected, 460

P

past, 73, 138-139

people pleasing, 180-181

perception, 17, 88

perfectionism, 194

perseverance, 462

perspective, 172, 180-181, 337

possibilities, new, ix

power, 100, 213, 258, 412, 415-416, 532-534

powerlessness, 78, 80

practice, 147, 280, 537

pray, 425, 511-515
   for others, 514, 515
   knowledge of God's will, 529-531
   when, 514

prayer, 91, 120, 153, 217, 263, 306, 341, 403, 451, 488, 508-510
   affirmative prayer, 518-519
   answered prayer, 517
   benefits of, 524-528
   connection thru prayer, 516
   for power, 532-534, 543, 599, 655-66

preparation, 396

principles, xii, xiii
   (spiritual), 199-201
   of the 12 Steps, 578-581

process, 105-106, 136-137

procrastination, 175

program, 3, 7-8, 66-67, 108-109

progress, 10, 474, 479-480

R

readiness, 274-278, 419

reconciliation, 417

relationships, 437-438, 466

release, ix

reliance, 497, 530

religion, 66, 144

repetition, 461-462, 579

responsibility, 184

restitution, 413

restoration, 105-106, 110-114, 116, 136, 146, 413

rituals, 36-37

S

sanity, 102, 112-114, 447

searching, 192-193

secrets, 75, 245

seeking, 501-507

self-abuse, 16, 19, 362, 363
    see also *harm (self)*

self-care, 25-26, 368-370, 442-443

self-love, 141-142, 206, 258, 334

self-responsibility, 256-257

self-talk, 39, 103, 436

self-will, 129

serenity, 174

Serenity Prayer, 290

service, 8, 254, 584-587
    benefits of, 586-587

shame, 234

sharing, 79-80, 150, 240
    Step 12, 552, 575

shortcomings, 320-322
  removal of, 324-326, 330-335

spiritual, 48, 551

spiritual awakenings, 135, 551-562

spiritual awareness, 565-566

spiritual experience, 569

spiritual growth, 496

sponsor, 252-253, 467

Step 1, viii, 71-91, 205, 277, 313

Step 2, viii, 96-120, 205, 277, 313

Step 3, viii, 127-153, 205, 277, 314, 375, 527

Step 4, viii, 157-217
  purpose, 168, 173, 277, 314

Step 5, ix, 221-263, 277, 314

Step 6, ix, 269-306, 314, 328

Step 7, ix, 311-341

Step 8, x, 345-403

Step 9, x, 407-451

Step 10, x, 457-488
  Benefits of, 481-482, 538

Step 11, x, 493-543

Step 12, xi, 538, 549-599
  written in past tense, 563-564

Steps in general, 592-594

stories, 35, 181-183

strategies, 25-26, 205

success, 149-150

support, 26, 188, 279

surrender (see *let go*), 129, 134, 148, 273, 335, 376

T

telephone calls, 8

thankfulness (see *gratitude*), 590

thoughts, 229

time, (present), 31, 35, 40, 99, 136-137, 275-276, 281, 325, 464

tips tricks and tools, 31-41

tools, 7-8, 28, 31, 33, 41, 212, 254, 301-302, 398, 508, 518

transformation, x, 88, 248, 271, 284, 299, 397

trauma, 12

triggers, 32

trust, 15, 16, 99, 249-251, 283-285, 314, 433-434, 499

truth, (honesty), 37, 73-74

turning it over, 130-133, 136-137, 140

Twelve Step path, vi, 465

Twelve Steps, xv, xvi, 51-52

Twelve Traditions, xvii-xix, 54-56

U

unmanageability, ix, 82-84

V

victim, 78-79, 189

vision statement, 5

W

"we", 65, 75-150, 184, 253, 272

we count, 88

wholeness, 110-111, 147

will, 129

willing, 129, 131, 314, 336, 375-379, 350-351

witnesses, 77

working the steps, 32

writing, 167-168, 246

wrongs, (nature of), 230, 232-233, 237, 243

www.ingramcontent.com/pod-product-compliance
Lightning Source LLC
Chambersburg PA
CBHW070926010526
44110CB00056B/1939